A FLY ON THE WHEEL

A FLY ON THE WHEEL,

OR

HOW I HELPED TO GOVERN INDIA.

BY

LIEUT.-COL. THOMAS H. LEWIN

GYAN

Published by

Gyan Publishing House
5, Ansari Road
Daryaganj, New Delhi-110002
Phone: 011-47034999, 9811692060
E-mail: books@gyanbooks.com

Distribution Network
gyanbooks.com
India, USA, Canada, UK, Australia

ISBN: 978-93-6208-439-2 (HB)
First Published, 1884

2nd Impression 2024

Printed at: Gyan Press, Delhi.

A FLY ON THE WHEEL
Author: THOMAS H. LEWIN

A FLY ON THE WHEEL

OR

HOW I HELPED TO GOVERN INDIA

Captain T. H. Lewin (Thangliena) with the Lushai Chiefs.

A FLY ON THE WHEEL

OR

HOW I HELPED TO GOVERN INDIA

BY

LIEUT.-COL. THOMAS H. LEWIN

AUTHOR OF "WILD TRIBES OF THE SOUTH-WESTERN FRONTIER,"
"HANDBOOK OF THE TIBETAN LANGUAGE,"
ETC., ETC., ETC.

LONDON
CONSTABLE & COMPANY LTD
10 ORANGE STREET LEICESTER SQUARE WC
1912

PREFACE

It is now more than thirty years since I published this book of my youth in India; from the Mutiny into which I was plunged, a boy fresh from Addiscombe, to the end of the first Frontier War against the marauding Lushai tribes on the South-Eastern Frontier of Bengal, during which last operation I acted as political officer.

India has greatly changed since those days: changed as I myself am changed. I read the book in its new edition and wonder at the boy who so lightly went forth to face the unknown.

I can only add here that the book was entirely written from diaries, kept carefully for my home-folk, and that if there are mistakes or misconceptions I cannot alter them now. Such as they are recorded here, so they were real and true to the young fellow who wrote them down long, long ago, with no views as to publication. The "old fellow" who now reads the book over for the last time feels that he cannot touch this fresh young work without marring it: they are the vivid impressions of his youth.

> "Naught feared this body of wind or weather
> When youth and I dwelt in't together."

T. H. LEWIN.

Parkhurst,
January 26, 1912.

CONTENTS

ILLUSTRATIONS

"Jours à la fois heureux et triste, jours devorés par le travail et l'enthousiasme, jours comme on n'en voit qu'une fois dans la vie."

LACORDAIRE.

A FLY ON THE WHEEL

CHAPTER I

LOOKING BACK

1857–58

I HAVE arrived at the midmost stage of life; and now, before quitting the table-land of maturity and striking down to the lower level of old age, I am minded to look back, while I am still able to gaze at the past, with vision undimmed by age or infirmity.

I come of old Kentish stock, who for three generations had sent sons to India; and therefore it was a natural start in life when one of my Indian uncles obtained for me a cadetship in the East India Company's service, and I was in due course started out with a dozen other youngsters, my college-mates from Addiscombe, bound for Calcutta, on the 9th September, 1857, the year of the Indian Mutiny.

We had heard rumours in England, before starting, of insurrection in Bengal, but the disturbance was thought to be local, and not of general importance; and after the final wrench from home ties, and the quick ensuing superlative wretchedness of sea-sickness, we reached the Mediterranean, our youthful minds much elated with the sense of our own individuality, and troubled only by insatiable appetites; sea and sky, present and future, alike undimmed by any fleck of cloud, any presage of evil omen.

At Malta, however, serious news awaited us, news that struck home to our boyish hearts, and brought us face to face with the stern realities of life and death. The province of Bengal was in a flame of revolt from end to end; the entire Bengal army was in open mutiny; and, what stirred us most, the batch of cadets which had preceded us to Bengal by a few months only, young fellows we had all known, and with whom we had played cricket within the year—they, our schoolfellows, had been surprised and massacred at Allahabad, as they sat at mess. The knowledge and fear of death as a thing possible to ourselves had hitherto been unknown to us; but now it came very near as we realised the dreadful scene. The cheerful mess-table, with its lights, and white cloth sparkling with silver and wine; and then in a flash the windows filled with the black threatening faces and murderous eyes of the mutineers, as they surrounded the mess-house, from which not one of the poor lads escaped alive. The fun of our voyage was gone. The glories and wonders of Alexandria and Cairo; the crossing of the pathless desert sands, strewn with skeletons of animals and shapeless masses of rock, over which we jolted heavily in our mule-drawn vans; the dry burning heat of the Red Sea and the moist clinging warmth of the Indian Ocean and Ceylon; the strange new human creatures that swarmed round the ship, importunate for alms, as we stopped for coaling: all passed before our eyes like a dream, as obstacles and delays in our now tedious journey. The fever had seized us; the desire to fight, the wish for vengeance was in our blood. We wanted one thing only—to reach quickly the land where our comrades and friends had so treacherously been murdered.

It was a relief when at last the low, muddy banks of the Hoogly came in view. The pilot climbed on board, and we slowly steamed up the river and dropped anchor off the City of Palaces. I even now shudder to recall the chill feeling of loneliness and home-sickness with which I sought the bare, cheerless room assigned to me in the cadet's quarters in Fort William. Alone in a strange land; my fellow passengers had scattered and gone their respective ways on landing; my fellow cadets even, had found friends to meet them, while I went alone to the Fort Adjutant, to report my arrival, and inquire to what regiment of the Bengal army I was likely to be posted.

"Army!—regiment!" was the reply. "There *is* no Bengal army; it is all in revolt. You will be sent off to the front at once, and perhaps attached to some Queen's regiment. Provide yourself with a camp-bedstead and a chillumchee, and wait for orders."

I saluted and left the presence of my superior officer, deeply pondering as to the possible nature and qualities of a "chillumchee," but not venturing to inquire further. However, I must obey orders; so with some misgivings I entrusted myself to some palanquin-bearers, who jogged off with me to the bazaar, whence I returned triumphant, with my chillumchee, or brass washing-basin, borne helmet-fashion on the head of a dusky porter, who followed in the wake of my novel conveyance. The bedstead I did not purchase, grudging the expense out of my slender purse.

Next morning I learnt that I and four other cadets were to proceed to Chinsurah, to join Her Majesty's 34th Regiment, which was under orders for Cawnpore. We were each allowed 150 lbs. weight of luggage; and I ruefully parted with the rest of my belongings, which I did not see again for a year and a half.

On reaching Chinsurah and reporting myself to the Adjutant of the 34th, I was posted to C company, and the same day we were booked by railway to Raneegunge, and marched to a standing camp. There, two other cadets and myself were allotted an empty tent, and, rolling ourselves up in our cloaks, we lay down on the bare ground and slept profoundly.

From Raneegunge, I set off with a lieutenant and fifteen men of the 34th Regiment, by horse-dâk, in wretched jolting vehicles. The order was given for the men to load their rifles, and we pushed on night and day, changing horses every ten miles. At Benares we joined forces with a detachment of the 82nd Regiment, and, leaving our horse-dâks, we proceeded in bullock-wagons.

I engaged a servant at Benares, who added much to my comfort, and at Allahabad I had the satisfaction of drawing my first pay—my last, too, for many months—and invested promptly the greater part of it in the purchase of a pony.

I had found the slow, dusty progress of the bullock-train most weary and monotonous, and one evening, to beguile the tedium of the way, I rashly displaced the driver of my wagon and determined to try my hand at driving the quiet-looking beasts. There was no driving-seat, the driver having to squat on the pole to which the oxen were yoked. I seated myself accordingly, and sought to apply the simple means I had seen the driver use to increase our speed. It looked so easy, to screw the tail round a bit and give a gentle dig with the goad. I had no difficulty in setting them going; but, alas! it was the old story of the salt-mill over again. I had no power to stop them. Away went the heavy wagon, swaying and groaning in the ruts of the road. The lieutenant from the wagon in front turned in astonishment to see what had happened; but I, luckless charioteer, had enough to do clinging to the pole, where I with difficulty kept my seat. The road lay along a steep embankment, and, checked by the wagon in front, down the slope my bullocks plunged, dragging me and the wagon after them. Shouts filled the air as we left the track, and I, thrown from my uneasy perch, clung on for dear life underneath the pole, with the great wheels thundering on either side of me, while in front lay the deep precipitous chasm of a watercourse, in which we seemed doomed to end our career. To my inexpressible relief, the beasts seemed to object like myself to this conclusion, and wisely stopped short on the brink, while I hastened to recall the driver, and, much crestfallen, lay down meekly inside the wagon, sore with kicks and bruises, and fully convinced that I had no vocation for driving bullocks.

The driver resumed his place, and we were soon jogging along again on the right track, and with the bullocks' bag of bran for a pillow, and all the wraps I could muster to keep out the cold night air, I made myself as comfortable as circumstances allowed. It was all so strange and new. In the dim light of the swinging oil-lamp I could see my sword and revolver hanging to the wagon-tilt over my head, along with the wood-pigeon which I had shot just before dark, while at the far end of the wagon, the dusky form of my servant squatted motionless on my solitary portmanteau. Outside the stars shone brightly, throwing a pale light on the gloomy jungle and waving trees, which formed a black wall on either side of our long train of wagons. All was silent, save for the groaning of the heavy lumbering vehicles, and the guttural sounds by which the drivers cheered and urged on the patient oxen, or an occasional order given among the soldiers who guarded our train. So short a time it seemed since I was in England, among the dear familiar faces; and now how changed, how strange! But it was best not to encourage such thoughts, and, resolutely knocking out the ashes of the pipe which had recalled them, and, closing the heavy canvas curtain of the cart, I betook myself to sleep.

When I awoke it was early morning, and the cart was standing still. I pulled aside the curtain and looked out.

The long line of dusty-tilted wagons had halted in a quiet stretch of white sandy road; the drivers were squatting together in groups, smoking and warming themselves round a *small fire which they had lit from straw and wayside rubbish*; while the great white oxen, who had toiled so patiently through the night, stood sleek and silent, munching their chaff. All was quiet, strangely quiet, in fact; for where were all the soldiers? I jumped out, buckling my sword and revolver hastily round my waist, and sought my comrades. We had halted near a group of low whitewashed huts, built native-fashion, with closed court-yard. At the main entrance stood the stump of a large tree, round which our men were grouped, their excited gestures and low voices showing that something unusual had occurred. I walked hastily towards a group of my brother officers, who stood near the mouth of an old well.

"What is it?" I asked. "Where are we?"

The answer startled me by the cold intensity of its tone. "We are at Cawnpore, and this is the Slaughter-house!"

It is many years now since I stood beside that well, and saw the mass that lay down in the darkness, which I knew to be the bodies of my countrymen and women. Clothes and other rubbish had been thrown down after the thin covering of earth which the first relay of soldiers sent to relieve Cawnpore had thrown over the poor bodies, and to us it seemed that we saw the actual white-clothed women and children who had been thrown into that dark pit. The shock remains with me, a never-to-be-forgotten horror.

The court-yard was about forty feet square, with numerous small rooms opening off it. It was still strewn with shreds of clothing, leaves of books, and some human hair. On the walls were splashes of blood and marks of sword-cuts, many so low down on the walls that they must have aimed at little children, or at poor crouching women shrinking from the blows.

Is it possible to wipe out the memory of that fatal 15th of July, 1857, when, with the sounds of the British guns in their ears telling of help near at hand, these hapless helpless ones were ruthlessly slaughtered? Outside, the English soldiers anxiously pressing on to help, fighting against fearful odds, ten to one against them; inside, two butchers, Mahomedans by religion, told off to their ghastly work. The doors were shut; two were enough against those helpless, starving, unarmed people. Presently one wretch came out to get a fresh sword, his weapon being blunted, returning quickly to complete his task. After another interval the blood-stained butchers reappeared, carrying two wounded children, leaving behind them no living thing. Shall these two die also? Alas! there is no mercy; and the Nana's emissary, standing at the door, orders the executioners to dash out their brains against the old tree, so that not one may escape. The English troops under General Havelock came too late. There was no help for the dead.

The horror of this place laid hold on us all, soldiers and officers, most of us newly arrived from England. The men clustered together, swearing deep oaths of vengeance against the whole race of those who were guilty of such atrocities. I had never before seen men stirred by strong passion, their faces white and set, and their eyes gleaming with fierce blood-eagerness. Who can wonder if the revenge taken was stern and pity was scanty! Inside the slaughter-house, kicked into a dark corner, lay a Bible (I have it beside me now), dirty and blood-stained. In it was written the name "Anthony Dickson Home," and the words, "Read Psalm lvi. J. E. H." I turned to the Psalm and read, "And they cried unto God, and there was none to help them."

Next morning I went to see General Wheeler's entrenchment, where our folk made their first stand. It was wonderful they had held out so long. The place was literally riddled by shot and shell, and had been ill-chosen for defence. Poor things! poor things!

We marched slowly on, and camped close to the town of

Cawnpore. Tents were provided for us by the Commissariat department, and here we waited for the rest of the regiment, which arrived rapidly in small detachments.

Sir Colin Campbell, with the main army, had pressed on to relieve the beleaguered garrison at Lucknow, leaving General Windham, of Crimean renown—"Redan Windham," as he was called—at Cawnpore, with a small but daily growing force, to guard the bridge of boats over the Ganges, and maintain communications with Allahabad.

Windham's task would have been comparatively easy as far as the rebels were concerned, as they were fully occupied at Lucknow; but he was threatened in flank by a formidable foe—the native army of the State of Gwalior, which sided against us, and 10,000 strong, was now said to be on the point of attacking our position at Cawnpore.

General Windham's force to oppose this attack may have numbered, all told, some 1,500 men. It was made up of small parties like that with which I had arrived, drafts from the 34th, 82nd, and 88th Regiments, and from the Rifle Brigade, which had been pushed up from Allahabad as fast as possible. There was also a small contingent of Madras troops, under General Carthew, with four 9-pounder guns manned by Madrasees, and two 9-pounders with English gunners. This small force was encamped on the glacis of an entrenchment, or *tête-du-pont*, which had been thrown up hurriedly on the riverside to protect the bridge of boats.

On the 17th of November, General Windham marched his whole force out and took up a fresh position some few miles nearer Gwalior, where the road crosses the Ganges canal. Here we remained quiet until the 26th, when we fell in before daybreak for the attack. We ate what was left from the last night's rations, drank some hot tea, and then marched in the dark across the canal bridge into the open country beyond, not knowing where we were going or what we were going to do, but with a growing feeling that we should soon see fighting. We marched along cheerily in the excitement of this thought for some two miles, when the day began to break, and the band was heard to play at the head of the column.

"We shall be at 'em directly," muttered the weather-beaten

captain who commanded my company. "The General would never play the music were we not in sight of the enemy."

Presently we halted, and "the music" marched to the rear, and with the 88th Connaught Rangers leading, on we marched again. Bang went a heavy gun, and over our heads came the whizz of a round shot, a greeting from the enemy. The details of General Windham's engagement are well known. What follows here is taken from my diary, and is given as the purely personal experiences of a young lad of eighteen, recording his first fight.

I felt my heart jump as the shot rushed past, and watched my neighbours, tightening my waist-belt as I saw them do. I recalled all that I had been told of the sensations of others, and our old Major's dictum, that "in going into battle we are all of us frightened, but we don't all of us show it," so I resolved not to show it. The Colonel now gave a loud command, in obedience to which our left wing moved rapidly off to the left. Bang went another gun. This time they had got the right range, and the round shot tore through our column, knocking over two or three poor fellows. The cries of strong men in agony are very dreadful to hear; but there was no time to think, or to offer help.

"Extend into skirmishing order to the left!"

Away we went, extending our line, but at the same time rushing on at the double, advancing on our unseen foe. In front was a high bank, and as our long line of men clambered up and over it, a small bugler-boy at my side fell forward.

"Hold up, my lad," said I, stretching out my hand to help him to climb.

Great God! the boy was dead. Without a sign or cry he had fallen on his face, and as I raised him the blood welled forth from his mouth on to the green earth. "Forward!" was the cry, while the bullets hissed through the air so close and quick that death seemed certain. The flask at my side was smashed by a ball, and men began to drop right and left as we ran forward.

But now we saw our enemy. In front of us stretched a broad sandy plain, and some five hundred yards off, on the further side, were hundreds of dark men in red coats, looking like toy soldiers in the clear distance, who ran hither and thither, with little puffs of white smoke breaking out at intervals along their line. It was a curious spectacle.

The noise of the musketry was tremendous. I heard someone say that the enemy were retiring, and still we pressed on. Suddenly there was a cry of "Cavalry! cavalry! Form square!" and hurriedly our scattered companies formed themselves into square, the front ranks kneeling with fixed bayonets, while the men behind them kept up the fire.

"Reserve your fire, men!" shouted the Colonel; and as he spoke, out of a field of high mustard or sugar-cane, I know not which, came a mass of horsemen, urging their horses at full speed straight on to the square. Surely, I thought, this means annihilation.

"Stand firm, my lads!" came the Colonel's voice. "Ready!" Then, after a slight pause as the cavalry neared us, "Fire!"

When the smoke cleared, there lay many men and horses on the ground, and the rest were scattered and flying right and left of us. Then on again, advancing in skirmishing order, till we arrived tired and breathless at a wall, where we were allowed a brief respite. Some fifty or sixty of us stood behind the wall, regaining our breath, and surveying ruefully the ground on the other side, where for a few hundred yards it was literally swept by three of the enemy's guns, busily served, as we could see, under cover of some mud huts beyond. Clearly, those guns had to be taken, for their fire, passing over our heads, raked heavily the main body of the troops; but our men did not like the job.

"Here comes the Colonel," said a man beside me; and looking back, I saw Colonel Simpson of "ours" on his grey horse crossing the plain. For a moment I thought he was down, as a well-aimed round shot fell right between his horse's legs, raising a cloud of dust; but on he rode safely, and was soon with the rest of us under the wall. The officers clustered round for orders.

"Rally the men," he said. "Those guns must be taken, and there is no time to lose."

Away went the officers down the line. Then with a cheer

and a long breath, off we went from our friendly shelter into the iron hailstorm of grape-shot and bullets. No matter who fell; on, on with a rush,—and the guns were ours!

After this we got scattered. No one seemed to know what was to be done next. I followed those about me, and found myself in a village. A shot from the houses killed one of our men.

"I see the beggar!" shouted a soldier, and the house was quickly surrounded. There was a cry of "Here he is!" answered by the yet fiercer demand from the men outside, "Don't kill him!" and the poor wretch was thrown from the parapet or roof of the house on to the glittering bayonets fixed to receive him.

"Damn it all, men, don't be cowards!" shouted the Adjutant. "Kill, but don't torture."

We now got into order to retreat on our old quarters, whence we had set out in the early morning. Weary, and thirsty, and exhausted by the heat, I saw four or five men struggling for a mouthful of muddy water in a roadside puddle.

Great talk had we young cadets over the day's doings, as with infinite zest we fought our battle over again. Chief among the incidents of the day was the cavalry charge, and much did we admire the bravery of the dusky officer who had led his men right up to the muzzles of our guns, paying forfeit with his life. We reached our camp between four and five in the afternoon, and at six o'clock I lay down in my clothes dead tired, and thankful that it had not fallen to my lot to go on picquet duty, as some of my less fortunate comrades were required to do.

At six o'clock the next morning we were paraded, and stood on our stiff, weary legs until ten o'clock, waiting with piled arms while General Windham reconnoitred the enemy's movements. Soon after ten the sound of guns reached us as they attacked our position, and the 88th and 82nd Regiments moved off to the left, leaving us, the 34th, to hold some mud houses, to skirmish to the front, and to try and pick off some of the enemy's gunners.

We left our camp standing, and I cast a lingering look on the tent that contained all my worldly belongings, which; alas! I never saw again. The time went on, and the grape and musketry fell thick among us, not doing much harm, until at midday came the order to retreat, and it gradually dawned upon us that we were getting the worst of it. A rumour spread that the Nana Sahib had joined the enemy with 25,000 men, against which force we were powerless. So we marched back through the deserted streets of Cawnpore, catching a glimpse here and there of some affrighted native scuttling away for bare life, and reached the entrenchments as night fell. A handful of biscuits and some rum and water were served out for supper, and we slept on the ground rolled up in our cloaks, each man at his post. I was restless from an intense feeling of dirt and discomfort. Never had I remained unwashed for so long a time; but why think of washing, with barely enough water to drink?

In the early morning we were marched out by companies, and piled arms under some trees just beyond the glacis of the entrenchment. We were to have another hard day, it was said. Very soon came the command in a hoarse whisper, "Fall in! Stand to your arms!" And off we marched, to occupy and dispute the passage of the main roads leading to the entrenchment. My regiment was stationed close by the bridge over a small stream, beyond which lay the church of Cawnpore—or, rather, its walls, for the church had been plundered and wrecked during the first defence under General Wheeler.

Company after company defiled right and left along the bank, and we comprehended that the stream was to be our line of defence, and this bridge the key of the position. On the far side of the stream extended a wide sandy plain, with no cover but the church walls and some mud huts, and clumps of trees at about 800 yards' distance, among which we could see figures moving. We were soon employed in making a barricade across the bridge-way by means of broken carts, with planks, railings, or whatever we could lay our hands on. I and some others were carrying the wheel of a cart to add to the obstruction, when whiz! a round shot came into the midst of us, and we fell about like a heap of wooden soldiers. I staggered to my feet again, much surprised at finding myself alive, and even more astonished that none of my comrades were hurt. We had been knocked over by the rushing wind of the shot, which must have passed right through the midst of us. Among the distant trees we could see the enemy's guns, which thenceforth kept up a steady fire on our position, and we watched the round shot as sometimes, after striking the ground, they came hopping towards us like lively cricket-balls.

"Arrah! the playful little varmints! they hops about like St. Patrick's pig in a thunderstorm," quoth an Irishman who was sitting close by under cover of a mud wall; when crash came one of the "varmints" through the wall, knocking him head over heels, and breaking his fire-lock "all to smithereens," as he expressed it, but without doing him any further injury. The fire grew hotter as the day wore on, and we on the bridge were ordered to lie down, while two Madras guns were brought up to return the fire, without much effect in checking that of our opponents.

Towards four o'clock we began to get the worst of it, and being largely out-numbered, our small force was driven in on both flanks. The enemy now came pouring down, and occupied the church on our left, where they brought a gun to bear on the bridge at close quarters, loading with grape, pushing the gun out round the corner to fire, and drawing it back to reload under cover. From the church, from the houses, from every available cover, the fire concentrated on the bridge, while our men replied with spirit, although we had many casualties. Three of our subalterns were hit, one killed. The noise of the firing, the shouts and cries, were terrible. The men, so long exposed to this terrific fire, began to waver.

"They are surrounding us!" came the cry.

"Never mind, my boys!" cried the Colonel. "We've got to keep this bridge, if we die for it!" and he, standing up in the midst of the shower of bullets, lit a cheroot as quietly as if he had been at home. I admired that man, and he certainly gave us new courage. The hardest sort of fighting is to stand still and be shot at. One can fight or fire, but to do nothing is a severe ordeal for nerve and courage.

Our surgeon had established himself under cover of a mud wall hard by, and was tending the wounded as calmly as if he were in Netley Hospital. The Brigadier, General Carthew, was brought in to have his wound dressed, just as I was helping to carry one of our poor fellows who had been badly hit. I ran off to fetch water for him, glad to have anything active to do, instead of waiting passively among the bullets.

It was getting towards sundown when we got orders to retire to the entrenchment. An Englishman does anything better than retreat, and when the order to fall back was given, most of the men ran for it; but they had held a difficult position under heavy and deadly fire during the whole weary day, and this disorderly retreat was covered by a small party of officers, non-commissioned officers, and a few of the best men. Fortunately, our opponents were not inclined for close quarters, and we all reached the fort in safety. How any of us survived that storm of death on the bridge is still a mystery to me, and the feeling of finding myself alive and unhurt that night was little short of ecstasy. In our regiment alone we had three officers killed and eight wounded, with a heavy list of killed and wounded among the men.

We had been thirty-six hours without food, and we further learnt that our camp of the previous day had been plundered and burnt, so for myself and many others the clothes we stood in formed all our possessions.

That night Sir Colin Campbell, with a few of his staff officers, galloped across the bridge of boats into the entrenchment. He had got news of our disaster, and had hurried forward in advance of the main body of the force, with which he had just relieved the garrison of Lucknow. A hearty cheer we gave him as he rode in, bringing with him the promise of succour, and reviving our drooping spirits with fresh hope of victory.

On the 29th of November the enemy opened fire on the bridge of boats with a battery of heavy guns; but Sir Colin Campbell's horse artillery silenced them from the Lucknow bank of the river, and soon the van of the main army crossed the river to our entrenchment, bringing the ladies and children rescued from Lucknow.

I went round to the hospital that evening to see some of the wounded of my company, and hoping to be of service. I found there a young officer of our regiment, for whom I had felt a strong friendship. He had been hit in the side, the ball passing through the liver, and he lay there dying. He knew no one, but tossed restlessly on the narrow hospital cot, while his Madras servant sat at the foot crying, and flapping away the flies in a helpless manner. Poor lad! he was but eighteen, tall, dark, and handsome; but there was no help for him. I smoothed back his hair and arranged his pillows, while he muttered something about "Fix bayonets and come on!" As I left him, full of sorrow for his untimely fate, a man on a neighbouring bed cried out to me, "For God's sake, Sir, ask the doctor to do something for me! This is hell-torment!"

I spoke to the doctor, who glanced hastily round.

"Oh! that fellow there. He'll be dead in an hour or so. I can do nothing for him. He is shot through the stomach, poor fellow, and must suffer dreadfully."

Yet another fine young soldier close at hand lay dying, shot through the chest. He was not suffering, it seemed, yet knew he was going. As I stood behind him, he said to the comrade who supported him, "Give my love to my dear wife, Jack, and say"—here he raised his arm—"say that I died for old England, and I'd do the same again."

I left the hospital full of sad thoughts. Evidently men still could willingly die for their country, and suffer gladly for her sake. It was strange to think that only a few months before I had slept quietly in my white college bed, while now I was thankful to sleep on the bare ground, with a pistol for my pillow. Four hours' sleep at a stretch was all I could take; at the expiration of this time it was my duty to visit our sentries and see that all were on the alert. We lived, for the most part, on hard biscuit and rum and water; standing, marching, running, and fighting in the broiling sun; but by way of compensation, I had a wonderful appetite and perfect health, enjoying the mere fact of existence the more, perhaps, from the uncertainty of life from day to day.

Our late opponents, the Gwalior Contingent, consisted of four companies of artillery, two of cavalry, and seven regiments of infantry, in all about seven thousand men. To these must be added the soldiers of the various native regiments which had mutinied in and about Cawnpore, together with a considerable auxiliary force furnished by the Rani of Jhansi, the whole body, amounting to little short of twenty thousand men, nominally under command of the Nana Sahib, but actually directed by a much abler soldier, Tantia Topee.

To oppose this force, Sir Colin Campbell had five thousand infantry, six hundred cavalry, and thirty-five guns, and at the head of this little army he issued forth from the entrenchments on the 6th of December, attacked, and completely defeated them. We who had been fighting under General Windham were left behind to recuperate after our late hardships, and it was with feelings of the profoundest satisfaction that we saw our enemies routed. Our regiment now moved out of the fort and took up quarters in the Masonic Hall, a large building some thirty feet high by a hundred and fifty long, where, before these troubles "the Craft" had carried on their mysteries. A large hole in the roof, made by a round shot, afforded perhaps too much ventilation, for the nights were cold; but after our recent hardships we were more than content, and thought the accommodation palatial.

It was with truly thankful hearts that we fell in for church parade on Christmas Day, and well do I recall the cheerful strains of the band playing "Hark to the merry Christchurch bells," as the Colonel walked though our open ranks making his inspection. The message of "Peace and good-will towards men" was read to us by the white-robed clergyman in the roofless church, whence, a short time previous, the rebels had trained their guns on to the bridge, and I gazed curiously on the blackened and shot-torn walls of the building, which I had last seen filled with the dusky, red-coated enemy, and sending forth volleys of fire and smoke. After the service, I, with two or three more, went to the corner round which they had slewed on us that accursed 9-pounder gun. The marks of its wheels still showed plainly on the ground.

A few days later I was officer in charge of the guard when four natives were hanged. The gallows was prepared for them close by the dreadful slaughter-house, and they met their death calmly; but it was a terrible sight. This was the first time I had done regular guard-duty, and I had hardly got settled into my quarters in the guard-room, when two of my men appeared to claim a "footing," to drink my health, which I had to pay out of my slender purse.

We rested a fortnight at Cawnpore, recruiting our strength, getting new clothes, and making ready for a fresh start, and the end of January saw us on our way to Lucknow, where the rebels still mustered in great force. My regiment, the 34th, was directed to occupy Bunnee, a village midway on the road between Cawnpore and Lucknow, to furnish guards for convoys, and keep open Sir Colin's communication with the rear.

Shortly after our arrival, great excitement was created in our camp by the body of one of the men being brought in dead, and horribly mutilated. He had loitered behind to get water during the march, and had been taken by the villagers and tortured to death. This incident still further excited the ferocity of our soldiers, and a number of them swore to give no quarter to any native who should fall into their hands.

Convoy after convoy arrived and was pushed on to the Alumbagh, before Lucknow, bearing provisions and siege materials to the main army. Some of the bullock trains extended over three miles in length. In one I counted fourteen hundred camels and nine hundred carts. It seemed strange that so long and so scantily-guarded a procession could pass unmolested; but, save by an occasional and easily-repelled raid of a few horsemen, no attempt was made by the enemy to cut off our supplies.

Towards the end of February, Sir Colin Campbell, having collected sufficient stores in the fortified camp at the Alumbagh, proceeded to send out flying columns to right and left, with a view to dispersing the scattered parties of the enemy, and concentrating the whole nest of hornets in Lucknow, where he hoped to strike a final blow and end the campaign.

The 34th Regiment was detailed to form part of one of these columns under command of Sir Hope Grant, consisting of two batteries of horse artillery, the 9th Lancers, a wing of the 7th Hussars, and the 38th and 53rd Regiments, in all about three thousand men. We moved straight into the country, going north-west, without regard to roads, our baggage being carried by camels, crossing broad sandy plains, or treading a wide path through fields of standing corn.

Our first day's march of twenty-five miles under a broiling

sun, was somewhat trying, and as on the following day we did twenty-three more, it became evident that we had some definite aim in view, and were not making a mere reconnaissance. Rumour had it that we were in pursuit of the infamous Nana Sahib, the cavalry having been sent forward, and when at evening we reached the strongly fortified town of Futtehpore, we found that rumour for once was right.

The Nana narrowly escaped capture, having been there the night before. We only succeeded in taking his baggage, containing papers and valuable jewels, and two of his confidential servants, but the villain himself escaped us. His servants were hanged, and the fort blown up when we left next morning.

The column now moved on by easy marches towards Futtehghur, searching on the way any villages where the insurgents could have found shelter, and destroying defences or fortifications that might be turned against us.

On one occasion, when we were searching for rebels, I had a narrow escape. I went into a house through a dark entry, where was piled a heap of brushwood, over which I trod, passing to the courtyard beyond. Finding the house empty, I returned and idly prodded the brushwood with my sword as I passed over it. To my amazement the whole mass uprose, and a sepoy came at me with fixed bayonet. I parried with my sword, and firing my revolver with my left hand, shot him through the body. I silenced my remorse for so doing by the reflection that it was only a question of his life or mine.

We met with but little resistance. At one place only, the fortified village of Meahgunge, the enemy mustered in force and made a stand. We took the place, with a loss of only one killed and five wounded, but the mutineers suffered severely, being cut up in their retreat by our cavalry.

Among the prisoners were found two who had in their possession articles of European clothing. Our men, in consequence, jumped at the conclusion that these had been concerned in the late massacre at Cawnpore, and got completely out of control, giving vent to their pent-up feelings of revengful ferocity. The officers, after trying vainly to bring the men to order, had the prisoners, half dead, forcibly taken from them by an armed guard.

After this we marched steadily back to Lucknow, and rejoining the main army late in the day, after a long and tedious march, attacked the rebels posted in the gardens and houses near the Alumbagh. The fighting was not at close quarters, and our skirmishers had no difficulty in driving the enemy before them.

When our regiment at last halted and piled arms, I saw the General and his staff riding towards a large turreted house a short way off, and wishing to see as much as possible of what was going on, I followed. In front was a long high wall, and making for a gap, I stood spell-bound by the sight which broke upon my gaze.

We were standing on the summit of a hill, and below, spread out like a panorama, lay the city of Lucknow, and the army of the rebels. Far away, perhaps a mile beyond the gardens and groves of trees that filled the middle distance, glittered the domes and palaces of the King of Oude. Nearer to us, like a fringe to the city, were swarms of dusky natives, dressed for the most part in white, working like bees at the entrenchments, while here and there the sharply-cut shadow of embrasures, or the muzzle of a gun caught the eye.

To our right rose the fantastic pile of the Martinière College, thickly manned by red-coated sepoys. From this college the ground rose with an unbroken slope to the turreted house, from the roof of which the General was surveying the position through his glasses. The house was a pleasure-house belonging to the King of Oude, and called by him "Dilkhusha," or Heart's Delight, in front of which our men speedily began to throw up earthworks.

Far down the valley came a puff of white smoke, followed immediately by the roar of a round shot, which passed over my head and killed a horse picqueted behind me—a visiting-card from our adversaries on taking up our new position. At sunset our regiment marched up to the rear of the Dilkhusha to bivouac for the night. Some of the officers' servants came up, and I looked anxiously for mine, hoping he might bring with him a cloak or some of my belongings. We had been fourteen hours without food, and night fell and the stars came out, and still no signs of rations, nor even the shelter of my familiar tent. So with inward grumbles I lay down on the stone steps of the Dilkhusha and fell asleep.

" Oh blessed sleep ! " as Sancho Panza says. " God's blessing on the man who invented sleep. It fills the hungry, and covers the weary as with a mantle." But I was soon roused up.

" Eh—what ? A night attack ? "

" No ; two tots of regimental rum."

" Thanks, thanks, good Corporal ! " and with one gulp I swallowed the welcome draught, and with a sigh of contentment sank back on my stony couch. The morning found me full of cramp, but considerably rested by my sound sleep. We now settled into camp life, and the second siege of Lucknow commenced. There was plenty to do for all. For five consecutive nights I was on duty, sometimes at the Dilkhusha, sometimes on picquet over the artillery park of siege guns. Such guns ! My head fitted easily into a howitzer.

The enemy's round shot began to fall with unpleasant frequency into the camp. At night one pitched some two feet from my tent, killing a native servant who was asleep there. It is easy to write or to read about round shot, but it is difficult to convey the extreme sense of discomfort and uncertainty experienced when, lying dead tired on one's bed, one hears a mass of iron, weighing eighteen pounds or more, come hurtling through the air with a grim indeterminateness of destination. To sleep is difficult.

On the 9th of March the Martinière was taken by assault. Our regiment did not take part in the attack. Sir Colin told our Colonel, who was eager to join, that no regiment better deserved a front place, but that one regiment must remain to guard the camp, and in view of the smallness of our numbers, only four hundred strong, he was obliged to detail us for this duty. So we looked on as spectators at the attack, and a very pretty spectacle it was.

When the order was given to advance, the 42nd and 93rd Highlanders gave a cheer, sprang over the entrenchments, and under a heavy fire went straight at the enemy's works. With the Highlanders went a Punjaub regiment, who raced them neck and neck, and looked quite as fine fellows as the Scotsmen. As they stormed the earthworks, the rebels abandoned their first line of defence, but held very obstinately a second line of entrenchment thrown up in rear of the Martinière, till they were driven out at the point of the bayonet, with heavy loss on both sides.

I was on inlying picquet, and ought, of course, to have remained in camp; but at eighteen years of age curiosity is a powerful agent, and the excitement was too much for me. I secretly saddled my old white mare, and with the saice holding on by my stirrup, I made for the Martinière, which had just been taken. I rode as fast as possible over the open ground, provoking a personal salute of a couple of round shot from some attentive sepoy gunner, and, on reaching the building, I left my horse with the saice, and quickly made my way to the roof of the house, where, from a high pinnacle or turret, I had a splendid view of all that was going on.

Underneath my turret the roof formed a broad flat terrace, and here was Sir Colin Campbell with his staff, consulting maps, despatching orderlies, watching and directing the fighting, field-glasses in hand. I had my pinnacle to myself, as Sir Colin would come no higher, the great altitude making him too giddy to stand there.

Below I could see the Highlanders slowly fighting their way, driving the rebels from a number of mud huts in front, while on the right the Punjaubees and a company of one of the Highland regiments were running as hard as they could go towards a very strong earthwork, swarming with sepoys, and protected by two heavy guns. It was a nasty-looking place, with a deep ditch in front, and flanked by bastions. I saw the enemy crowding towards the left of their work, to meet the attack of our main column, and not seeming to see or suspect the advance of the Punjaubees, who were hidden from them by some trees and houses, and who evidently were bent on a flank movement in surprise.

For a time I lost sight of them; but soon they came again in view on the extreme right, clambering down into the ditch, and up the steep parapet on the other side, quite unnoticed. Then, with a cheer, they rushed down the inner face of the work, taking their opponents unawares. There was some sharp hand to hand fighting, and I saw men fall right and left; but the rebels gave way, as our main column attacked the face of the work, and were soon in full flight towards the city.

I found now that my excitement and involuntary shouts of jubilation at the success of our side had drawn on me the unwished-for attention of the Commander-in-Chief; so, with all possible speed, I flew down the slender staircase, and across the little bridge that had led to my lofty perch, and, remounting my nag, made the best of my way back to camp. As I rode off I saw the tall form of a staff officer occupying my late post of vantage, and congratulated myself on escaping a wigging.

Next day the attack was pushed still further. The Ghoorkas captured Banks' Bungalow on the left, while General Outram stormed and took the Secunder Bagh, with a terrible slaughter of the enemy.

Other and more able writers have written the history of the Sepoy War, so that I shall confine myself to relating such scenes as came under my personal observation, or in which I took active part.

Our regiment moved on with the rest of the army, furnishing guards and doing auxiliary duty, but seeing no actual fighting for the time being.

I had the misfortune to break my sword, and had previously lost my revolver at Meahgunge, so that when, on the 18th of March, our regiment was warned to lead the assault on the Kaisa Bagh for the next day, I found myself in a somewhat defenceless condition. Fortunately for me, the Kaisa Bagh, having been heavily shelled on the two previous days, was taken by accident that very night. A small party of our men effected an entrance through the wall of an unguarded part of the enceinte, and, as our force poured in through the breach, the enemy fled panic-stricken, and on the next day commenced to evacuate the city, taking with them their guns and stores.

Why they should have been permitted this honourable retreat was a mystery to the army, as we were ready and able to cut off and destroy them, having with us a splendid body of cavalry, and an enthusiastic spirit among all concerned.

For two or three days a great deal of private looting went on, for, in spite of strict orders, it was almost impossible to prevent the soldiers straying into the city. I met one man carrying under his arm what looked to my ignorant eyes like a French ormolu clock, studded with bits of coloured glass, which he had found in the private apartments of the King of Oude. It turned out to be made of pure gold, set with jewels of large value. Many stories were told of lucky plunder, and some (both officers and men) were rumoured to have realised large sums by such fortunate finds. Soon, however, prize agents were appointed, and the gates guarded day and night, when plundering rapidly became more difficult and much less profitable.

Our regiment was quartered in the Kaisa Bagh, a pleasure-garden of the King of Oude, and here, the day after the capture, was a scene of extraordinary confusion and wanton destruction. It was a vast square garden, walled all round, with handsome florid gateways, or rather, gate-houses. Two sides of the enclosure were flanked by gorgeous summer palaces, containing saloons for music and dancing, while throughout the grounds were scattered marble kiosks and fountains of most elaborate workmanship.

In all parts of the gardens we found heaps of costly things that had been destroyed by the rebels during their occupation. Large plate-glass mirrors and valuable china smashed to atoms; silks and rich Indian fabrics torn and burnt; guns and rifles, with barrels bent and stocks broken; furniture and precious knicknacks thrown about in disordered heaps. The buildings had all been lavishly and magnificently furnished with a strange medley of gorgeous Indian products, tawdry French gilding, and ill-assorted coloured prints and pictures. Everything, without exception, had been injured or destroyed.

I took up my quarters in a small white marble pavilion, at the corner of the great saloon in the centre of the gardens. This saloon was also of white marble, with gilded domes, hung round with a fringe of small golden bells, which tinkled pleasantly in the morning breeze, while the many-coloured tame pigeons thronged round the fountain outside, learning too late their altered condition as they were knocked over by hungry men.

These gardens would have been a paradise to us, but for the swarms of mosquitoes which devoured us by night. Against this enemy we had no defence.

I took the first favourable opportunity of visiting the Residency, which had been so heroically defended in the first siege by its small English garrison, and where had died "Henry Lawrence, who tried to do his duty," as his simple tombstone, erected later, records. Here also my own cousin, Edward Lewin, of the Bengal Artillery, had lost his life, gallantly serving his guns in the Cawnpore battery, till, like many another brave fellow, he fell at his post.

The walls of that Residency, pitted by balls and shattered by cannon shot, are, to my mind, the grandest monument of the supremacy of our race that India furnishes.

Not for long were we permitted to sojourn in king's palaces at Lucknow. The end of the month saw us once more on the road, with that delightful ignorance of destination or intention, which struck me throughout as one of the most curious features of the campaign.

Our start was made in a secret and sudden manner, for we were aroused from our sleep at one in the morning, and marched off straightway into the darkness, as if on mighty mission bent. To my reluctant arms were entrusted the Queen's colours—reluctant because the honour involved walking for miles along the dusty road, carrying a heavy weight, instead of jogging along comfortably on my pony with my fellow officers. However, there was no escape, and I toiled along in the heat until midday, when a halt was called, and I went off with my company on outlying picquet duty. At sundown we were relieved by another company, and I found a welcome shelter for the night in a curtained palanquin, a certain number of which accompanied each regiment for the transport of sick and wounded.

The weather was growing very hot, the thermometer often marking 100° in the shade, and marching now became a great toil. The object of our expedition, it transpired, was to succour some of our countrymen who were shut up in the fort of Azimghur, and sorely pressed by the rebels. We had but one skirmish with the enemy during this march, when we took two guns and killed over a hundred of our now disorganised opponents. Our own loss was slight, but a nephew of General Havelock was shot in the affair.

While our main body thus advanced to Azimghur, to attack and disperse the rebels, who, under Koer Sing, had invested that place, three companies of ours (of which mine was one) were detailed to strengthen the garrison of Jounpore, and to take up our quarters there for the hot weather.

We reached Jounpore at the beginning of May, and were most hospitably received and entertained at breakfast by two officers, who were in garrison at the fort with a detachment of Madras Infantry. Only those who have been upon the war-path can realise the luxurious feeling of physical comfort which pervades the human frame, when, after months of hardship and privation, one comes again in contact with a real white-clothed, civilised, square meal of well-cooked food, served in a comfortable room, with pleasant hosts, and plenty of leisure to discuss it. Not that we had fretted about the absence of these comforts; but, as the proverb says, "The dog in the kennel barks at the fleas; the dog who is a hunting does not feel them."

We were assigned quarters in some empty bungalows in the vicinity of the fort, and quickly subsided into the ordinary humdrum life of an Indian station.

A new character now, however, appeared on the scene—the Divisional Pay-master, and a hard master he proved to be. We had been living, it seemed, upon credit, and he now called upon us to square accounts. To my credit I found had been placed a sum of one hundred and eighty rupees for each month since I reported myself in Calcutta; but against me was a heavy score for daily rations that I, too often, had never seen, and a monthly charge of fifty rupees for a Government tent, occupied by me certainly for not half the time, and rarely, if ever, alone. There was a further charge of forty-three rupees a month for cart-hire for the conveyance of my modest kit; so that, after paying my servant, and counting up the advances that I had from time to time received to purchase clothes, horse, fire-arms, and the necessaries of life, I found, not only that I had nothing to receive, but that I was actually a considerable sum in debt to Government.

The tent and transport charges now ceased, and I had only to pay a monthly charge of fifteen rupees to Government for the two rooms I occupied while at Jounpore. But, on the other hand, I found it necessary to employ and pay five servants, viz. a khitmutgar, or table-servant, at ten rupees; a bearer, or house-servant, at six rupees; and a saice and a grass-cutter at four rupees each, besides four more rupees monthly to the regimental 'bheestee,' or water-carrier; so that my small income was barely sufficient for my actual needs, even without the burden of debt to start with.

It was now the middle of May, and the heat began to be intense, the thermometer often reaching 104° in the house. The men suffered terribly, perhaps from the reaction after the hardships and excitement of the campaign. But, from whatever cause, the fact remains that, whereas, while in the field the cases of sun-stroke were extremely rare, now, in comfortable summer quarters, with nothing to do, the men went down in numbers. In a few weeks we lost fourteen by solar apoplexy alone; a mysterious ailment, that slew swiftly and silently, making no sign of its coming. A man was hale and well in the morning and buried at sundown.

There was but little to do. I rose daily at six o'clock for parade, and, after inspection and drill, mounted my pony and rode off to the station bath, or "gossip corner," as it was rightly termed. The road was beautifully smooth, and bordered with green grass, that invited a canter. A double avenue of acacias cast their shadow on either side of the way, the long feathery foliage swaying gently in the morning breeze. Groups of natives passed me, going towards the town; fat, white-clad attorneys and office clerks, who salaamed respectfully to the Sahib; or at times, wild-looking, dusty villagers from a distance, going to market, or bound for the judge's court to plead their causes. The judge-sahib will not, however, be ready to dispense justice at so early an hour; he, like the rest of us, is bound for the bath-house, the white walls of which gleam pleasantly through the trees. Horses and buggies, with attendant saices, congregate outside, while their masters disport themselves within. Here, in twelve feet of cool green water, are performed manifold feats of agility; diving through small cane hoops, fetching up eggs from the gleaming white floor of the bath, or riding tournaments in the water, seated astride "mussocks," or inflated goat-skins. A cup of fragrant coffee and a cigar accompanied the leisurely toilet; then home to breakfast before the air grew too hot to be pleasant for the ride back. This was perhaps the pleasantest episode in the twenty-four hours. After breakfast, I worked hard with a moonshee, preparing for the rigorous examination in the vernacular, which must be passed before I had any chance of staff employ.

On the 1st of October we left Jounpore to join the headquarters at Azimghur, where a small brigade was forming under the command of our Colonel, to sweep up the scattered embers of the rebellion in that part of the country. A planter friend gave me a small old pall tent, which I had patched up into serviceable condition, and which rendered me independent of the Government tentage, and, being absolutely my own, gave me privacy.

On reaching Azimghur, we found the small force all ready and eager to start; so, being joined the next day by the Jath Horse, some four hundred strong, we set forth on our travels once again. For the next few weeks my journal contains simply records of marching and countermarching, destroying forts, dispersing or preventing any collection of armed men, but nothing of interest. The rebellion was practically dead.

Many of the village strongholds that we visited might have been troublesome, had they been well defended. One place, called Tandah, struck me as very original in its fortification. It was built in a square, with bastions at the corners, the walls of sun-baked mud, some twenty feet high by twenty-four feet thick. It was surrounded outside by a dense thicket of bamboo, impossible to penetrate save by one hidden tortuous path leading to the fort. Inside was a central stronghold; a masonry keep, well loop-holed, and surrounded by a ditch fifteen feet deep.

A large comet was visible each night on this march from Azimghur into Oude, looking grandly beautiful against the clear dark blue of the sky. Before we started I heard that I had been posted as a Lieutenant to the 31st Native Infantry, and was to join as soon as practicable. This regiment was one of the few corps which had remained faithful to their colours.

It was stationed at Saugor, in Bundlecund, far away in Central India. Our Colonel, however, held out no hope of my being allowed to join before the end of the year.

On the 2nd of November we held a solemn full-dress parade, when the Queen's proclamation of amnesty to the rebels was read, and the assumption of the direct sovereignty of India was proclaimed. A royal salute was fired, and three cheers given. The Indian Mutiny was at an end, and good old " John Company " was no more.

CHAPTER II

CENTRAL INDIA

1859

THE beginning of the year 1859 saw me on my way to join my own regiment, the 31st Bengal Native Infantry.

I bade adieu to many kind friends and comrades in Her Majesty's 34th Regiment at Fyzabad, to which city our wanderings had finally led us, and took my way alone with my servants to Futtehpore, where I fell in with a detachment of the 31st, which had come there on treasure escort, and was halting for a time before returning to Saugor.

On my way I visited Cawnpore, where we had passed through such stirring scenes. Even in so short a time the place had greatly changed. The house of the massacre had been demolished, the well filled up, and a tablet was being prepared to the memory of the unfortunate ones who lay buried there. I revisited with the greatest interest the old positions, and identified the places where we had fought—the bridge which we had held all day under that tremendous fire, and the Masonic Hall in which we found such comfortable quarters after our hardships. The hole in the roof, through which the morning sun used to stream in and awaken me, had been repaired. The wall near the bridge, where the surgeon had tended his wounded, had been pulled down. Even the friendly tree which had sheltered me from the fierce hail of bullets was felled; but I patted his stump with grateful feelings, and cut off a chip as a remembrance of that day.

On the 13th of January, 1859, our detachment marched for Saugor. Some commissariat doolies, or palanquins, accompanied the party, and I occasionally varied the tedium of the journey by a ride in one of them. The bearers kept up a strange monotonous chant as they carried me along, which may be translated thus—

"Who is this we carry here? Hinda ka tinda!
A Sahib very big, we fear. Hinda ka tinda!
Alack! he is a heavy one; weighing very many stone.
Surely 'tis an elephant. Hinda ka tinda!
Let us drop him in the mud, drop him with a heavy thud.
Oh but he'd be angry then, and would beat us all, my men.
Come then, let us trot along; run along, jump along;
Singing merrily our song, Hinda ka tinda! Hinda ka tinda!"

On the march we met a Sikh regiment, who were going to our late quarters at Futtehpore, and I was most kindly entertained by the officers, after the hospitable custom of the country. The Sikhs were extremely fine-bodied and handsome men. Many of them wore polished circlets of steel, sharp-edged, around which their many-folded turbans were twisted, and when at sundown the men were amusing themselves with games in the cool of the evening, I learnt how these were used. The sharp-edged disc was thrown quoit-fashion, skimming through the air, and at a distance of two hundred yards these men planted their discs very accurately in a tree trunk. The missile in its flight took first a slight upward curve, and then swooped down with a slant upon the object aimed at. A deadly weapon indeed to descend upon an unwary head! Afterwards a war-dance was performed, to the music of drums and a sort of clarionet, the sound of the latter instrument closely resembling that of the Highland bag-pipes. The dance was executed with great animation, time and rhythm being well marked, and the effect was enhanced by the dancers occasionally breaking out into a rough martial chorus, clashing their swords the while. As I gazed on this strange scene—the circle of Orientals, in loose flowing robes, with their long dark hair and hooked noses—my imagination ran back to the old Jewish history, and I seemed to see the Israelites on their journey through the desert, under their great captain, Moses.

We passed through Banda on January 18th. M——, the magistrate in charge, like many another, had narrowly escaped on the outbreak of the Mutiny. When the storm burst, he was the only European left in Banda, the other residents having already sought refuge in Futtehpore. The Nawab of Banda, although at heart in sympathy with the mutineers, yet preserved to the last an appearance of loyalty. M—— had been warned that a rising was imminent, and went to the Nawab to exhort him to use all possible influence to quiet the people. Even as they sat talking, there reached them a murmur from the town without, swelling into a shout as the tumult came nearer. A dead silence fell in the room, and on looking up M—— saw that the Nawab was smiling. He knew then that his only hope lay in prompt action; so, drawing his revolver, he seized the Nawab by the collar and placed the muzzle against his forehead.

"Is a carriage likely to be soon ready for me to depart?" he asked quietly.

"Yes, yes, Sahib; one is now ready," vociferated the affrighted attendants.

"Then we will go at once."

Without relaxing his grasp, they emerged from the palace, and the immense mob outside hushed their clamour, in terror for the life of their Nawab, and in amazement at the daring of this solitary Englishman.

"Now," said M—— to the Nawab, "tell them that if I hear a hoot or an insult, or if any man's hand is raised against me, that moment will be your last!"

The Nawab entered the carriage with him, and they drove off, no one daring to interfere. At twelve miles from the city, M—— had a horse waiting for him in case of a sudden emergency; so here he left the Nawab, politely thanking him for the pleasure of his company, and rode off unharmed to Futtehpore.

On the 25th we halted at Chutterpore, and in the afternoon, as I was strolling round with my gun, hoping for a wild duck or any small addition to our scanty larder, I found myself in immediate proximity to a sort of parliament or general assembly of the largest and most human-like monkeys I had ever beheld. There were at least two hundred of them, great "lungoors," some quite four feet high, the jetty black of their faces enhanced by a fringe of snowy whisker. With sparkling vivacious eyes, black hands and feet, and long sweeping black tails, they made an imposing spectacle. I walked slowly towards them as they sat under a group of trees, expecting them to decamp on my near approach. None of them stirred, however, or showed any sign of fear. I then shouted and threw a stone amongst them, but at this they only began to gibber and show their gleaming white teeth at me. I thought it, therefore, better and more polite, not to say more politic, to take my departure without further disturbance, and accordingly I left the council to their deliberations.

The road from Chutterpore rose steadily as we pursued our way. We were gradually ascending to the table-land of Central India. Such a road! strewn with boulders, varying from the size of a sheep to that of a man's fist, and so steep, that it was a wonder to see how the patient bullocks dragged their loads over it.

On gaining the plateau at the top of the pass, the nature of the country quite changed from that which we had left behind us. We now traversed wide flat plains thickly strewn with boulders, and bounded on either hand by low hills, showing darkly blue in the evening distance. The rocks and stones were clothed with a beautiful sort of lichen which lent a general warm purple hue to the foreground, while the broad disc of the setting sun deepened all the tints, until the country seemed to glow blood-red. As our long line wound along to the camping ground the lines rang in my ears—

> " Rest, rest, for ever rest, spread over brow and breast,
> Our face is towards the West—the purple land."

By the beginning of February, I had settled down at Saugor, with my regiment, one of the few Bengal native regiments which remained loyal during the Mutiny. When the rebellion broke out at Saugor, the 31st, although a Poorbea regiment of the same stamp as the rest, turned out to a man and beat the mutineers out of the station. The explanation of this curious fact could not be attributed to any special influence of their English officers, for as good, and better, had been murdered by the natives under their command, giving their lives in the vain attempt to maintain the allegiance of their men. The secret lay, I think, in the exceptional ability of the two senior native officers, men of the bluest Hindu blood, true Brahmins, and to their influence over the regiment the loyalty of the men was mainly due. The regiment was almost entirely composed of high-caste Hindus, and only those who have lived among these people can realise the power caste has over them, especially when combined with force of character.

Sewbakus Awusty, one of these two native officers (who afterwards became aide-de-camp to the Governor-General), was subadar-major of the regiment, and the other officer, Ramdeen Tewary, who was his closest friend, was senior jemadar of the regiment. Both, mentally, were strong men, who had the courage of their opinions, and were formed to influence their fellows. It was through my subsequent friendship with both these men that I was able to gain a closer insight into the springs of native character, and also to attain a much higher proficiency in, and familiarity with, the language, than I could otherwise have hoped for. Circumstances threw me greatly into their society, and Ramdeen Tewary initiated me into all the mysteries of Indian wrestling, club play, and gymnastics.

Of the English officers of the corps, none specially commanded my respect or admiration. The two seniors were old Indians of the most pronounced type, steeped in that atmosphere of moral Oriental enervation which consumed so many of the previous generation in India; cognisant of only the worst side of native character; fussy, luxurious, and weak.

One really great officer the regiment had possessed—Henry Norman; but he had quickly emancipated himself from the weary monotony of regimental life, and had been translated to the happy hunting-grounds of Staff employ, whither all energy and talent in India inevitably tended.

The Adjutant was a high-minded gentlemanly soldier; and if the loyalty of the regiment had depended on him, he would have implicitly believed in the fidelity of his men, in spite of all evidence to the contrary, and would have been shot down at his post, as many a brave fellow was in those days.

I found the routine of regimental life very dull work after the late stirring and eventful campaign, and particularly resented being put to learn my drill all over again, standing in the ranks firelock in hand, with a Brahmin on either side of me. This was sufficiently mortifying to one who had commanded and drilled a full company of Europeans, but the most unbearable part to me was that my rank-fellows thought it necessary to eat largely before encountering the fatigues of the parade-ground, and in the heat of martial exercise, they literally stank of garlic to such a degree, that my shuddering and unregenerate nature almost sank under the appalling effluvium.

Part of my duty was to take charge occasionally of the fort guard. This fort was a most picturesque place, situated on the banks of a large lake, the waters of which laved its walls. On one hand, the shores were closely covered by a crowd of Hindu temples with gilded pinnacles and long white stairways graded to the water's edge. Beyond these lay the native town, the roof-lines broken here and there by groups of trees, feathery palms, and shining, long-leaved bananas, becoming gradually lost in a long stretch of purple moorland, which was bounded on the horizon by a range of low jungle-clad hills. Looking down from the high windows of the fort into the clear lake, I could see great turtles the size of a small dining-table, with here and there a green-brown alligator, disporting themselves in the water. Morning and evening and at noon, or at any other time or season when it pleased or amused the priests, there came from the temples of the gods all manner of strange sounds—clanging of many cymbals, the clashing of bells, or the scream of the conch-shell trumpet by which evil spirits were affrighted; truly a noisy worship, and not the contemplative "cultus" one associates with the great name of Brahma.

Shortly after my arrival the bachelors of the station gave a ball, at which, of course, I attended—my first ball since leaving England. I had hitherto associated the word "ball" with an entertainment in which a large number of pretty young girls played the chief part, and men were in the minority. Here the dancing men, or men who fain would have danced, abounded, but the ladies were, for the most part, matrons no longer young, and the two spinsters of the station were so deeply engaged, that a youngster like myself had no chance of a turn. The Brigadier-General commanding at Saugor was himself an old bachelor, and quite an original in his way. He headed the ball-committee, and was enthusiastic in promoting amusements of all sorts. His anger was great against the advocates of temperance, and one day at mess he burst out fiercely at an officer who ventured to suggest that for men in the army, subject to the Indian climate, total abstinence even might be advantageous, "Pooh, pooh, my good Sir. God bless me! a glass of good sherry, Sir! where's the harm in a glass of good sherry?" Then warming to his subject, he took a higher flight. "A glass of really good sherry, Sir, why it brightens the eye,—er—er, it—er lightens the heart, and makes a man look well in the eyes of his mistress!"

The Brigadier was pleased to issue an order that no officer should appear in any place of public resort save in uniform, and this decree caused much grumbling and many attempts were made to evade it. One evening, at the Band-stand, where the usual evening gossip was going on, under cover of the strains of the regimental band, the Brigadier was present, and on the alert to see if any disregarded his orders. It was a warm evening, and his eye soon caught sight of an individual dressed in the thin black alpaca coat which takes the place of broadcloth in India. Moved by an uneasy conscience, this person abandoned the promenade and hurried down a by-way to avoid the chief's eagle glance. Away went the Brigadier to his Brigade-Major, and on getting within hailing distance, vociferated, "Gully! Gully! take care, Sir! have a care, Sir! my God, Sir! there's an alpa-a-a-ca about!"

Good old Brigadier, peace be to his memory! Many a good game of racquets have I played with him, and many a round oath has rolled harmlessly about my ears when I played badly.

My turn as officer of the fort guard used to come round pretty frequently. The duty was solitary enough, but I did not dislike it on that account. I used to make up my bundle and march off with my bull terrier "Grabby" into our temporary exile.

I utilised the enforced leisure thus afforded by studying the language, in which I daily gained greater proficiency. When evening came, Grabby roused himself to remind me that it was time to amuse him a little, and as the sun sank in the west, off we went: past the guard-room filled with lounging soldiers; past the great heaps of shot and shell, stored-up munitions of war, which set one wondering when and under what circumstances those quiet-looking black balls would take wings of fire and smoke, and speed forth on their errands of death; past the old fortified gateway, whose ancient magnificence recalled the days of forgotten Indian Rajahs, whose castles we now occupy with our men and guns; past the native sentinel who saluted stiffly, and so on to the native town, and down the narrow street which skirted the lake.

In the doorways of the squalid mud houses, each streaked on the lintel with sacred red paint, men sat smoking the hubble-bubble, while here and there a woman, with a lean dusky child astride on her hip, would shrink back and draw her scarlet "doputta" over her face as I passed by. Sometimes I would encounter a line of commissariat bullocks conveying grain up to the fort, and experienced much difficulty in inducing Grabby to pass these horned monsters; or great, red, and terrible pariah dogs would pounce forth as if to make a meal of my terrier, and I had to come to the rescue with a well-aimed kick or two, while the natives gazed in tranquil amazement at the activity of the "sahib."

My boatman would usually be found smoking peacefully in the bosom of his family. When I appeared the family fled in every direction, as if I were a wild beast, while the man approached me with a low salaam, and led the way to a long dangerous-looking dug-out canoe, in which he paddled out to fetch my English boat, lying moored at a little distance in the lake. On one occasion, while seated on the low parapet of the ghaut, awaiting his return, my attention was arrested by the proceedings of a strange-looking person who was employed in crawling on his hands and knees around a small shrine close by. This devotee was clothed in dirty saffron-coloured garments, and being likewise adorned with a thick coat of white ashes, streaked here and there with vermilion, he had somewhat the appearance of a clown at a circus.

"O reverend one, how many times are you going round?"

"Five hundred, Sahib."

"Why are you performing this rite?"

"On account of my great sins. Mohabir be merciful to me!" Here he nearly tumbled over Grabby, who, much perturbed at these unusual proceedings, was investigating his legs.

The shrine was a mean-looking little building, containing an image of the elephant-headed god, Ganesha, or as the people here call it, Mohabir. Both the image and the shrine were plentifully besmeared with vermilion, which looked unpleasantly like fresh blood.

When my boat at length arrived, after a slight demonstration of unwillingness on Grabby's part, we would take our places and pull slowly away from the shore out into the glassy stillness of the deep lake. From the native town the cry of the Muezzin could be heard as the twilight closed in, calling from the Mohammedan mosque, "Great is God! To prayer! To prayer!" And quickly following, as if the Hindu deities were jealous of this invocation, came an infernal clamour of clashing brazen cymbals, booming of gongs, braying of conch-shell trumpets, and bellowing of horns, proclaiming that in these temples also, men sought for and worshipped "the unknown god."

Early in the month of March, 1859, intelligence was received that the rebel chief, Tantia Topee, commanding the remnants of our old enemies, the Gwalior Contingent, had been driven southward, and was in the Saugor district at Rathghur, some thirty miles distant. Our Brigadier accordingly marched out with all the men he could muster, and I accompanied him, in command of a detachment of the 31st Native Infantry.

Our first march was a hurried and long one, the Brigadier's object being to surprise the rebels before they could get notice of his approach. Oh, how tired I was on that march! walking until my blistered feet compelled me to mount my pony; then falling asleep as I rode along, and waking with a start and a frenzied clutch at the mane, in the very act of tumbling off.

Towards midnight we halted for a short time, and flinging our wearied limbs on the hard but friendly bosom of mother earth, we took literally forty winks, rousing up to repeat the march, the halt, and the hasty doze, till the early dawn showed in the east, and we halted to camp.

As might have been anticipated in this wonderful country, where whispered rumour flies like the telegraph, the rebels got wind of our approach, so our thirty miles' march was of no avail; but we were up and away before dawn the next morning, and while it was yet dark we found ourselves on the banks of a river. My pony not being sure-footed, I led him through, wading bare-foot, and cutting myself a good deal with the sharp stones of the river-bed. It was a strange scene. Against the dim sky-line moved the mighty silhouettes of a line of elephants carrying the tents, while, in the stream below, the wagon-drivers made terrific hubbub in getting their beasts through the dark water. Then, as the dawn broke, I saw the long scarlet line of our irregular cavalry, like a brilliant-coloured snake pushing its sinuous way through the green fields ahead of the column.

As an officer commanding a detachment, I found myself during this expedition far higher in the social scale than I was wont to be. Hitherto in my campaigning I had been accustomed to regard Brigadiers and Brigade-Majors as bright particular stars, far above my humble subaltern sphere; but here, thanks to my command, and also to the kind-heartedness of the Brigadier, I messed with the head-quarters' staff, and found them all very genial and pleasant.

The officers of the Queen's regiment which accompanied the expedition gave themselves great airs, not associating with the rest of us, nor even inviting the Brigadier himself to their mess, because, forsooth, we were "Company's" men. I had already met with this sort of feeling during the siege of Lucknow, and then, as on this occasion, it struck me as remarkable, seeing that the officers of both services are drawn from the same class of men in England, and receive precisely the same sort of education.

Our vain pursuit of Tantia Topee and his band lasted over a week; we, marching as hard as we could go, and daily expecting to come up with them. I do not myself think we had ever any chance of overtaking them, on account of the long train of baggage and ammunition-carts which accompanied us, and the slow pace of the bullocks which drew both carts and guns. The British soldier, moreover, no matter what the urgency of the expedition, must be fed on wheaten bread, with rations of beef and rum, all of which had to be carried about with us; while the enemy marched without luggage or impedimenta, save what each man could carry on his back, trusting for their food to the country they might be in. Further, about half their number were mounted on ponies, and went ride and tie with their comrades, so that our heavy lumbering pursuit amounted almost to a joke.

At last, Tantia Topee was reported to be encamped on the top of a hill, from which vantage ground he quietly watched our movements. We halted about eighteen miles from his camping-ground, and report said that a combined movement with General Napier on the other side of the hill was in course of projection. Of course the heads of affairs only knew what was doing, and we waited in patient ignorance till we were warned for a night's march on the 11th of March.

Having had my dinner, and seen that all was in readiness for a start, I lay down to sleep while I might. I was wakened by my orderly. The moon was shining brightly overhead, gleaming white on the long lines of the men as they fell into rank, and contrasting strangely with the red glare of the camp-fires, which always blaze up brightly just before a start, in a final conflagration of odds and ends. This was to be the grand combination movement; but this also, like our manifold previous detours, was fruitless. We marched thirty-two miles, only to find that our foe had again escaped us, and I sincerely wished he might feel as tired as we did.

After this effort, the Brigadier left the bullock-guns in the fort at Kirwai, and I and my detachment were left behind to guard them, while the column moved off again on their wild-goose chase.

When the Brigadier finally relinquished the pursuit of Tantia Topee, we returned to Saugor, and I shortly afterwards successfully passed the first, or colloquial, examination in Hindustani. I found no difficulty in this, as for months past I had been in the habit of talking to every native I could meet, and had acquired considerable fluency of expression.

In April my regiment changed its quarters to Calpee, while I was detailed with two companies on detachment duty to

Hamirpore, parting from the main body at Chutterpore. I marched off in all the dignity of my first independent command, and halted the detachment at a comparatively early hour that evening, as the weather was sultry and unsettled, and my Jemadar, Ramdeen Tewary (the fine fellow of whom I have already spoken as keeping the men true in the Mutiny), opined that we ought to make ready for the coming "túphan," or tempest. It was oppressively hot, not a breath of air was stirring; but clouds were gathering ominously on the horizon, heralding the coming storm.

We hurriedly pitched the tents, driving in the pegs as firmly as possible, and cutting trenches outside to carry off the rain and prevent the men's bedding being flooded; for of course all slept on the ground. The earth from the trenches was banked up against the sides of the tents to keep out the wind. In my own little tents, whither I repaired after seeing my men all settled, I found that extra precautions had been taken to render all secure. The tent-ropes were tied to bushes or boughs of trees, and these had been buried about a foot under ground. This, my servant explained to me, was much safer that to trust to tent-pegs in a storm; for if there was much rain the pegs became loosened, and were liable to be drawn out by the strain of the wind, while with the ropes thus bushed it would take an elephant to draw them.

I just looked round my little habitation to see that all was snug—my gun safely tied to the tent-pole, and my boxes raised by big stones under the corners, to guard them from the night attacks of the all-devouring white ants—and then I went out again, with a vague feeling of impending disaster.

The spectacle without was grand but ominous. From the north-west a canopy of dark indigo-coloured clouds, shot here and there with red-brown reflections, was rapidly approaching us, mounting higher and higher in the heavens. There was still no wind, and no living thing was to be seen moving, save one stray crow, which was hurriedly and uneasily seeking shelter. Presently there was a slight rustling in the tree-tops, and my cheek was fanned as with the breath from a furnace. But how shall I describe what followed? A mighty wall, hundreds of feet high, of dark brown dust, extending right and left as far as eye could see, advanced upon us. It impressed one with an indescribable feeling of helplessness and terror. Darker and darker grew the air, though one could still see the bright sun shining overhead; it chilled one's blood to think that we must enter and be submerged by that advancing gloom. With a mighty roar, as of floods let loose, the tempest was upon us. I stood fascinated. The tall trees bowed down as the fury of the storm-wind touched them, the air was filled with thick dust, with leaves, sticks, small stones, and even branches wrenched from the living trees. My bearer seized me by the arm. "Come in, Sahib; come inside the tent. It is not good to look out on the tempest; it might anger the evil spirits that walk therein if they saw you watching them."

A darkness that might be felt, and that no lamp could illumine, shrouded our camp. The wind roared and yelled. It was a hurricane. My little tent stood bravely; but soon cries of distress reached me from the men's quarters, and darting out from my shelter into the hurly-burly, I found that one of the tents had been blown away. It was not possible to do anything while the storm lasted, so all hurriedly sought refuge in the still standing tent and waited till the fury of the tempest should be spent. Before very long a steady gale replaced the violence of the hurricane, and a heavy rain fell, accompanied by thunder and lightning; then this too passed, and the air became delightfully cool; the sun showed again in glory setting in the west, leaving behind him a surpassingly grand pageant of piled-up beds of orange and golden clouds with fiery edges too bright to look upon, and scattered wreaths of rosy red with streaks of amber and pale green sky between, fading into a tender pale primrose, as the stars came out, like silver spangles in the dark blue overhead. The thoughts of all, now joyfully turned towards dinner. Damages were soon repaired, fires lighted, pots put on to boil, peacocks began to cry in the jungles, and partridges to call to each other in the fields, every bird and insect fell to making a joyful noise, for the storm was over and gone. I sat down at my tent-door to enjoy a pipe, with the feeling of comfort which follows a relief from violence, when Jemadar Ramdeen Tewary stepped up to me with a very grave face, and saluting, said, " Sahib, the cholera is in our camp ! "

A sad night followed, wrestling against a worse foe than the tempest. First one poor fellow and then another was stricken by the dire disease, and before morning two lay dead. We did all that could be done for them, applying mustard poultices and hot fomentations, and giving doses of opium and ginger. Having no doctor with us, I felt keenly the responsibility, as all came to me for advice and assistance. But no human aid was of any avail against the terrible disease.

Early the next morning as I was taking a few moments' rest after the troubled night, I was roused by a deputation from my men. I had intended halting during the day where we were, to burn or bury the dead, but the men had been frightened by the events of the previous night, and insisted that the cholera demon had ridden into our camp on the wings of the storm, and unless we moved our camp forthwith we were all dead men.

Putting aside the question of the demon (although Ramentour Panday averred that he had himself seen the evil one ride into our camp on a white pony, scattering ashes, just when the tent was blown down)—putting aside this difficult question, I made no objection to an immediate start, as we should thus no doubt run less risk of further infection. By midday all was ready, and we moved on, a crestfallen company, bearing our dead with us.

We halted for the night in a grove of trees in the vicinity of a large village. I strictly forbade any communication with the villagers for twenty-four hours, until we saw if any fresh cases would occur. Here the bodies of our dead comrades were duly burnt, and their obsequies performed by men of their own caste, I, of course, not interfering in any way with their religious ceremonies.

As no further sickness showed itself, I ventured to accept an invitation to dinner, sent me in due form by the Thannadar of the village. I was at first doubtful what rank of life was indicated by the word " Thannadar," and whether it would be consistent with my dignity to accept his invitation; but curiosity, and the wish to add to my stock of information in regard to native life and manners, prevailed, and I went.

My host's name was Muhammed Syud Khan, of Bareilly, in Rohilcund. He received me at the gate of his dwelling, and conducted me inside with many demonstrations of polite welcome, to which I responded as far as my limited acquaintance with the forms of Eastern etiquette would permit.

He then led me by the hand to a raised dais at the further end of a long low room, whereon were spread a rich carpet and some cushions. Here I was seated, and supplied with a "gurgurie" or water pipe, while a small tray of sweetmeats was handed round.

As we waited for dinner, my host, by way of showing his importance, his zeal, or his ability, busied himself with hearing and deciding several small cases of larceny and assault. Then a report was made to him about a woman who had fallen down a well, and it seemed doubtful whether it was an accident or a case of suicide. I listened attentively, but being ignorant of the civil administration of the country I preserved a judicious silence, and smoked my "hubble-bubble" with all possible gravity.

Presently the dinner was served, and as it came in on a succession of small plates, each borne by a separate servitor, the operation was imposingly lengthy. There were pullaos, curries of various sorts, fresh chutney, kabobs, fruit, and half a score of other dishes—all very nice. I was much disappointed that my host requested me with all politeness to eat, but did not himself sit down to eat with me. He smiled, bowed, expressed himself honoured by my desire, but would, however, content himself with the pleasure of attending to my wants.

I had been warned that it would be well to take with me my customary beverage, and had accordingly gone provided with a bottle of beer and my large pewter mug. All my proceedings had been closely observed by a crowd of retainers, who remained at the lower end of the apartment during the meal, and the interest culminated when I quaffed a deep draught from my glittering tankard, and suppressed murmurs of "Wagh! wagh!" ran through the room. The only strong drinks known by the lower orders are our English spirits and a coarse strong spirit which they distil from rice, and I doubt not but that they imagined I had poured down my throat a quart of raw alcohol, hence the murmurs of admiration at the strength of the "foreign devil's" head!

After dinner was over, the "Tehsildar" or Government revenue collector, and the "Moonsiff" or Small Cause Court judge, dropped in, and were introduced to me in due form. The conversation turned chiefly on the strange manners and customs of the English. I was asked, "Do the English eat kite's flesh, or camels, or monkeys?" and "Do the gentlemen of the Queen's household ride sideways on their horses?"

I explained that our little island did not possess kites, camels, or monkeys, but with regard to the equitation of Her Majesty's household I failed to convince them.

"Why," said the Moonsiff, who was evidently regarded as a great authority on all matters of etiquette, "is it not true that the Queen herself rides sideways?"

I admitted that this was so.

"Then," said he, conclusively, "of course the Emirs must do so also; to do otherwise would be indeed indelicate."

After a time a couple of nautch girls were ushered in and commenced dancing and singing before us, and their monotonous current of song flowed on interminably, until in very weariness I took leave of my host, and giving a small present to the dancers, I sought the quiet seclusion of my tent.

It is a common thing among these people for a nautch to go on for twelve or fourteen hours at a stretch—one girl relieving another. The spectators sit, or rather squat, round, placidly chewing betel-nut and smoking for hours together, with apparently endless satisfaction, although to European taste both the singing and dancing of these girls is not only uninteresting but even disgusting.

I could not help thinking, as I took leave of my polite host and his smiling companions, how different would have been my reception among them a few months back, during the Mutiny, when, as I afterwards learnt, a poor English fugitive had been hacked to pieces close to this very village, and his naked and mutilated body dragged through the streets. Now we bowed and smiled at each other, I with my knife and pistol under my garments, and my orderly, Ram Gholam, close by with his sword; for, as he had said on setting out, "One can never be too careful in dealing with Mussulmans." It was this mutual distrust and suspicion of the various races in India which enabled us to conquer in the Mutiny. Had all combined against us, the English rule must have been annihilated.

The native opinion of Englishmen has been thus summarized. They regard us as an unclean people who eat cow and pig, and whose common beverages are intoxicants; as a species of curious devil, gifted with much brute courage and some human perceptions of an elementary nature, such as the love of justice, the power of making money, and the like—creatures not altogether evil but most unaccountable, whose presence in India must be endured as an ordinance of Providence or a scourge of Fate.

I was awakened early on the morning after the dinner with the Thannadar by the preparations for our last day's march into Hamirpur. There was the familiar sound of the men striking tents, and the strange grumbling gurgle of the camels protesting against their loads.

The camel is, I think, of all domestic animals the most offensive. It is ugly to look upon, it is full of strange fierce noises, its odour is fœtid, and it has, moreover, a fiendish trick of spitting in the face of any person objectionable to it. As a beast of burden it is only valuable on dry and sandy ground, for if driven loaded on wet or slippery places, its great cushioned feet fly sprawling from under it, and it lies prostrate and helpless.

I rose reluctantly and dressed. The faint morning light scarcely showed in the glare of the camp-fires, round which stood the men, belted and buttoned for the march. I swallowed a hasty cup of tea, the bugle sounded, and by evening we were settled into our new quarters at Hamirpur.

I found myself the occupant of one-seventh part of a large tumble-down bungalow, the other tenants being officers of a detachment of Her Majesty's 48th Regiment and of the half-battery of artillery, which, with my men, made up the garrison of the place.

My new comrades soon introduced me to the pleasures of the station, foremost among which was bathing in the river

Betwa. We rode off on our ponies, five white-faced men among a crowd of dusky fellow-creatures, who scowled or salaamed according to their mood as we passed through the crowded bazaar, where the merchants spread their wares—cloth and grain, and heaps of golden green melons. I looked with interest at one Alexander (Ram Jan) the coppersmith, who with his apprentices was clinking away vigorously, hammering into shape an image of the great goddess Diana (Kali). A little further on, a man, plentifully sprinkled over with white ashes, sat on the ground in the midst of an array of brass pots, squatting before a pot-bellied image of "Maha Dev," the great god, clanging away with two cymbals in an ecstasy of devotion.

We plunged into the cool green river as the sun threw its level setting beams into our eyes. What a delight it was, like a shoal of young porpoises, to wallow in the clear water, diving, floating, lying on our backs, looking up into the far-off blue sky, with here and there a fleecy speck of floating cloud—then a long breath and down, down, into pellucid river depths, to open your eyes and look around, like Schiller's diver! The most noticeable subaqueous feature that I was able to discern was my own legs looming large and white in the dark-green beneathness. Ah! what was that? A dark mass twines around my leg. Horror! I strike up to the surface with quick convulsive strokes, mindful of alligators, to find nothing worse than a yard or two of river weed round my ankle. Then, dressing quietly, we walked our ponies home, calling by the way at the canteen to take a glass of beer and drink to the health of our good queen Vic., who provided so well for her soldiers in the far East.

This season of rest and recuperation at Hamirpur lasted for only one month, by the end of which time I was again under marching orders in pursuit of one Bajawul Singh, a rebel leader.

My detachment numbered fifty tried soldiers, and in addition to these, Captain S——, who commanded as senior officer, had with him about two hundred of a raw police levy. S—— was a very Scotch man, and a good fellow into the bargain. He had served for ten years but was still Lieutenant, being only Captain by courtesy.

Our first march was to Bewar, a dreary place, where the heat was so intense that I felt quite glad we had no thermometer wherewith to measure our discomfort.

We next halted at Raat, and here I was occupied in resting after the march, when S—— burst into my tent, exclaiming, "They have come!"

"Who have come?" I replied, testily, for flesh is weak, and I was hungry and tired.

"Why, Bajawul Singh and all his men, about a thousand strong. They have been driven by our troops from the other side, and are now within fifteen miles of us. What is more, we must attack them to-night, before they learn the smallness of our force."

We started in pursuit once more, but the fifteen miles proved misleading information. We marched all night and halted in the early morning near a village, where we hoped to gain more exact tidings of the enemy's whereabouts.

Presently a scout came in to report that Bajawul Singh had actually been close by, but that on hearing of our proximity he had hastily decamped.

The manner in which S—— paid his scouts struck me as original and characteristic. If any man brought in a really valuable and reliable piece of intelligence, a large bag of rupees was placed before him, into which he was allowed to thrust one hand and take for his reward as many rupees as he could clutch, literally a handful of silver. It was amusing to watch the diverse expressions of countenance with which the men approached the bag. Some pounced upon it greedily; others came up with an off-hand don't-care manner; and others again would seem bashful and shy at this novel manner of payment.

On the night of the 13th of June a note came from the officer commanding a detachment of Madras troops at Joorum, twenty miles off, saying that the enemy were close by, at a place called Bagora.

"Weel," said S——, relapsing into broad Scotch in his excitement, "A'm no a mon o' mony worrds, but A think we've just trapped these tods the noo!"

I was extremely glad that there seemed some chance of a successful termination to our hitherto fruitless expedition; but my ardour was somewhat cooled on finding that we must start instanter, it being then 8 o'clock P.M., and the rain falling in torrents.

"Never say die, my lad," said S——. "Three things in India kill a man, a hot sun, a hot supper, and a love trouble. We have none of these to contend with, so let's be off!"

Down went the tents, and down came the rain. In half an hour's time we were wet to the skin, plodding on through the mud and the darkness, but more than ever determined to put an end to the author of our woes—the iniquitous Bajawul Singh.

I rode my pony, as he was clever at avoiding the cracks and holes which made this part of the country dangerous in the dark. We marched on wearily till 2 o'clock in the morning, when the men became so discontented that S—— began seriously to think of halting and letting them camp.

Accordingly, we plied arms, while a horseman was sent to Joorum asking the officer commanding there for news. We were all glad of a rest, and I curled myself up in my cloak, under a tree, and was soon sound asleep.

"Sahib, Sahib, the Captain Sahib sends his salaam, and he is going to move on." Thus spoke my saice, shaking me by the arm, and I arose wet and aching. The grey dawn was streaking the sky as we prepared to start after our two hours' rest.

"Here," said S——, handing me an open letter, "was I not right to hurry up?"

The letter was from Joorum, and stated that not only were the rebels close by, but that they were making themselves comfortable, building huts, and cooking their food. This it was clear could not be allowed. What! must we go wet and supperless while the accursed Bajawul Singh had a hot meal and a dry pillow?

As we moved on the rain ceased, and S—— pointed out to me the hill at Bagora where the enemy were encamped, and, sure enough, two or three small columns of blue smoke were rising straight up in the still morning air, showing that our foes were even then preparing that breakfast of the enjoyment of which we hoped to deprive them. We reached Joorum at seven in the morning, and found there a company of the Madras Rifles and a detachment of Madras Cavalry.

A council of war was held, and our course of action speedily determined. Then, a swallowing of scalding cups of tea, accompanied by some knobs of hard biscuit, and with a hasty buckling on of revolvers we were off again.

I led the advance with my men, having the guide fastened to to me by a rope. The cavalry were to make a detour right and left to take the enemy in flank.

Our guide seemed cool and composed enough in his post of danger, for the leading man of a column is pretty sure to be knocked over by the first volley. He walked quietly in front of me, scrutinizing the path and kicking the stones as he went. Presently, as we entered a thick overhanging jungle, he stopped, and pointed out the fresh footprint of a man who, he said, must have just gone in front of us, running.

Running meant bearing tidings of our coming, so there was evidently no time to lose, and we too pushed on at the double, and in a few moments firing began on both sides, we advancing as we fired, and the enemy retiring as fast as possible.

On we went, running and panting, up precipitous rocky paths, through the beds of watercourses, scratched and torn by the thorns of cane and bamboo, bleeding and bruised from heavy falls ; but with all our haste we found on reaching their main position nothing but their deserted fires, not even their dinners had been left behind !

We had killed two of their rear-guard and, happily, lost none of our men.

We returned to Joorum in the afternoon. The Madrasees, both officers and men, were much exhausted ; but S—— and I, with our Bengal party, prided ourselves on showing no fatigue, although I may confess that I felt well-nigh extenuated, and would have given all my worldly goods for a bottle of beer.

There was, I need hardly say, no beer in that thirsty land. All supplies were finished, and at the rate at which we moved about there seemed small chance of replenishing our stock of luxuries, for we seemed daily to get further and further from civilization.

We did not abandon our pursuit of the rebels, but, co-operating with the Divisional Police at Alipura, dispersed the band. The Police Commandant, with a party of his men, succeeded in cutting off from the rest of his companions a handsomely mounted and armed horseman, who, finding himself isolated, leaped his horse into a clump of brushwood on some broken ground difficult of access, and holding his long silver-mounted matchlock in one hand so as to guard his left side, and with his sword in his right, he struck an attitude, and called after his flying comrades, "What, brothers! will you desert me? Come back! come back! and we will make these dogs of Feringhis eat dirt!" He called in vain, poor fellow, and as he could not well be taken, he had to be shot as he stood. This man was a brother of Bajawul Singh, and his arms, sword, matchlock, and dagger were very handsomely ornamented.

His death completed the discomfiture of the band, some of whom joined the following of a higher class of leader, one Desput Singh, a very popular outlaw, a sort of Robin Hood among these people. Desput was descended from the great Raja, Chutter Saal (founder of the Bundlecund dynasty), and had quarrelled with the British Government, before the Mutiny broke out, on some question of his own independence, claiming the power of life and death over his people. He confined his depredations to the rich, befriending the poor, robbing only rich usurers, tax collectors, and unpopular Rajas; so that he had the sympathy and protection of all the country folk, and was altogether a more formidable antagonist than Bajawul Singh, who was only a vulgar freebooter.

I was now sent with my men to Jeitpur, where there was a Government Treasury, in charge of which I found a Bengal civilian, who was much relieved by the advent of military protection. He had been living for some time past in a highly-fortified condition, prepared, if necessary, to stand a siege. He inhabited the Treasury, and was surrounded day and night by a cordon of matchlock-men whom he entertained at his own expense. He habitually carried a short thick cudgel attached to his wrist by a cord, so that when he came to shake hands with me he had to disengage himself, with much difficulty and labour, from his stick.

While we were at Jeitpur I had a brush with Desput Singh, who had encamped on a hill not far off, called the Black Mountain. My friend the Assistant Magistrate produced his maps, and we marked out a bee-line to take through the jungle, as by experience I had found all the roads and paths were watched. We kept the attack a profound secret up to the moment of starting, only sending a letter to the officer commanding a Madras regiment at Pipera, on the other side of the hill, to be ready to intercept them in case we drove them down his way.

We made a good march and reached the place at dawn. They fired a volley at us over a rough breastwork of stone, which had been thrown up at the entrance of their camp; but we climbed this defence, killing or dispersing the defenders. We captured some men and horses and a quantity of provisions in the camp; but their legs were fleeter than ours, and after a few hours of ineffectual pursuit we abandoned the chase, and returned to Jeitpur.

I learnt subsequently that the Madras detachment had never stirred from Pipera, and further, that the rebels had taken the exact road I had indicated in sending information of our attack. Desput's band numbered five hundred strong. I kept for myself one of the horses we had taken; the rest of the booty was sold, and the proceeds divided among the men.

In July I was relieved at Jeitpur by a company of the Shahjehanpur levy, commanded by a Sikh gentleman, holding what was at that time, for a native, the unique position of Captain in our army. His name was Golab Singh, a brother of the Sikh Sirdar, Shere Singh. He was a handsome man, and wore handsome weapons. His sword, he said, had belonged to one of the Ameers of Scinde; it was a beautiful weapon, the blade all engrailed and damascened with gold, and bearing an inscription in the Persian character: the hilt was of silver gilt, and studded with jewels. Making over charge to this gentleman, I set out with my detachment for Calpee, where the regiment was waiting for us to join, before taking up fresh quarters at Shahjehanpur.

On reaching Shahjehanpur we were surprised and gratified by a most enthusiastic reception being accorded to us, as one of the two loyal regiments of the late Bengal army. The band of Her Majesty's 82nd met us and played us into the station, where the men were assigned most comfortable quarters, and the European inhabitants vied with each other in hospitality to the officers of our corps.

I and a brother sub. agreed to chum together, as Government found quarters for the men only, and we united our resources in the purchase of an estate ! Our domain comprised three mud huts and a small tope of mango trees, not too far from the parade-ground. We promptly ejected two large scorpions and a larger black snake, who were the previous tenants ; my chum took possession of one hut, I of another, and the third was shared by our servants.

All was done to our new abodes that broom and whitewash could effect, and it was with feelings of proud satisfaction that we assumed occupancy as proprietors. We were to pay the modest price of our purchase by instalments from our monthly pay.

My friend was wakened early one morning by being dragged unceremoniously out of bed by his head ! Being a man of prompt action, he at once knocked down his native servant who had taken this liberty. Indignation changed to a gentler feeling on seeing erect upon the bed he had left a large cobra with expanded hood, from whose deadly bite he had been saved by his servant's presence of mind.

One of our men—a madman, I think—was confined soon after our arrival at Shahjehanpur, for seditious and mutinous language. He was promptly arrested, having openly incited his comrades to rebel as other regiments had done ; but the Colonel simply directed him to be dismissed the regiment. I was astonished at this leniency ; but our Adjutant informed me that it was thought advisable, as otherwise the scoundrel would have had to be tried by court-martial, and the prestige of the regiment would have suffered.

I worked hard at Hindustani, to qualify for the higher standard examination, and had for my instructor the old regimental moonshee, an excellent old gentleman, full of old-fashioned politeness, and replete with legendary lore. Our lesson would proceed something in this wise—

"Good-morning, Moonshee Jee !"

"Hazrat Salaamet ! It is a very fair morning, God be praised !"

"Pray take a seat. Shall we resume the perusal of the 'Bagh-o-Bahar,' or will you take the 'Gulistan' first?"

"Whichever your Highness desires; but the 'Gulistan' is perhaps best, since it is more difficult."

"Perhaps, Moonshee, you would first relate to me that history of Abraham, which you alluded to the other day, when we discussed the affinities between Christianity and the faith of Islam."

So, after a little hesitation, my respected teacher would proceed to relate the following story:—

"Father Abraham was once going upon a journey. He halted on the banks of a river to make his ablutions and to pray. As he did so he saw a melon floating down the stream, and being very hungry, he reached forth his hand, took the melon from the water, and ate it. After he had eaten the fruit, he thought in his heart, 'I have committed a great sin; I have eaten this melon without the permission of the owner. This is surely the road to become a thief.' So, to obtain forgiveness for his transgression, Abraham went to the village which was on the other side of the river, and began to wander about crying out, 'Whoever has a melon-garden on the banks of the river, let him inform me.' But all the people thought him mad, and paid no heed to him. At last the Zemindar of the village, who was sitting at his threshing-floor, heard him, and called out, saying, 'What word is this?' So holy Father Abraham related how he had eaten the melon, and how he now hungered for forgiveness. Then the Zemindar answered, 'Of a surety it is my melon that you have eaten, and I shall consent to forgive you, on one condition only. I have a daughter whose eyes and hands and feet are all awry, and whose body also is misshapen. If you will marry her, then I will grant you my forgiveness.' Abraham bowed his head meekly and answered, 'I will accept and marry your daughter.' But when he had married her, he found her very handsome, and with no defect whatever. Her name was Sara."

"O Moonshee Jee!" I exclaimed, "this is much better than reading for examination. Besides, your language is so flowing and elegant, that I feel sure it is extremely beneficial for me to listen to you. You do not mind my writing down your story; and can you think of another such a one?"

The old moonshee stroked his white beard, and looked at me with a twinkle in his eye, as if saying to himself, "You are young—very young." Still, flattery is sweet, and human nature prevailed, for it is pleasant to relate stories to an appreciative audience.

"Sahib," he continued, "we have a proverb that 'Too sweet words leave a bitter taste,' so do not flatter your servant any more; but, if you wish it, I will tell you another small story, on the understanding that your studies shall begin immediately it is finished.

"An old man with his old wife and their son were sitting together in the jungle. They were miserably poor, having, indeed, only one piece of cloth to cover the three of them; and so it came to pass that, at the hour of prayer, one of them put on the cloth and performed devotional exercises, while the other two hid their nakedness by burying themselves up to the waist in the earth. One day his Highness Moses happened to pass by, and seeing the sorry plight of these poor ones, he stopped and asked them why they did not all pray together? Whereupon they all three made petition that he would, in his kindness, grant them two more chuddars, so that all three might pray at once. Having heard their petition, his Highness Moses represented to Allah that, 'To thy slaves in the jungle, two sheets are wanting for purposes of prayer.' Whereupon the order came, 'To those three are given three wishes; what each one wishes, that shall be.' His Highness Moses explained accordingly to these poor ones the orders of the Almighty, and then proceeded on his way. Then said the old wife to her husband, 'If you are disposed to be kind, then I shall wish to become young again'; and she became so, as at the age of fourteen or fifteen years. Now at this moment, the Governor of the province came by, hunting in that direction, and seeing the beautiful young girl, he became enamoured of her, and placing her in a palanquin he carried her off to his dwelling. The husband then said to his son, 'O my son, that wicked woman was glad at being taken away by the Governor; say you, therefore, "O Allah! grant that she may become a pig!" The boy said, and it was so. Then the palanquin-bearers who were carrying the woman said among themselves, 'This is not a woman in the palki. Hark the noise, kush ! kush ! kuh ! It is a devil !' So saying, they dropped the palanquin and ran off. Then the pig, having got out, ran back through the jungle and rejoined the old man and the boy ; and when they saw the pig they became sorry, and made supplication, 'O Allah ! that she may return to her human form again !' So the old woman returned to her original shape. After some days Highness Moses was again passing that way, and he saw from afar off that one old man, wearing a sheet, was praying, and the two others were buried in the ground up to the waist. Having seen this, he made supplication, 'O Allah ! these unfortunates have not then got their sheets ?' The answer came, 'O Moses ! I have fulfilled the desires of these three persons.' Highness Moses then went to them, and having heard their story, he put his hand to his mouth and became thoughtful, and said, 'Allah is great ! Allah is all-powerful ! Who shall tell His praise ? Al humd-ul-Allah ara-bil-ahl-min !' "

The 8th of October was the festival of the Ram Leila, a Hindu festival held in commemoration of the taking of Ceylon (or as they call it Lunka), by a popular hero, since deified, of course, Raja Ram Churn. On this day, an enormous image is set up, a presentment of Ravan, King of Ceylon, the opponent of Ram Churn. This image is treated much as boys at home treat Guy Fawkes, being pelted and abused by the vulgar till sundown, when it is finally blown up with gunpowder, burnt, and made an end of.

It was a wonderful spectacle to watch. The people, thick as ants on a disturbed nest, crowded around the enormous black demon-faced image, which towered above them to the height of twenty feet or more, with straddling legs and threatening arms. Just such a scene as might have been when Elijah saw the worshippers of Baal cutting themselves with knives and crying, " O Baal, hear us ! "

Thanks to my good friend the moonshee's instruction, I successfully passed my examination in the native language, and became eligible for Staff employ. I wished to give up regimental life, which was in no way suited either to my tastes or my ambition, but before seeking any fresh employment I took a year's leave to England "on private affairs."

I parted regretfully from my chum J——, with whom I had shared the mango tope (which we had christened the groves of Blarney), and with whom I had formed a deep and lasting friendship. We exchanged souvenirs, and I left with him my faithful bull-terrier "Grabby," the companion of so many lonely hours.

CHAPTER III

THE INDIAN POLICE SERVICE

1861–62

AT the beginning of 1861, I was back again in Calcutta, after a short but most invigorating interval of furlough in England.

In returning to India I had resolved to avoid, if possible, going back to regimental duty. I had found the close subordination of military life unbearable; it seemed, indeed, like going back to school again, with a commanding officer in place of the master. I had learned what there was to learn of practical infantry soldiering; I knew my drill thoroughly, and could handle either a company or a battalion respectably in the field. I was acquainted with the internal economy of both native and European regiments, knowing how the men were equipped and fed, and how the accounts were kept. I longed now for some fresh field of action, some outlet for energy and individuality, where I might think and act on my own responsibility, and not be merely a cog in a fighting machine.

With this end in view I set to work busily to look up all personal or family friends who might have a word of advice or goodwill for me in this emergency, and after a few weeks of waiting I was successful in obtaining an appointment as Adjutant and second-in-command of one of the newly raised police battalions, with which Government was supplementing the native army. These battalions were, in fact, native regiments, in all but the name; for they performed no police functions, save the keeping of the public peace, and were drilled, armed, and regulated in the same way as regular troops. I was indebted for this appointment to the good offices of a connection of my family, Mr. Arthur Grote, from whom I have always received great kindness.

The second battalion of military police, to which I was appointed, was stationed at Rampur Bauleah, the centre of the great Bengal indigo industry; and here, as in so many other parts of India, the great spasm of the Mutiny had dislocated old commercial arrangements, and caused friction between employers and employed. Hence came disturbances and breaches of the peace, between English indigo-planters with their servants on the one hand, and the native cultivators on the other, which rendered necessary the presence of the military police battalion with which my lot was cast.

The cultivation of the indigo plant had been for many years a source of large profit to the English merchants in Calcutta. Their custom was to buy a comparatively small plot of land, on which they set up a factory and built a house for their agent, trusting to the surrounding peasants for the plant, which was grown in large quantities, in consideration of certain moneys paid in advance by the so-called indigo-planters.

So long as indigo fetched a high price in the market this was a very good arrangement for both parties; but when from various causes the price fell, then the system no longer answered, and the native cultivators refused to sow indigo when they could get better prices for their corn, mustard, or other produce. Hence arose many disputes, ill blood, enmity, and at length open riots, the planters enforcing and the natives refusing the old terms. Things went so far that the planters, in defiance of right or justice, commenced ploughing and sowing the fields where their indigo had been wont to grow; but at this the owners of the land banded themselves together, armed with clubs, to resist the oppression, and my police were sent to keep order in the district.

By the middle of March I had fairly settled to my new duties. The battalion was about six hundred strong—a very mixed lot of men, Hindus, Mussulmans, and Sikhs, of various sorts, but all fairly drilled and disciplined.

Soon after my arrival an event occurred which aroused me to a lively sense of the wildness of the country in which I dwelt. At a short distance from the mat huts which formed the police barracks were a few hovels, occupied by some villagers who carried on a small cultivation in the vicinity. One morning, while the men-folk were away at their work, a leopard quietly entered one of these huts, and seizing by the arm a child six years old, was walking off with it, when its mother and grandmother coming to the rescue, caught the poor little creature by both its legs. Then ensued a horrible scene, the great cat snarling, and the poor human creatures screaming, till some of my police, hearing the noise, came shouting to the spot. On this alarm, the leopard struck the poor mother senseless to the ground with one blow of its paw, and, counting the grand-dam as naught, carried off the child into the jungle. The police pursued, and forced the creature to abandon its prey; but the unfortunate child died the same night.

On the 24th of May our loyal community was unusually full of life and gaiety in honour of the Queen's birthday. The Rajshaye Volunteer Cavalry, nearly all of them indigo-planters, mustered in great force to celebrate the occasion by a full-dress parade, and afterwards, in Anglo-Saxon fashion, to dine with the Commandant at his house, the Burra Koti; this was the largest house in the district, and occupied, of course, by the largest and most influential indigo-planter, who was also the Commandant of the corps.

I was one of the guests at this great celebration, and having neither liking nor capacity for wine equal to the occasion, I heartily wished I could have emulated the example of my own grandfather under similar circumstances. He, when serving in India, used to have beside him a cut-glass sherry decanter filled with golden-brown toast and water, and in this, unremarked and unchallenged, he pledged his friends and yet kept his head.

"India is a fine country," sagely remarked my neighbour at dinner (an Irishman), as the fun waxed furious; "India is just the finest country in the world. But a pack of young fellows come out here, and they eat and they drink, and they drink and they eat, and then they die; and then they write home to their friends that the climate has killed them!"

A ball followed the dinner, at which the gentlemen numbered thirty-eight and the ladies eight, and, great powers! what a tyrannical minority they proved!

It was at Rampur Bauleah that I had the satisfaction of

killing my first tiger, winning my spurs in sport, as it were. I made one in a party of four. We had heard of a tiger skulking round, dangerously near human habitations, and killing a cow at a village some ten miles distant. We set off with six elephants, and for the first day we ineffectually beat the neighbouring jungles, without catching a glimpse of the beast; so we camped for the night in the hut of a friendly villager, and early in the morning we again mounted our behemoths and went forth in slow pursuit.

For some hours we plodded through the dry nullahs and long grass, still unsuccessfully, until I began to feel very tired of this so-called sport. The afternoon sun of the day before had burnt my neck and hands till they felt raw, and the continuous joltings of the elephant had rendered every joint stiff. Suddenly the shout "Bagh! bagh!" (tiger! tiger!) roused me, and put new life into our party. We pushed on as fast as our elephants could go, sending a pad-elephant out to turn the tigress from a field of corn for which she was making. We left our second pad-elephant in the rear, to head the beast back if we should over-run her in the ardour of our pursuit.

I had just turned my elephant in order to beat a patch of jungle on the left when there was a shot, and a fierce ough! ough! from the tigress, showing that she was hit. I pressed on, and coming to an open space in the jungle, I met the beast face to face, as I may say, crossing the open from cover to cover, and bleeding from a wound in the shoulder. I took as cool an aim as I could manage, but it was more by good luck than good guidance that I hit the animal in the head, rolling her over for all the world like a shot hare. She rolled down into a small watercourse, whence we extricated the striped carcass and bore it home triumphantly.

Snakes abounded at Rampur Bauleah, and I had there an opportunity of practically testing the powers of a snake-charmer, which I had hitherto somewhat doubted. One morning, while sitting in the verandah, I heard a sound much resembling the noise made by bagpipes, and presently, as it came nearer, I descried a strange-looking figure coming towards me, playing on a curious double pipe. His hair was long and matted in elf locks, like strips of thick felt, and he carried over his shoulder a long springy bamboo, from either end of which depended a reddish-yellow bag.

"Salaam, Sahib!" he said.

"Who are you, and what do you want?"

"Hazoor! your servant, is a charmer of serpents, and desires to exhibit his skill for your amusement."

This seemed to me a favourable opportunity for testing the pretentions of these persons, and I proposed to the man certain conditions under which he should work, promising him a liberal reward if he were successful in capturing a poisonous snake within a certain distance of my bungalow. After some demur he assented to my proposal, stipulating only that if he failed, he should receive half the promised sum of money.

Accordingly, I first had him stripped naked, and assured myself absolutely that he had no snake concealed about his person. I examined his hair, searched in the folds of his dress, and even looked inside the gourd-pipe. He was then allowed to resume his garments; but I kept a close watch upon him, not allowing him to approach his reddish-yellow bags, which contained baskets, and doubtless also tamed snakes. After this examination he was told to begin his performance, and so, taking his pipe and accompanied by me, he began his peregrinations, playing his doleful wild music the while.

First he searched the house, then the small piece of garden in front thereof, after which he turned towards the cook-house, and my servants' huts which lay a short distance in the rear. Midway between these huts and my bungalow was a small weedy patch of rose-garden, and towards this patch he first directed his steps, making wails and groans issue from his pipe, and keenly peering about as he went; not a corner seeming to escape his eye. Suddenly he left off playing and commenced an exhortation in an unknown tongue, the purport of which might be gathered from the varying tones of his voice, running through a gamut as it were—coaxing, exhorting, commanding, threatening. Then he ceased speaking, and fixing his eyes upon a spot among the rose-bushes, he recommenced playing on his pipe. Slowly, very slowly he drew nearer and nearer, his pipe keeping up a very soft monotonous droning sound, when—whish! with a plunge and a dart he thrust his arm into the grass and drew forth a wriggling cobra!

I gave him his reward; but as I had still a doubt lurking in my mind as to whether he might not have placed his snake where he found it, I tempted him with another reward to catch for me one which had often been seen, and was known to reside behind my bearers' house. Thither we accordingly went, and the same incantations recommenced, when I saw to my astonishment, as he swayed to and fro, playing on his pipe, a snake slowly raise its head from beside a ditch or gutter which ran behind the servants' houses. In an instant he caught it by the neck and jerked it out among the crowd of native onlookers, who fled precipitately on every side as the snake fell in their midst. The snake-charmer then caught the creature, and forcing open its jaws, passed a fold of his turban into its mouth and round the two poison-fangs which lay in the upper part of the mouth, tearing them out with a dexterous jerk. He then spat down the snake's throat and deposited it in his bag. As he did so I noticed that his thumb was bleeding.

"Have you been bitten?" I inquired in some trepidation, as I did not desire a tragic outcome of my curiosity.

"Yes, Sahib," he replied calmly; "the last snake was a vicious one, and it has bitten me. But there is no danger," he added, extracting from the recesses of his mysterious bag a small piece of white stone. This he wetted and applied to the wound, to which it seemed to adhere. He then took a piece of some other curious substance from the bundle, put it to his forehead, and drew an imaginary line with it round the wrist of the injured hand. This completed the treatment, and he apparently suffered no inconvenience or material hurt. I was thus effectually convinced that snake-charming is a real art, and not merely clever conjuring, as I had previously imagined. These so-called snake-stones are well known throughout India; when applied to a snake-bite the stone appears to adhere to the wound, by some sort of capillary attraction, I suppose. It is placed afterwards in milk, where it discharges the poison which has been absorbed into it, and thus becomes cleansed and again fit for use. The milk, it is said, turns colour and becomes corrupt.

I still felt unsettled in my work, and seized the opportunity offered by Government to all officers in the old East India Company's Service, to exchange to a Queen's regiment, hoping thus to be sent to China, where war was then going on, and so eventually to return to England. I therefore volunteered for general service, and after some delay was appointed a Lieutenant in the 104th Regiment, although retaining, for the time being, my police command.

Towards the close of the year some disturbances occurred in the adjacent district of Pubna, and I was sent thither, with a strong detachment of the battalion, to preserve the public peace.

I found Pubna the quietest of small stations, the European society being limited to the magistrate in charge of the district, who was a Bengal civilian of sporting proclivities, and the surgeon. The latter gentleman was distinguished by his bulk. He weighed twenty stone, and was one of the largest and most good-natured men I have ever met. No horse could carry him, no carriage contain him, so he daily mounted by a ladder a very stout and docile elephant, and thus made his professional rounds.

The country round offered rare opportunity for sport, and was good both for shooting and for riding. The neighbouring indigo-planters were, as a rule, good shots and good pig-stickers, and most hospitably inclined into the bargain.

Shortly after my arrival, the magistrate and I arranged to go together to Dilura, an indigo factory about twenty miles distant, where the manager, Mr. P——, was the best spear in the country side, and his good wife the best hand at pastry. We had also a warrant out against an outrageous female tiger, whose tyrannous and carnivorous behaviour had caused the villagers in those parts to present a petition of complaint, requesting the Court to make an order!

We were hospitably received by Mr. and Mrs. P——, and early on the following morning we rode off, a party of four, in search of pig, our host quoting gaily the distich—

> From tusk of boar, though hurt be sore,
> There is not much to fear;
> But horn of hart, though light the smart,
> Will bring thee to thy bier.

We were provided with three horses apiece, to allow for hard running or accident. Each man carried a spear heavily weighted with lead at the butt-end, the point being shaped like a laurel leaf. Our servants followed, leading the spare horses and carrying fresh spears, and with them came a crowd of beaters armed with sticks and drums.

We beat through the fields and coverts for some two hours, without finding anything save quail, which rose, here a bird and there a bird, as our horses pushed breast-high through the crops. Suddenly, as we were walking our nags through a tall field of mustard, our host stopped and raised his hand in warning. We joined him quickly, and saw on the ground a hemispherical heap of dry grass and mashed stalks, with just a sprig of fresh green on the top.

" The old gentleman is at home," said P——; " see his card outside," pointing to the green stalks outside the lair; and with that he plunged his spear into the heap. Ough! Humph! Humph! Out rushed a tumultuous boar, straight between my horse's legs. My nag gave a tremendous leap into the air; but I stuck to him, and in another moment we were off in pursuit as fast as our horses could go, racing for first spear. On we went, through high grass, over rough ground full of holes, trusting to our horses' sureness of foot. Down, down plunged the boar into a deep ravine. With a rush down and a scramble up, we followed him, but the veteran, turning with admirable tactics, charged us on the opposite side as we came up, with such vigour that the first horseman rolled back into the nullah. The second spearman quickly followed, delivering his thrust with so much energy that he could not withdraw the spear, but had to leave it quivering in the boar's body. My turn came next; but as I thrust at him, the beast jumped and caught my foot in his mouth, biting the toe of the boot completely through, but fortunately inflicting no further injury.

The boar was now hard hit and could run no farther; so, choosing a piece of broken rocky ground, he stood there at bay in the midst of a clump of bushes. Every bristle stood erect; his small eyes gleamed with fury, and as he champed his teeth the foam flew on to his dark hide, and, mingling with his blood, gave him a most formidable appearance.

Vainly we tried to get at him. The ground was so bad, and his position so well chosen, that not one of the horses would face the savage rush with which he met any attempt at approach.

At length we rode at him together, one from each side, and thus gave him the final stroke. He died bravely, fighting to the last. A large boar, thirty-four inches and a half high at the shoulder, with a fine pair of keen curved white tusks, and so heavy that it took four men to lift him. Truly a most game and courageous animal, and fully bearing out Shakspeare's description in "Venus and Adonis"—

> "On his bow-back he hath a battle set
> Of bristly pikes, that ever threat his foes;
> His eyes like glow-worms shine when he doth fret;
> His snout digs sepulchres where'er he goes;
> Being moved, he strikes whate'er is in his way,
> And whom he strikes his cruel tushes slay.
> His brawny sides, with hairy bristles armed,
> Are better proof than thy spear's point can enter;
> His short thick neck cannot be easily harmed;
> Being ireful, on the lion he would venture.
> The thorny bramble and embracing bushes,
> As fearful of him part; through whom he rushes."

We had more good sport, killing a couple of pigs; neither of them, however, made so gallant a stand as the first one, until at last a most unfortunate incident put an end to the day's sport.

While we were in pursuit of a fine boar, a native who was at work in a field hard by, saw the hunt approaching, and ran to hide himself in the ditch which bordered his field. As ill luck would have it, the angry hunted beast entered this very ditch in his flight, and coming upon the crouching man, fell upon him, and with repeated tusk-strokes literally cut the poor fellow to ribands before we could come up to his assistance. We did all we could; but one of the main arteries must have been severed, for he bled to death in a very short time.

This sad accident cast a gloom over our party, and we returned to the house much downcast.

On my return to Pubna, I received official notice that the military police was to be disbanded, and a civil police established on an entirely new footing. I had to decide whether to return to regimental life or to become a real policeman, and weighed the matter carefully in my own mind.

Should I "become a dog for the bone's sake," as the old proverb has it? But the bone was a good bone, and several of my friends had already thrown in their lot with the new dispensation, so I decided to do the same.

I returned with my detachment to Rampur Bauleah in April, sailing down the Ganges in native boats, and soon had my hands full of work in making up all the books and regimental accounts, preparatory to the disbandment of the corps.

A terrible tornado visited the district before I left, culminating, or rather centred, at Gadagari, some eighteen miles from the station of Rampur Bauleah. Three villages were entirely destroyed, and over three hundred human beings besides, killed, and heavy losses in flocks and herds.

I had to go out to the relief of the poor folk, and the sight was indeed awe-inspiring. A regular pathway had been clean swept by the storm, and upon this, for at least five miles, not a stick was left standing—every house, every tree razed to the ground, as if a raging fire had swept along. Fish had been taken up by the fury of the wind out of a small lake in the vicinity, and strewn broadcast over the fields, accompanied by a shower of mud. Only about twenty per cent. of the inhabitants along this track of the storm escaped alive. A man's dead body was found jammed in the cleft of a tree eight feet from the ground; others were missing altogether. Only those survived who had had the presence of mind to throw themselves flat on their faces when the storm came. One man told me how he had been forcibly lifted off the ground by the wind, and then as violently dashed down again. I found the air deadly with noxious emanations from the dead carcasses of cattle, and many people were suffering from fever and want of food. The district magistrate did what lay in his power to help, and many of the sick were sent into the Government Hospital at Rampur Bauleah, but the distress notwithstanding was very great.

At the end of April I was appointed District Superintendent of Police, on a salary of five hundred rupees monthly, which was exactly double my regimental pay as Lieutenant. I was directed to proceed without delay, and assume charge of the police in the district of Bhaugulpur. The military police battalion to which I had been attached was ordered to march to Patna, under charge of the Commandant, there to be disbanded. I accordingly took leave of my friends, and of the men I had commanded, and made the best of my way to my new quarters, assuming charge of the Bhaugulpur police early in May.

The first noteworthy circumstance that struck me in the place, was finding the worship observed of an Englishman who had been revered and deified by admiring natives. This was a new and refreshing point of view, after having for the past five years considered my countrymen only as the hunters or the hunted, fighting either to save their own lives or take those of others.

He was long dead, this good Englishman; but in bygone years, when our Government assumed charge of the Bhaugulpur District, he had been the first representative of the East India Company; and so well, so wisely had he exercised his power, that after his death the natives built a shrine to his memory, and worshipped as a god the memory of Cleveland Sahib.

I found the duties of the new police scarcely yet defined, and travelled about the district trying to learn what was doing. I was camping one evening in the vicinity of a village, when I was called upon to try and condemn to death a very hardened criminal.

A respectable-looking native came to me as I sat smoking my evening pipe. His clothing was rent, and dust was upon his head, sure signs of woe.

"Protector of the poor!" he cried, prostrating himself at my feet, "help thy most unworthy and wretched slave! An unblest and evil-minded alligator has this day devoured my little daughter. She went down to the river to fill her earthen jar with water, and the evil one dragged her down and has devoured her. Alas! she had on her gold bangles. Great is my misfortune!"

Other villagers came up and confirmed the man's story. This alligator, it appeared, had become the terror of the neighbourhood, haunting the bathing-places, and seizing on any living thing that came within reach of his ugly jaws. Like the tiger, alligators habitually avoid human beings, but once they taste blood, they rival the striped man-eater in cunning and ferocity.

I had often before seen the mud banks of the Ganges bordered, as it were, with the sprawling handprints of the great saurians; and once during very hot weather I had sighted, and carefully concealed myself from, a great alligator wandering across country, probably in search of a pool, his own having dried up. I watched him out of sight, waddling slowly, with ungainly lurching gait, crashing through the dry reeds and grass. From my lurking-place I could have dropped a stone on him as he passed, his small, dull, malignant eye gleaming from under his mud-caked hide; but I had never hitherto been the death of an alligator, and the present opportunity was a good one. So, dismissing the villagers, I sat myself down to excogitate a plan for the circumvention of the foe.

Boyish books of adventure recurred to me, in which one favourite hero, I remembered, had stunned his victim by a discharge from a powerful galvanic battery; another had laid an artful mine of gun-cotton; while a third had concealed a charge of powder in a floating bait. A floating bait! The very thing for this greedy monster. "Hi! Chaprasi! Go and procure for me two very strong fish-hooks."

"Hazoor! this poor place possesses no worker in iron."

I explained, however, that the hooks I must have; so presently a man was brought over from another village two miles distant, who, constructing for himself an impromptu forge, in a grove of mango trees close to my camp, soon hammered out and tempered a couple of rough hooks, strong enough to hold a shark.

Meanwhile, the villagers informed me that there was no further sign of the alligator; probably he was lurking in some hole in the bank, gorged by his dreadful meal on the poor child, a portion of whose garments had been found floating among the river weeds.

At daybreak the next morning all were astir, and curiosity was rife among the dusky crowd who followed me to the water's edge. Silently they followed, for an enemy was being approached; fearfully they went, for rumour had it that this alligator was no alligator, but a devil. Here, however, was a real live Sahib, and all the village knew that the Sahibs were white devils of a most powerful description.

The river rolled down its yellow turbid flood, tinged by the faintly golden light of the early day. A slight morning breeze ruffled the tops of the feathery palms, while the crowd of villagers, each close-wrapped in his white sheet against the chill of the morning air, seemed like a company of spectres flitting with naked noiseless tread over the sandy ground.

I had devoted a fat duck to the honourable post of decoy-bait, and the bird quacked in an uneasy, protesting manner as we went along. Under each wing I had firmly attached a strong hook, to which was fastened a stout cord buoyed at intervals by fishermen's net floats.

Having reached a high bank under which the alligator was said to lurk, I cautiously approached the water's edge and loosed the struggling bird, which sailed away down the current, flapping and quacking just over the enemy's den.

For a few moments we watched it in breathless expectation; then two long smooth waves in the dark current parted before a snouted head; there was a splash and a swirl in the pool, and the duck had disappeared.

The line now began to run out at a rate that kept all hands alert. What a hubbub and a shrieking! What yells and execrations! The parents of the poor child, who had been seated on the ground at a short distance wailing and muttering curses on the alligator, caught the excitement and joined actively with the rest. The rope had been made fast to the stump of a tree, and all hands tugged at it, paying out the slack and pulling in whenever the strain of our fairly-hooked fish was eased. Once the beast made for his hole under the bank and tried to sulk, but he was soon routed out from this refuge by repeated pokes of long bamboo poles, and at last I had the satisfaction of seeing the soft yellow white skin over his heart as he wallowed helpless in shallow water. His mighty tail still circled dangerously, lashing the water into foam with tremendous force, until I shot him in the head; immediately a dozen spears were thrust into him, and his hideous, ungainly carcass was hauled to shore in triumph.

I could not restore the poor child to her parents; but I had avenged them on her destroyer, and I think that the recovery of the gold bangles, which were found in the animal's stomach, afforded them considerable consolation.

At Bhaugulpur I frequented the swimming bath most assiduously, and, shortly after my arrival in the station, I there made the acquaintance of the judge, Mr. S.——, somewhat unceremoniously.

The bath was in close contiguity to this gentleman's house, and his custom was to array himself in bathing-drawers in his own bedroom, and then, throwing a dressing-gown over his shoulders, he would walk ponderously (being a heavy weight) to the bath-house, where, instead of entering by the door, he took a nearer way by plunging head foremost through a small window which opened on to his grounds. It was a favourite amusement of his, thus to surprise any unsuspecting acquaintance with a ducking.

I, who had never met this gentleman in my life, was quietly enjoying the cool bath one morning, and floating lazily on the water, when an enormous white body projected itself suddenly through the window on top of me, and proceeded, to my great indignation, to hold me down under water. Being myself of a somewhat irascible temperament, I at once retaliated by punching the offending body with all my might, and we rose to the surface panting, puffing, and glaring wrathfully at each other. I had been mistaken for a friend, and did not appreciate the greeting of amity!

I was inordinately fond of bathing and diving, and from this latter amusement I contracted an abscess in the ear, which for a week gave me the most intolerable pain. I could neither eat nor sleep, and thought I should go distracted, having never before been ill in my life.

Towards the end of May I was ordered to go to Mozuffurpur, and there to organise and introduce the new system of civil police, pending the arrival of the Commandant of my old military battalion, who was busy at Patna disbanding the corps, and for whom I was to act as *locum tenens.* I was glad of the opportunity, feeling that the work to be done would give me fuller knowledge in my own special district, when it should be deemed fit to give me a district of my own.

The new Bengal police system was one of the many reforms introduced by Her Majesty's Government on taking over India from the Honourable John Company.

Under the old system, the magistrate of the district, a Bengal civilian, was the head of the district police. The force usually consisted of a few score of Burkundazes, as they were called, who were stationed at the different Thannahs—each station being in charge of a Thannadar or Police Darogah. The Darogah worked directly under and with the magistrate, reporting crime and sending up cases for trial, or making inquiries as directed. He was responsible to the magistrate only, just as the magistrate himself was responsible to Government, for the good order and well-being of his district.

By the new regulations, the police throughout the whole province of Bengal was now constituted a distinct and separate department, directed by an Inspector-General of Police, who had his central office in Calcutta, with Deputy-Inspectors in charge of divisions, and District Superintendents under them again, over each district.

The Burkundazes of the old police were either pensioned off, or incorporated with the new force; fresh rules and regulations were issued, and, in a word, a great new machine was constructed for the repression of crime. Like other machines, it did not at first work quite smoothly, and perhaps the most fruitful source of dissension (which has since been remedied) was the making district police superintendents independent of the district magistrates.

Most of the new superintendents were, like myself, young military men, entirely without experience in criminal investigation, and not inclined to subordinate themselves voluntarily to the civilian magistrates in charge, for the two Services had from time immemorial been antagonistic and jealous one of the other. As a natural consequence, the magistrates were prejudiced against the system from the commencement, and viewed its officers with disfavour and suspicion.

At Mozuffurpur I made a full investigation of the police

records, and extracted therefrom some curious information. I found that dacoity (that is to say, robbery with violence) was generally brought home to the offender by means of the so-called voluntary confessions of one or more of the band; but the devices to which the police had recourse to procure confession were often extremely ingenious if not particularly humane.

They would fill the nose and ears with cayenne pepper; stop the circulation of the blood with tight ligaments; suspend their victim head downwards in a well; and, in cases of great obstinacy, immerse repeatedly in the water until insensibility (but not death) was produced. These were a few of the feathers from the wing of justice in dealing with criminals. A few minor amenities were observed in dealing with women and children, such as hanging them up by the hair or suspending them by a cord tied to their thumbs.

In the old golden age, when it was usual for a police Darogah to leave a handsome fortune to his heirs, there was no difficulty about money. In a difficult case, where evidence was wanting money would be well spent in suborning a witness or two. "Ha!" the magistrate would say, "the case is deficient in evidence. Remanded for a fortnight." And as the police officers were judged mainly by the success of their criminal inquiries, and a man's promotion depended on his proving his cases, it happened usually that at the end of a fortnight the requisite evidence was forthcoming.

All we, brand-new military superintendents, set to work to bring about a different state of things. Full of zeal and destitute of experience, thinking more of drill and discipline than of detecting and punishing crime, we were very new brooms indeed. The old functionaries of police in the districts assigned to us, disgusted at the wholesale changes, and hating the very names of drill and uniform, for the most part resigned, while the police stations were hastily filled with batches of raw recruits, or by men from the old disbanded military battalions, who were ill fitted for the intricate and complicated investigations of crime among the acute criminals of Bengal.

Great also was the difference between the aspect of a magistrate on the bench, trying a case which had been directed by his own police, and that of the same functionary called upon to decide in one brought forward by the new system of investigation. Sternness and judicial severity in the latter case were apparent in every wrinkle of the magisterial brow, a demeanour fully sufficient to indicate to the witnesses what the Sahib's views might be; consequently, evidence which had in the first instance been given firmly and clearly to the police officer would quaver and shake, waver and be wanting, under the dread glance of the presiding magistrate.

It was astonishing what accuracy of statement was now required from plaintiffs. They must be acquainted fractionally with the weight, size, and shape of each article of their property which had been abstracted, even if weeks, or perhaps months, had elapsed since the theft, otherwise the plaint was dismissed.

I struggled hard to keep both heart and temper in the seemingly hopeless task of putting new wine into old bottles, and was at length rewarded for my efforts by an approving letter from the Inspector-General of Police, and the intimation that I had been appointed permanently as District Superintendent of Hazaribagh. So making over charge of the Mozuffurpur police office to my quondam Commandant, who arrived from Patna early in July, 1862, I set off for my new appointment.

CHAPTER IV

HAZARIBAGH

1862–63

I PERFORMED the journey to Hazaribagh by palki-dâk, travelling by night as well as by day. One morning I woke in my palanquin with the sound of a hammer in my ears. I put my head out to see what it might mean. The dim grey dawn was breaking, barred with streaks of darker cloud, and the rain poured down steadily.

"Ohé! where are we? What is this noise of hammering, O unblessed ones?"

"Your Highness, behold! There in front of us lies Hazaribagh. We have gone bravely the whole night through, and trust that we may be considered worthy of your favour."

This was a hint at "baksheesh," which indeed they deserved, poor fellows.

"Yes, but why do we stop? and what is this hammering noise?"

"We stop, Hazoor, on account of the stream, which the heavy rain has caused to rise above the head of a man; and while we waited for the water to go down, Ram Dhyan, my brother, was repairing a stay in the palki, which has given way during the night's travel."

I sent a man across the stream, swimming, to carry a letter to Major B——, my new chief, the Deputy Commissioner of Hazaribagh; for this was a non-regulation district, a happy Eden where the Bengal civilian had not as yet intruded, and where an army officer could still be a magistrate and head of a district.

I was very hungry, and ached much from the jolting of a night's travel. "Bothersome little torrent!" thought I, as I went down to the water's edge, fourteen feet deep, and running like a mill-sluice. Nothing for it but patience, commingled with hunger, for I had eaten nothing for sixteen hours.

The day wore on, and at length my eyes were gladdened by the sight of my messenger returning. Soon he reached the opposite bank, and arranging carefully a bundle on his head, proceeded to swim across. Precious bundle! What might it not contain? My anxiety was intense as I watched his efforts. Ah! the stream is too strong—he will be swept down. The bundle must be wetted or lost! Confound the fellow! he is not worth his ears full of water. No; he recovers himself, and all is well. Gravely he approaches me, dripping from his swim.

"The Major Sahib sends his salaam, and this letter, and this bundle."

What! a pie! O pie, accompanied as thou wast by two bottles of pale ale, even at this distance of time, I regard thee as a green spot in memory's waste!

Major B——'s note was most kind. He bade me welcome, and offered me a share of his house and table. Strange, this *esprit de corps!* Here, as from one soldier to another, I had a kindly and hospitable reception, and, dweller in tents and dâk-bungalows as I had been, I felt my heart warm as if coming at last to a home.

My pleasant anticipations were fully realised. I found in Major B——, not only a chief, anxious for the good of all those under him, but also a warm personal friend, who did all in his power, both to make me comfortable, and to put me in full possession of my work and responsibilities.

I was most anxious to learn all that I could of the place and people among whom my lot was cast, and to this end, although the rainy season was then at its height, I started off, as soon as I could get together the necessary camp equipage, to visit every police station in the district.

After inspecting and making myself known to my police, I returned to the station. Her Majesty's 77th Regiment was then quartered at Hazaribagh, and the officers of the regiment courteously made me an honorary member of their mess, a convenience which I much appreciated.

These evenings at the mess formed a welcome interlude after my day's work; for I had plenty to do in introducing and organising the new police. New forms, new returns, new methods of account-keeping, had to be introduced, and required endless explanation and supervision; the old Burkundazes had to be dismissed and new men enlisted and drilled, clothed and disciplined; whilst I had, in addition, to acquire an accurate knowledge of the written Persian character, in which all the reports were made, besides endeavouring to pick up the still more intricate dialects of the Kols and Sonthal tribes who inhabited the Hazaribagh district in great numbers.

When the pleasant cold weather came, I arranged with the Deputy Commissioner to make a joint tour of inspection in the district, and we started in December, with full camp equipage.

Tents in India are many in form and size, and in purchasing one for myself I was much exercised to decide among their various merits. There was the great double-poled tent, used by our soldiers during the Mutiny, cool and spacious inside, but heavy and cumbrous to carry; the simple pall tent, such as the friendly planter at Jounpúr had given me; the single-poled tent, and the béchoba, or tent without a pole; and finally, there was the "Swiss cottage" tent, on which I decided, as it had the advantage of being divisible into two compartments, with, in addition, a small bathing-room, and large outer flaps which served as shelter for my servants. I hired also a professional tent-pitcher, or kilassee, and purchased various articles of camp furniture of the *multum in parvo* order.

We travelled by easy stages, enjoying the cool mornings and the immunity from office work. Our way lay through level cultivated fields, interspersed with an occasional thicket of bamboo, and as we rode along, followed by my police sowars, we chatted pleasantly of old England, and compared our experiences during the late Mutiny.

"One picture remains on my memory," said Major B——, "a scene during the Sonthal Insurrection in these parts in 1856. We had had a sharp bout with the rebels, and had put them to rout. I had got separated somehow from my party, and reined in my horse at the edge of a wood to look round for my men. Before me lay a field of trampled corn, the ripe ears stained here and there with blood, or flattened under the weight of a dead body.

"I heard a rustle on my right, where some of the corn was still standing, and saw a young man, a fugitive Sonthal. He was dark, almost black in colour, nearly naked, with wild, matted elf-locks hanging over his face. With one hand he cautiously pushed aside the corn; in the other he grasped his bow and arrows. He was followed by a woman bearing a child in her arms, and an old man; these were probably his wife, son, and father. I watched them silently, hoping they might make good their escape, when a rushing sound announced the arrival of a horseman. The fugitives hastily hid themselves as he appeared, a native soldier, in gay uniform, cantering through the field, the scarlet pennon on his lance all draggled and dark with blood. For a moment I thought he would go by without seeing them. But no; some movement caught his eye, and with a yell he checked his horse. Wheeling round, still at a hard gallop, he passed his spear through the body of the younger Sonthal. With a graceful turn of his wrist he withdrew the lance, and the man fell dead; but as he cantered heedlessly off, a sudden fury seized the old father, who grasped the dead man's bow, and sent a shaft from it straight between the horseman's shoulders, rolling him also over on the ground. The whole thing was over in less time than it takes to tell it; but it impressed me greatly, and even now I seem to see it, as I stood, a silent and unwilling spectator, at the edge of the wood."

We halted a couple of days at Chatra, where in 1858 the mutineers were worsted after a very stiff fight with Rattray's Sikhs. The Mahunt of Chatra is the head of the Sikh religion in this part of the country, whither the faith of Guru Nanak (which prevails throughout the Punjaub) has travelled and found votaries and an abiding place. Here is strictly observed the ritual of the sacred book, the "Grunth." The high-priest must not marry, but adopts a boy as a "cheyla" or spiritual son, who inherits his sacred office and his worldly wealth. The holy man, with whom we had a ceremonious interview, was a young fellow of not more than nineteen years of age, whose spiritual father had died about two years previously.

The district offered fine opportunities for sport. There were plenty of partridges, hares, and such-like small game, while deer of all sorts and big black bears weıe also common. On one occasion I killed a large hyæna, which surprised me by the enormous size and power of its teeth and jaws, breaking with one bite the stock of a gun. Wolves, too, were very plentiful and destructive, in spite of a liberal head-money paid by Government, and they committed cruel outrages on the inhabitants. They were more cunning and ferocious than tigers, and many painful incidents were recorded against them. One that was reported to me at Burhee by my police, struck me as extraordinarıly shocking.

A poor woman was walking home with her two little children, having taken her husband's dinner to him in a field where he was working. One child she held in her arms, while the other toddled along holding her dress. A great wolf sprang from the thicket, seized the child by her side, and carried it off into the jungle. The distracted mother laid her infant on the grass, and pursued the robber with shrieks and stones, till a cry behind made her turn—a second wolf was bearing off the babe.

Another anecdote I recorded which shows the astonishing power of combined attack often displayed by these dangerous beasts. Two men were returning home by a jungle path after attending a neighbouring market. One of them stopped for a moment to adjust his load, and on again proceeding found his way barred by a large wolf, which, however, did not seem inclined to attack him. He shouted to his companion, and stooped to pick up stones to frighten away the animal. As he did so, a second wolf sprang on him from behind; and had not his friend, who fortunately was armed with a spear, come up quickly on hearing his cries, he must have been killed. Between them they killed one of the wolves, and the other made off.

This camp life made me acquainted with all manner of expedients for procuring food. One day we camped on the bank of a small stream, and our men got us a dish of capital fish, by damming up the outlet to a pool and throwing therein the leaves and bark of some tree, which had the effect of stupefying the fish. They floated in great numbers on the surface of the pool, and were in no way injurious when we came to eat them. While the men were thus employed, I amused myself in feeding an ant-lion, a curious small creature with a formidable name, but with a body not larger than a flea. There were scores of them in the sand, their dwelling-places indicated by small funnel-shaped depressions, at the apex of which the insect lay in ambush for any ant or other small game which might chance to pass by. If any such unwary one strayed near the treacherous margin of these declivities, it was at once assaulted by a tiny shower of sand from the unseen foe; and should this attack cause it to lose its foothold and slip downward, there was no hope of escape. The miniature lion flirted forth volley after volley of bewildering sand-grains, till he could seize his victim and drag him into his den. After an interval the sapless carcass, sucked dry, would be ejected with a flip from the hole, and the small ogre would readjust his trap for the next comer.

We visited the great pilgrim road which lay to the extreme north of the district, along which passed crowds of devotees on their way to the holy place Deoghur, where an annual gathering takes place in February. A conducting and directing priest headed each company of pilgrims, who shouted as they passed us "Bhúm! Bhúm Byjnath!"

This camp life was further made pleasant to me by a visit from my brother, who came from England to see me. Major B—— had returned to head-quarters, and my brother and I continued our peregrinations together. He was much interested in my strange surroundings, and often strolled off alone to see the country and its people, whilst I was occupied with other matters. One evening, towards sunset, I had finished my work and went out to look for him. I had with me my single-barrelled rifle, on the chance of seeing any deer, and sauntered along hoping to meet him on his way back to dinner. About half a mile from camp I heard a rustling among some "bair" bushes on my left; thinking that probably it was a cow from the village, I turned and peered through the bushes. There I saw a fine black bear, making his supper on the bair-berries which grew plentifully there, and of which these animals are inordinately fond.

I at once cocked my rifle, and without reflecting on the probable failure of a single ball, I aimed through the leaves at his shoulder and rashly fired. With a grunt and a plunge out he came, tearing through the bushes, rearing on his hind legs, and angrily looking round for his assailant. I had a short glimpse of his white teeth and cavernous red mouth, and then, remembering that I had an empty gun and no knife with me, I turned and fled. I had no idea before that I could run so fast; but the fierce and vengeful gumph and growl at my heels was a great incentive to speed. A man with two legs is, however, no match for a bear with four; and I should have probably felt the ardour of Bruin's hug, had not my headlong flight brought me to a deep and precipitous cliff, down which I tumbled, and lay for a while half-stunned by the fall, but rejoicing at my deliverance: for the bear, whether it was that he was hard hit and could not follow me, or that I vanished from sight with a suddenness that he could not comprehend, certain it was that he retired to his jungle, and I reached camp with fortunately no broken bones. We went out after him better armed the day following, but although we found a slight track of blood for a short distance, it soon became lost in the thick underwood.

Early in February we pitched our camp in a large mango grove near the village of Kusmar, where was a shrine of the blood-loving goddess Kali. Here had lately been enacted a curious tragedy.

Five of the villagers of Kusmar had an enemy, a common foe, resident in a neighbouring village, and they agreed together to put an end to him. So one day an opportunity presented itself, and they caught their man in the jungle; and after taking council together, they determined that, since he must die, they might as well have the enormous merit of offering a human sacrifice to Kali. That goddess had not tasted blood for a number of years; as a matter of fact, not since those disturbing English Sahibs began to rule. So they took their enemy, washed him, perfumed him, dressed him in a saffron-coloured robe, with garlands of flowers round his neck, and then cut off his head before Kali, close by the ground we had chosen for our camp. Three of these fellows were hanged; the other two had escaped into the jungle, and there led a sylvan life as robbers and outlaws. The escapade which had brought them under my notice was of recent date, and of an unusual character; for, meeting the clerk of the district magistrate, ambling quietly along the high road on his fat pony, and bearing important official documents, they knocked him out of his saddle and stripped him to the skin. This ill-timed jest brought them again prominently under police attention, and they were accordingly tracked down and brought to justice · all except their leader, Ragwa Karmali, whom we shall meet later.

This part of the Hazaribagh district was closely studded with Sonthal villages. They are an aboriginal people, dwellers in wild and hilly places, having language, customs, and religion wholly different from their Aryan conquerors the Hindoos.

Their dances were also peculiar and characteristic, and offered many points of difference to the usual nautch. At Kusmar a dance was performed in my honour by the villagers which gave me the opportunity of studying its peculiarities. First advanced with measured steps a weazened old man, carrying a drum nearly as big as himself, under the burden of which he vainly strove to impart dignity to his bearing. He was followed by a long shuffling string of Sonthal women of all ages, sizes, and shapes, who proceeded with a flat-footed and ungraceful shuffle, holding each other's hands. After an heroic struggle to make a salaam to me, in which the big drum vindicated itself and came out victorious, the leading drummer passed on, and, joining the rank and file of those who closed the procession took his post with them on the left, to make music for the corn-dance of the harvest festival.

About two hundred women then formed themselves in rows of twenties, swaying backwards and forwards like a field of corn in the wind, and singing monotonously as the throb of the drum rose and fell. All were dark and swarthy in complexion, and although the shapes of the younger women were graceful, their faces, when visible, were not prepossessing. The old women, who seemed most thoroughly to enter into the spirit of the dance, were truly hideous to look upon. One old dame I could have sworn was in someone else's skin. So loosely did the integument clothe her shrunken body, that one felt, had a slit been made at the top, it would have fallen from her like a garment. All wore necklaces of small red beads strung in many rows, which enhanced the blackness of the skin, whilst on wrist and ankle heavy carved pewter bangles covered them six inches broad. Some of the more distinguished elderly ladies wore, attached to these bangles, small silver bells, and all wore the universal "sari," a long piece of home-spun cotton cloth, with one end twisted round the loins and falling to the ankles, while the other end was brought up over the head and shoulders, whence it depended in not ungraceful folds. The hair was taken lightly back off the forehead, and twisted up at the left side of the head, with fastenings of scarlet worsted and tufts of many colours.

The first dance ended, there was a pause, when another leader entered clad in a breech-cloth. He too was old and battered, but wild-looking withal, and with grey bristly hair that gave his head the appearance of a blasted heath. Having salaamed deeply, he signified that another band of women had arrived, and desired permission to join in the festival. I graciously assented, and after a short delay, the second procession entered headed by a flute-player, a swarthy old man of portentous gravity, whose whole attention was devoted to his instrument, from which he elicited sounds of the weirdest and most doleful description.

The lines of women now swayed to and fro in an indescribable manner, the heavy pewter anklets clanking with the rhythmic motion of the dancers' feet, and their white drapery flowing gracefully as they saluted the new comers. These quickly took their places with the rest, and the dance recommenced in earnest.

The women, old and young, were ranged according to age, the old crones on the right, passing down in order to small girls of five or six years old on the left of the lines.

There were now fifteen rows of dancers advancing, retiring, swaying, and treading the measure with their clanking feet. In front of each row male musicians played drum, flute, and cymbals, while leaping in the air and performing various monkey-like contortions. The old men of the village walked round and round the phalanx of women, keeping palsied time to the measure of the dance, and one old anatomy had strings of bells tied to his sharp withered shanks.

The drums were of various shapes and sizes. They were made of earthenware with wolf-skin stretched across. Some were semi-spheres like kettle-drums; others were long and cylindrical, tapering to the two ends. The exterior protection to the earthenware was made of twine, twisted and woven in strange patterns, and daubed with streaks of vermilion. The patriarch and director of the assembly stood in the midst, leaning on a staff, with long grizzled locks floating over his shoulders as he chaunted the harvest song.

There was also a clown or funny-man, who stood beside the patriarch and shot forth jests between strophe and antistrophe, yet reserving sufficient energy to lead the chorus with fit and proper emphasis. From time to time he appeared before my chair and favoured me with choice, but unfortunately incomprehensible *morceaux*, rushing back with renewed energy to posture and prank before the rows of dancers, to whom he sang with wondrous accompanying waves of leg and arm. The final measure of the dance imitated cutting the corn, and was specially pretty. I entertained the whole party with sweetmeats and strong waters, which I left them to enjoy while I sought refuge from the hum and clatter in the quiet of of my tent.

CHAPTER V

HAZARIBAGH (*continued*)

1863–64

"SAHIB! Sahib!" droned my bearer. A pause ensued, during which I slept vigorously and answered not a word.

"Sahib!" he reiterated, taking possession of one of my feet and proceeding to put a sock thereon.

"Oh bother!" I replied. "Jao! go away! There is no kutcherry (office) this morning."

Another pause, during which I regain possession of my foot and try to persuade myself that I am not awake. Alas! my persevering domestic captures the other foot, and I feel that I must rouse myself.

"Sahib, the Daroga has come."

"Tell him to go away again."

"He says his business is urgent and deserves attention."

"Well, well, don't bother. Fetch the chillumchee and some water, and order 'chota hazaree.'"

So, after a good sponging of cold water and a cup of tea, I am ready for an interview with the Daroga, my head police-officer in the neighbourhood, Rahmun Khan by name, Mussulman by religion, and Pathan by race. In he came, bearded and shawled, his tulwar (curved sword) slung to his side, and an old-fashioned flint-locked pistol in his girdle; an oldish man, with a grave expression of face and piercing dark brown eyes. His beard had been some days neglected, as witness the grey showing at the roots; but he ordinarily dyed it, first with indigo and then with the red mehdi root, together producing the jet black colour which it usually showed.

"Khodawunda, salaam!"

"Salaam, Daroga Sahib! What is your news?"

"Your Highness, I have intelligence that Ragwa Karmali, who robbed the Depti-Kampshner's writer, is in a village about fifteen miles from here. The bringer of tidings awaits your pleasure outside the tent. His name is Nimai, and he is a wood-cutter of that village."

"What do you think is his motive in giving information?"

"Ragwa wishes to marry Nimai's daughter, whether he will or no, and although he is a poor man, yet he would preserve his honour."

"Yes; and get the reward for Ragwa's capture also, eh, Daroga?"

"What shall your slave reply? The wise man does not speak of all he does, but does nothing that cannot be spoken of?"

The next question was how to capture the villain. The Daroga was in favour of commissioning Nimai's daughter to drug him, in which condition he could easily be taken. I represented however, that this expedient was not only dangerous, but contrary to law; we arranged, therefore, to try a surprise. There was no use setting off with a large party, as Ragwa would be sure to hear of it from some of his scouts; so I charged the Daroga to be ready at nightfall, with three of his best men, to accompany me.

"We will start to-night, after the moon has gone down, so have all ready and say nothing. The secret of two is a good secret," I added; "the secret of three is nobody's secret, so keep Nimai quiet and out of the way."

"My Lord, be it upon my head and eyes!" So saying, he departed.

My orders were faithfully carried out. Nimai's information proved correct. We surprised and captured Ragwa in his sleep, and had him safely handcuffed and locked up in a granary, before 6 o'clock the next morning.

My tents had followed us, and were pitched and ready before I had finished my work. I had to remain a day or two, to collect evidence and arrange for the witnesses attending before the magistrate at head-quarters.

The day had passed quickly and busily away, and the moon was sinking in yellow haze by the time my dinner was over, and I strolled out to the men's camp-fire to congratulate my good old Daroga, and have a chat with him about the old stories and legends in which his soul delighted. He rose at my approach, bidding the men pile on more wood, and bring a fresh bundle of rice-straw for the Sahib to sit upon.

"Khair! Well," said I, "I think, Daroga Sahib, that our little capture was very well managed. I will take care that you and your men are rewarded. That Ragwa was a dangerous miscreant. I hope none of you got hurt in the struggle."

"No, Sahib. He tried to knife me, but Asadullah here caught his arm in a trice."

"Well, well; it was a good business, and Nimai shall have his blood-money when I return to Hazaribagh. But now for pleasanter things. Who will sing me a song or tell me a story?"

"May it please you," said the Daroga, "Shaikh Jaffer is a singer of incomparable merit, and he will doubtless be proud to exhibit his proficiency."

Here Shaikh Jaffer modestly disappeared behind his comrades, but was pushed again to the front, complimented, and encouraged, and after many excuses about his "owl-like voice not being worthy to be heard," and difficulties on the score of accompaniment, he briefly recited the "Kulma," or profession of faith, by way of prelude, and started off in a high falsetto, "Ah! ay—y! ai—u!" with prolonged quavering. "Oh come to me!"—grand shake here in crescendo—"Come, come, flower of my heart; beauty is a flower that lasts but a day!"

"Eh—ah!" from the Daroga, as one experienced in such matters.

"Beauty, alas! is a frail flower. The beauty of woman endureth but a season, and then fades away like a plucked lotus. Come, then; come, now! We are young, and we have love."

"Ai—yi!" ejaculates the Daroga, with an emphatic clap of his hands, and a glance round the circle, as if ratifying the singer's sentiments with his entire approval. I also applauded, hoping the song was at an end. But no; Shaikh Jaffer, once set a-going, warmed to his work, and continued his high quaverings in endless contortions, until fortunately, in his fervour, he extended his leg too far and burnt it slightly in the fire, which turned his " Ai's " into another channel, and gave my ears relief.

I took advantage of the pause to ask the Daroga to tell us a story. He acquiesced more readily than I expected.

" Your servant, Sahib, recalls at this moment but one story, and that is about His Highness Suleiman (Solomon), the son of Daoud (David), and the hoopoes, showing why these birds wear a crown.

" Solomon the King sat in his treasure-house and beheld all his wealth and precious things which lay before him. Behold! there was silver and gold in plenty, even as stones, and cedar-wood like the sycamores of the vale in abundance. Yea; cunning work was there in gold and silver, in brass and in iron, with woven stuffs of crimson, blue, and purple, and the walls of the house were garnished with precious stones and gold, even the gold of Parvaim.

" One thing above all was precious in the eyes of the great King, next to his signet, the insigne of wisdom; he valued it even unto the worth of half his kingdom. It lay before him now at his feet. Only a small square carpet, glowing with colours, like as the sign-bow of the heavens, or the hues of the flowers in Paradise, or the tints of the forests under the ocean. In length this carpet was six cubits and in breadth six cubits, six cubits every way as it lay before the King. It was bordered with work of the flowers of lilies and of pomegranates, and the centre of each flower was a gem of great price, worth a king's ransom.

" Now, as the King gazed thereon, the sounds of the harps and psalteries came faintly from the Temple, the Holy Place, stirring the air of the treasure-chamber, and making it rich with floating waves of melody. And the King communed with himself and said, ' Verily, by the goodness of Hiram, King of Tyre, many of these precious things have been gathered together. It would be fitting that I see him and we talk together.'

" And Solomon summoned the slaves of his household and commanded, ' Gather me this carpet together and spread it upon the house-top.' So they gathered it, and the King reclined thereon; and lo! a great wind came, even a mighty wind, and the carpet rose and went upon the wind, and ascended up from the house-top, passing from the sight of the beholders. And they stroked their beards, placing the finger of astonishment in the mouth of wonderment, and saying, 'God is great, and mighty is the King, even King Solomon, the son of David!'

"Now it came to pass, as Solomon journeyed through the air, that the sun burned with a great heat, and the King was sorely oppressed, as from a flame of fire. He thought upon the shady gardens and fountains of Jerusalem, and as he did so, Shriknad, the King of the Vultures, swooped near and made obeisance. Then said Solomon, 'Summon now thy servants, and cause them to shade me with their broad wings, for the summer heat consumeth me.' And Shriknad replied, 'O my lord! thy servant is grieved that he cannot help you in this matter, for the vultures are gathered together at a carcass, and will not leave it.'

"Then the King saw that he was mocked, and he was wroth with Shriknad, and cursed him, saying, 'Lo! you, now, thy head and the heads of thy race shall be defenceless and bare to the sun, even as the naked rock, and the heat shall pursue thee, and where the sun beats most fiercely, there shall be thy abiding-place!'

"And Shriknad shrivelled within himself, and became as nothing before the wrath of the great King, and the feathers fell from his head and neck till he became hideous to look upon, and his wings failed him from shame and fear, and he fell to the ground.

"Yet a little while passed, and a flock of hoopoes came gaily fluttering by, and they saw that the King was consumed by heat. Then Luli, their leader, said, 'My brothers, it is not meet that the great King should faint with the heat whilst we feel it not. Let us hasten to do him service, and that right gladly, that the King's heart may be turned to his servants.' So the hoopoes banded themselves together, flying above King Solomon, and with their wings they sheltered him from the sun, even unto his journey's end. Then Solomon was glad, and called to Luli, saying, 'Truly thou hast well done, and I am pleased with thee and thy fellows. Now, whatsoever thou shalt ask of me I will give it.' And the hoopoes bowed themselves before the King, and said, 'O Light of the World! if thy servants find favour in thy sight, grant that we may have crowns of gold upon our heads and upon our children's heads for ever, so that all may know that we have served the mighty King.'

"And Solomon bowed his head, and said, 'Let it be so.' And it came to pass that on each bird's head there sprang up a tiny golden crown, which glittered and sparkled in the sunshine, and was very fair to look upon. So the hoopoes went forth from before the King, rejoicing greatly.

"Now the noise of this thing spread abroad among the children of men, and the lust of gain was in their hearts; and every man's hand was against the hoopoes for the sake of their crowns, and the slaughter was very great. Then with sad hearts they gathered together to take council about this thing which had befallen them.

"Then spoke Babek, a long-tailed bird, well stricken in days, 'Hearken, O hoopoes! There was once a poor man who had a white elephant, which he loved as his own son. Now the Raja of that country heard of that elephant, and of the many wonderful qualities which it possessed, and he said that if he did not become its owner he would die of grief. He therefore sent for the man and for his elephant, and spoke unto him, "What is the price of this elephant of elephants? Speak! My liver is perishing with longing to possess the beast of beasts. What wilt thou take for it?"

"'"Perfume of the Atmosphere!" returned the poor man, with seven thousand salaams, "my elephant is my mother and my father, my child and my children's children. By the eye-lashes of Indra, I will take nothing on earth for my elephant."

"'"So be it," said the protector of the poor. "Nothing shalt thou have, since it is thy wish. Slaves, lead the elephant to the royal stables, and dismiss this man with many kicks. So shall he have even more than he asks." See, then, O hoopoes, how wisely the Raja came out of this difficult matter. Let us, then, go and lay our case before Raja Suleiman, that he may decide for us.'

"So they went before him. Then said Solomon, 'What

will ye, O hoopoes?' And they told him how the hand of every man was against them by reason of their crowns.

"Then said the King, 'O foolish ones! I foresaw that this would come upon you, even on the day you made petition, on the day of the sun-shielding.'

"Then he smiled and waved his hand, and the golden crowns changed, and became as feathers that are of gold, but still are feathers, and no gain to any man. So the hoopoes departed rejoicing, and praising the goodness and the wisdom of Solomon, the son of David."

I thanked the Daroga for his story, and retired to my tent, having no mind for further vocal melody, but far into the night I was dreamily conscious of Shaikh Jaffer's shakes and quavers.

On returning to Hazaribagh, I found an unwelcome summons from my Colonel, calling upon me to rejoin my regiment, the 104th, as there was a lack of officers. I had no mind to return to the dull monotony of regimental life, and therefore submitted to Government a respectful application to be permitted to join the Bengal Staff Corps, and reported my action in the matter to the Colonel of my regiment, waiting meanwhile for further orders.

As the rainy season set in, the criminals of the district roused themselves to greater activity, hoping, doubtless, to escape pursuit owing to the difficulty of travelling. But

> Naught cared this body for wind and weather,
> When youth and I lived in 't together;

and I rode sometimes forty miles a day, investigating and following up serious cases of murder and robbery. There were hitches and difficulties also with the police, and cases of insubordination and mutiny requiring immediate repression and punishment. I was fairly successful in my work, taking prisoner sixteen out of a band of forty miscreants who had been committing serious highway robberies on the Grand Trunk Road, sixty miles of which I had to patrol and keep in safety for travellers.

On this expedition it was necessary to travel with extreme secrecy. I started off with only ten of my best men, all well armed. We went on foot, and, the better to escape observation,

I wore native clothes during the three weeks we were out, and fared in all respects like one of my own men, eating rice and chupatees, and marching an average of sixteen miles a day. Our final march, when we closed on the band was one of twenty-five miles. We carried no tent, but slept each night where we could, often under a tree in the jungle.

I returned to Hazaribagh in high spirits, for we had not only taken sixteen, but learnt the names of many more of the outlaws.

I greatly enjoyed riding quietly back after the capture, in spite of the torrents of rain that fell without intermission. The whole adventure seemed like a dream. The night marches through dense jungle; the surroundings of men's houses in the early grey dawn; the scuffles, fightings; the denials and searchings; and the patter-patter of the rain, which was a never-failing monotonous accompaniment of the whole expedition. I carried no luggage save a bundle of absolute necessaries; and one evening, when the rain was unusually heavy, in order to keep my one suit of outer garments from being absolutely soaked, I took off all my things, wrapping each article up in big leaves, and sat with only a waist-cloth on, the rain pouring down on my bare head and shoulders like a heavy shower-bath. But the rain brightened and refreshed the land, which bloomed out into myriad beauties. Insect life, too, was busy, and I often amused myself watching the tiny creatures. A green leaf seemed taking a walk; chameleons darted about with changeful hue; or an important cocked-hatted beetle occupied its time in propelling pellets of cow-dung, standing on its head and working with its hind legs.

My friendly superior officer, Major B——, greeted me warmly when I reached the station, and congratulated me on the success of our little foray.

My efforts at keeping order and promoting honesty had not always so pleasant a termination. One morning early I received a hurried note from a high-placed Government official, to say that a burglary had been committed during the night and his wife's jewels stolen. He asked me to investigate the case fully and at once, with a view to the recovery of the property and the punishment of the thief.

I proceeded accordingly to the house. The lady herself was in bed and could not see me, but her ayah informed me that the jewels had been kept, with some silver spoons, in a box under the bed occupied by her master and mistress, she herself sleeping in a small bathroom opening on the bedroom, and in the same apartment two pet dogs also passed the night. The box had been found in the morning empty beside the bed, and showed signs of having been forced open by some sharp-pointed instrument.

I thoroughly examined the premises, and set spies in the bazaar with curious results. In the first place, I found that the dogs had not barked, but passed a quiet night. It was true that the iron gauze outside the pantry window had been cut away, but no marks of violence or footsteps were visible outside, while in the bushes near, one of the police discovered a stout pair of scissors freshly broken, the points of which fitted into the marks on both box and window. On searching the house of the chief goldsmith in the bazaar the jewels were found in his strong-box. I pointed out to him the serious position in which he was placed by this discovery, and he then stated that the jewels were sold to him by the lady's ayah, who, in her turn, on being threatened with the law, confessed that she had sold them by her lady's own orders. The result was an unpleasant one to communicate to the lady's husband. It appeared that, being heavily in debt and afraid of her husband, she had sold the jewels, and tried to cover their absence, which he would be sure to note, by a pretended robbery. They shortly after left the district and I saw them no more.

The remnants of the band I had attacked, with their leader, a brave, clever scoundrel, named Jherria Rajwar were still at large, and one day I spent an hour vainly in trying to elicit information against them from a poor wretch whose house had been plundered; the only answers he returned to my queries being, "Ah! but I fear much, Sahib!" or, "They will be sure to come back and kill me if I say anything"; and lastly, "I am very poor, my lord; they have taken all!" To explain this last plaintive remark, I should add that the custom among the old police had been to exact a handsome gratuity from anyone who had been robbed, in default of which the sufferer was made to suffer more by long journeyings, tedious attendances, and providing food for the police during their protracted investigations, than by the original loss. So the poor man feared that I too meant to plunder him.

At last I spied his wife with a child in her arms peeping at me from an inner room, so I said in a loud voice, "Ah! they beat your little boy, the scoundrels!" The wife emerged a little from her obscurity to listen. "And you say they assaulted your wife, and made her show her face—the villains!"

"It is false! Who said so?" And with this out came the wife, forgetting alike both fear and poverty, and indignantly told me all she knew.

The robbers it appeared had, as their custom was, tied up their faces in cloths to avoid recognition; but the woman averred, and her husband did not contradict her, that the leader of the robbers was Jherria Rajwar.

Jherria Rajwar, therefore, must be hunted down. I collected all the evidence I could, and made a careful list of the missing property, and set to work. The task was no easy one. He was a convicted dacoit, who had been released when the mutineers broke open the prison gates at Gya, and made a general jail deliverance. When order was restored he continued living in the jungle as an outlaw, subsisting by robbery, and only occasionally visiting his native village, which was situated on the outskirts of the district, in a hilly gorge near the sacred place known as the Dripping Well.

I had to approach this locality very cautiously, in order to gain information of his whereabouts; so under pretence of returning to Hazaribagh, we left the village where the robbery had been committed, and after marching for some hours till daylight was spent, we took to the jungle and camped for the night.

As we lay under some trees, rolled in our blankets, a great black bear came grubbing for food close by. It was bright moonlight, and I watched his proceedings for some time without stirring, not wishing to attract his attention; but my men soon became aware of the unwelcome visitor, and raised the cry, "A bear, a bear!"

"Ahi! bap-ré bap! Oh, my father! go and drive him away!" said a timorous voice from under a blanket close by.

On this Rahmut-ullah Khan, a fine young Mussulman, who formed one of my party, arose, and seizing a large two-handled sword, with measured steps approached the bear, addressing the animal as he advanced.

"Ah! dastardly robber of honey, the skin of whose father is my sitting-place! Oh! white-livered son of a pig's mother! will you dare to abide my coming?"

Now, whether it was the gleaming sword which he brandished in a flashing circle round his head, or the torrent of abuse, which scared Mr. Bruin, I know not; certain it is, that the bear gazed for a moment, grunting uneasily, and then turned and fled.

Camp life has its unexpected luxuries as well as its hardships. I remember on this occasion a memorable bath, when on returning one morning to our camping-ground after a long and fruitless walk under a hot sun, I found my men had scooped out for me in the soft white sand of a clear streamlet an oval hollow, large enough to lie in at full length, and here the pure cool spring water, filled with sunlight and shimmering reflections of green leaves, seemed to bring new life into my wearied limbs. I lay there with my face only out of the water, watching the bright dragon-flies dance hither and thither round the gnarled trunk of an old semul tree, among whose roots my bath was made; while out and beyond, through the green boughs, was the intense blue of a cloudless Indian sky, telling of the glare and heat without and giving additional zest to the shady coolness of the streamlet.

The breakfast which followed was equally delightful in its way. Rice of snowy whiteness, boiled to a turn, and served on a large platter of green leaves; a cake of unleavened bread, hot and crisp off the wood embers; chutney made of fresh pepper and lemon-rind, some fruit, and a glass of sweet fresh milk.

We were getting hot in our pursuit of Jherria Rajwar, and hoped to surprise him by a night attack. I had learnt from a cow-herd that he was in the immediate vicinity of the Dripping Well of Mhaka with fifteen of his men, and we approached with caution, our party only numbering nine, including myself.

It was dark, and we lay down to rest for a few hours before attacking him.

"What hour is it, Rahmut Khan?"

"Your highness, I cannot exactly say, as there are no clocks in the wilderness; but I believe it to be exactly midnight."

"Why do you say exactly?"

"Because at that time of night only, does the air flow with even freedom through both of a man's nostrils."

I essayed this new mode of time-measurement, and found truly that I did breathe equally through both my nostrils; so we agreed that it was probably midnight. Our movements had been speedy, and we were within a mile of the robber's lair; still, great caution was needed, as they might have heard of our coming, and be on the look out.

"They would all be asleep now, Sahib, under ordinary circumstances; but with the rumour that your honour is out, you may be sure they will keep a good guard. We ought not to reach the Dripping Well until the morning star shows himself there," pointing to the eastern sky.

Before us lay a long range of low rocky hills, clothed from base to crown with thick jungle mixed with large forest trees, which stretched east and west as far as the eye could see, save for a break in the line just in front of us. Here the range suddenly fell in height, sweeping back in a great amphitheatre. The foot of the hills was belted with thick brushwood, through which we had to pass before reaching the well. We could almost follow with the eye the track along which our path would lie, until the steep ascent was closed by a perpendicular wall of rock, curving round in a semi-circle to where a large peepul tree marked the gully up which the path led to a natural terrace above. Here was situated a small cave, whence, out of the heart of the rock, welled forth, crystal-clear, the spring which gave the place its name of the Dripping Well. The spot was held sacred by the inhabitants of the village of Mhaka, whose dwellings were dimly discernible at the foot of the hills. The spring never dried up, even in the hottest season, and its waters were famed for the cure of all sorts of sickness and disease.

Here had collected the remnants of the nest of robbers which had for so long harassed the district. The rascals had with great astuteness confined their depredations to distant forays, or to robberies committed on strangers and wayfarers, and by so doing had preserved the goodwill of the country people in the vicinity, who doubtless benefited by the plunder, and who supplied them with food and helped to screen them from too pressing inquiries.

Acting on Rahmut Khan's advice, we remained quiet for another three hours, and then, the morning star having taken up the required position, we looked to our arms and cautiously made for the pass leading to the Dripping Well.

On commencing the steep ascent, one of the constables, who was somewhat corpulent and short of breath, took to puffing and groaning in a manner which threatened to frustrate all our precautions. I therefore pulled his ears heartily, and bade him stay behind.

We crept along so quietly that we gained the terrace before any alarm was given, and came in sight of the great tree, underneath which smouldered the embers of a fire. Then there was a shout, and, as we rushed in, a number of recumbent figures sprang up from around the fire, and two flashes with sharp reports told us they were armed.

There was a scramble and a scurry, and catch who catch can. I followed a man who had been lying a little apart from the rest, and Rahmut Khan followed me. The fellow tried to bolt along the terrace, but we were too quick for him, and cut off his retreat that way. He then faced up the cliff, but with a quick rush I caught him by the leg. He turned on me, and with a wrench and a twist sent me heavily down on to the rocks. I was stunned by the fall; and when I came to myself I found I was lying by the spring, with aching head and bruised shoulders, and a wet cloth round my temples.

Three of the robbers had been captured, and sat sullenly on the ground, each man's right thumb being tightly bound with small cord to his neighbour's left, and their legs tied in like manner. A villager or two, from Mhaka, disturbed by the noise, had come up, and stood with some of my men looking at the dead body of one of the robbers which lay at their feet.

"Well, Rahmut Khan," I asked, "have we taken Jherria?"

"No, Sahib," answered the Darogah, "the villain has, I fear, again escaped us. But I settled the man who threw you."

"My lord," said one of the villagers, pointing to the dead man, "this is Jhenia Rajwar!"

This expedition did much to check highway robbery, which had hitherto been conducted openly and with violence, even along the Grand Trunk Road, and in spite of police patrol. But I had still to deal with another class of criminals, who first drugged and afterwards robbed their victims.

Their mode of proceeding was ingenious. An insinuating and seemingly harmless wayfarer would join himself to a band of pilgrims, asking permission to do so, being solitary and afraid of robbers. He was seemingly a Brahmin, wearing the sacred thread and taking direction of the cooking, with an assumption that could only belong to the priestly class. For a few days all would go well, but one night, after camping in a lonely place, all the party after supper would fall into an unaccountable stupor. The insinuating Brahmin had drugged the food, and they are fortunate if on awaking they find even the clothes remaining to them on their backs.

In October, I undertook a thorough inspection of the Grand Trunk Road, with a view to making it safer for travellers; and as the Government executive engineer was bent on a similar errand of inspection, with respect to the bridges and metalling, we joined forces and travelled together in a dâk carriage.

From Hazaribagh to Burhee we were drawn by relays of men, who tugged the vehicle along; but at Burhee we struck the Trunk Road, and became dependent for locomotion on the dâk horses, which were kept at post-stages along the whole length of the road by contractors, who undertook the conveyance of passengers and goods up and down country. These horses, as might be expected, were of a soured and evil disposition, their faith in human nature gone, having indeed but one fixed idea—the determination not to drag a dâk carriage.

It was a curious sight to see the contractor and his grooms start our carriage. The horses were blindfolded in their stable, and in this condition were inveigled into the shafts. As soon as they recognised what had happened to them they commenced jibbing, and were only induced to reverse this process by forcibly backing the carriage, and thus making them believe that we wished to proceed in the contrary direction. They would then dash madly forward at a gallop, urged on by the driver to top speed; at this pace they were kept, if possible, for the seven miles which intervened between the posting stations.

We halted from time to time at the dâk-bungalows, which a beneficent Government had established at intervals along the road, where we cooked our meals by means of a portable Soyer's magic stove. The bungalow servant, who usually cooked for travellers, watched our proceedings with admiration and awe, keeping as near the door as possible, in case the evil spirit confined in our conjuring apparatus should escape control. On one occasion, when my companion spilt some spirits of wine and a blue flare-up ensued, there was a regular stampede among the on-lookers, who fled precipitately, invoking the protection of Allah.

We ascended Parisnath, a sacred mountain situated in the Hazaribagh district, which is the resort of pilgrims from far and wide. My companion had to report on a scheme which was then under consideration for establishing here a sanatorium for Europeans, the hill being of considerable altitude and within comparatively easy reach from Calcutta.

On the way, we passed through a mighty flight of locusts, in such numbers that the earth was shadowed for twenty minutes as if by a dark thunder-cloud. Their legs and bodies were red with black articulations, and metallic black-striped wings. It was an awe-inspiring sight, this host of insects; one felt that, had they chosen to settle on a man, their millions of small powerful jaws would soon make an end of him.

My friend Major B——, the Deputy Commissioner, with whom I had worked so amicably, had gone on leave, and I did not find his successor so pleasant to deal with. A new assistant magistrate had also been posted at Burhee, who seemed to regard all police and police superintendents as his natural enemies. I had never met this gentleman; but because I sent for some natives to take down their depositions in a robbery case, instead of myself riding some thirty miles to their various houses, he reported me to Government for having grossly infringed the law, and asked the High Court at Calcutta to authorise my trial for having illegally confined these persons.

The matter was referred to the Commissioner of the Division for orders; but in the meantime the natives were quick to notice and take advantage of difference of opinion among their rulers, and I very soon found my authority weakened. "What can your Sahib do?" asked a man whom my constables arrested for drunken brawling, "the magistrate Sahib will protect me. Look to yourself." And, in truth, it was woe to the policeman who was brought before that functionary.

In the East, where to bear false witness is the usual condition of things, it sufficed for the magistrate in authority to show any bias against the police and criminal investigation became paralysed. My policemen were afraid to act, for fear of the false charges which were sure to be brought against them, and the heavy sentences which were as sure to follow. With the departure of my kind friend Major B—— my luck seemed to desert me, and an unfortunate occurrence which happened about this time still further depressed my fortunes.

My assistant, Mr. E——, had gone out by my orders to investigate a case of robbery, and a man whom he had arrested died suddenly while in custody. The relatives of the deceased accused Mr. E—— of being concerned in the man's death, in having incited the police to administer the flogging under which he died. This was a terribly serious matter, and I at once proceeded to investigate it thoroughly. After a long inquiry, I came to the conclusion that although Mr. E—— had been grossly negligent in his supervision of the police under his charge, yet he had no personal cognizance of the illegalities which had been committed. There was, however, no doubt that the man's death had been hastened, if not actually caused, by the violence to which he had been subjected.

The case was to be heard and decided upon by the Deputy Commissioner; so I wrote demi-officially to my Deputy Inspector-General, giving him an outline of the case, and saying that I would report fully in official form as soon as the magisterial decision had been given. I did not report at once officially in my own department, hoping that at the trial things might prove more favourable for poor E——, who had not a sixpence in the world if he lost his appointment; and, remembering the proverb, "A bad wound heals, but a bad name kills,"

I did not wish until it became absolutely necessary to report the charge of murder against him. At any rate, I acted according to my lights; and so, doubtless, did the Duputy Commissioner, who brought the whole matter to the notice of Government, commenting most unfavourably on E——'s conduct, and doubtless on mine also, for I was thunderstruck one morning at receiving an official letter from the Secretary to the Government of Bengal, characterising my conduct as evasive and untrustworthy, and stating further that, in the opinion of the Lieutenant-Governor of Bengal, I was unfit to hold charge of a district.

I replied at once, respectfully but firmly setting forth my own views of the case, and I concluded my letter by saying that, should my explanation be deemed unsatisfactory on this the first time that any action of mine had been disapproved, I begged to tender my resignation of the Service.

It seemed hard to receive so sharp and sweeping a reprimand, after such unsparing efforts as I had made for the good of the district committed to my charge. At the worst, it was an error of judgment, which would not have occurred but for the known hostility of the civil servants, which prevented any consultation with them on district matters. Poor E—— was dismissed, and I saw him afterwards in London literally starving.

It is an old adage, "Kick a man when he's down," and, the Deputy Commissioner of Hazaribagh having been so successful in his attack, his subordinate, the Assistant Magistrate at Burhee, thought he would try his hand at a throw with the hated policemen. His first complaint, as to my illegal action in summoning witnesses, brought him only a sharp rap over the knuckles, in the shape of a communication from the Commissioner of the Division, saying that the tone of his letter was most objectionable. Smarting under this rebuke, and still further embittered against me, he issued peremptory orders for me to appear and give evidence before him in a case which I had investigated, but where the evidence of my subordinates was quite sufficient. Having received orders to visit the southern part of my district, I replied expressing my regret at not being able to appear in person, but that I would reply by post to any questions he might wish to put. On this the gentleman issued a formal warrant for my arrest! I at once placed the matter in the hands of higher authority, and the young official's warrant being quashed, he applied for leave on private affairs.

While I was waiting for the decision of Government, I sought to divert my thoughts from the cares which oppressed me, by going out against the outlaws in the southern part of my district, hoping to make a clearance of them there as I had done in the north.

He who measures oil gets some on his fingers, and the worry and trouble which had come upon me having told on my health, I found it a relief to leave the society of my fellows and enjoy the solitude of camp life. How delightful it was, instead of dining decorously at mess in formal dress, to sit in my little square tent and partake of a tender joint of the kid that but yesterday had been tethered to one of the tent-pegs, while the chickens destined for the cutlets and soups of my to-morrow's dinner clucked and cackled from a basket hard by. Whilst I dined, some villagers outside smoked a friendly "chillum" of tobacco with my saice and his attendant grass-cutter. They were Sonthals come to give me news of a bear or a deer, for the Sonthals are the great hunters of these parts, and are almost the only natives that are not afraid of the wolves, sweeping the jungles in great hunting parties of two and three hundred, killing whatever happens to come in their way, even the big black bear if they chance to start one. It takes five or six of their number to manage him, for while the bear pursues one of their number the others follow on either side, striking at him with the small axe which each man carries, and diverting his attention from one to another until they manage to cripple or kill the beast. No one man is a match for the great black bear, unless armed with a double-barrelled rifle. The bear, in attacking a man, always aims at the face with his great claws, and I have seen some horrible cases of disfigurement; but he is naturally a peaceable beast, and I will do him the justice of saying that he rarely, if ever, makes an unprovoked attack.

The Sonthals live chiefly on the proceeds of the chase, their wives cultivating the land in small patches for food. They are a manly race, and I had a criminal case to investigate on this occasion which was sufficiently striking to record here.

A young Sonthal, a fine handsome young fellow, standing six feet high, wished to marry, but unfortunately lacked the money to furnish the indispensable wedding feast. The natural Sonthal mode of earning money, of course, occurred to him, and so he waited and watched, searching the jungles early and late, until he slew a tiger and could claim the Government reward of ten rupees. Then the much-wished-for marriage was celebrated, with all the magnificence that ten rupees could afford, with much beating of drums, blowing of flutes, and libations of the juice of the "mowa."

The ceremony being concluded, the newly-wedded pair settled down to their joint life, she to cultivate the ground near her husband's hut, and he to hunt. One day, returning early from hunting, he saw a man, a former and, he feared, a favoured rival, standing talking with his wife. He concealed his suspicion at the time, but the next day, instead of hunting as usual, he returned after a short time and concealed himself in a tree which commanded the path to his house.

Soon the lover appeared, and glancing round cautiously, entered the house. The husband waited for a while, then, descending from the tree, grasped his spear, and going stealthily to his house, surprised and killed with one blow the two guilty ones. His wife he buried decently, with a groan and a sigh. He then cut off his rival's head, and casting the body to the pigs and dogs, he carried the head to the nearest magistrate, recounted what had happened, and requested to be hanged. He was imprisoned for life.

While I was still out in the district, the orders of Government reached me. My resignation was not accepted, but I was removed from the Hazaribagh district and ordered to take over charge of Noacolly in Southern Bengal. This involved not only change of scene, but complete change of language. In Hazaribagh all the work of the district was carried on in Urdu, with which language I was thoroughly acquainted; while at Noacolly the whole population spoke and wrote Bengali, which

I accordingly should have to master, if I wished to do any work to my own satisfaction.

I was sorry to leave Hazaribagh. I knew the whole district like a familiar face, and had grown much attached to my men and they to me. There was quite a scene at parting. My favourite, Rahmut Khan, and the old Lieutenant Panchkowrie, besought with tears to be allowed to follow my fortunes, and many of the others crowded round, wishing to go with me. What could I say to them? We were all but as pawns on the great Government board, moved hither and thither as best suits the game of our masters the governors.

I travelled as far as Calcutta with my brother, who was bound for England after his visit to me. At a dâk-bungalow on our road we fell in with two German missionaries, both of them quite young, who had come out to join the Ranchee Mission. Ranchee is the district adjoining Hazaribagh, and the Moravian Mission there is the only thoroughly successful work of the sort that I have met in India. The missionaries have addressed themselves, not to the Hindoos, but to the Kols and Sonthals, the aboriginal and simpler races, and count their converts by hundreds and thousands.

These two German lads, who had left home and country to give their ives to work among the heathen, were the kindest-hearted and most ingenuous of young recruits. They dined with us, and were full of wonder at the various new edibles presented for their consumption. Green peas were a novelty in their experience, and brandy they described as "a precious but breath-taking cordial." We parted with mutual good wishes.

It was on New Year's Day, 1864, that I bade farewell to my brother on board the good ship "City of Dublin," homeward bound, while I turned my own face southward, to start life afresh in my new district of Noacolly.

CHAPTER VI

NOACOLLY

1864–65

I LEFT Calcutta in a small coasting-steamer which plied between Bengal and Burmah, touching at Chittagong, the nearest port to my new district, Noacolly.

The passage across the Bay of Bengal was pleasant enough, the steamer having but one other passenger, a clever, amusing young fellow, who entertained me much with stories of his varied experiences. His had been indeed a chequered career. Starting first as a scholar at the École Militaire, at Boulogne; then at a public school in England; afterwards out to Australia, where he served in the mounted police, rising to be a Lieutenant, when he left the corps to go to the diggings, making and losing a fortune there, like many another. When news of the Mutiny reached him, he came to India, and served throughout the campaign in the volunteer cavalry, under "Hashed Richardson," so called on account of the many sabre-cuts he had received. Finally—if anything could be final with such a character—he got work as sub-editor to one of the Calcutta daily papers, and, his health having suffered from the desk-work, he was taking a sea-voyage for change of air. I parted company with him on reaching Chittagong, where I had to transfer bag and baggage into small boats in order to land. I had brought my favourite mare from Hazaribagh, and as she could not be taken in the boats, she was lowered into the water and swam to shore.

I was received at Chittagong by my *confrère*, the police superintendent of that place, a curious old withered, sun-browned stick of a man, with a fine expanse of shirt-collar, and a grey stubble of hair of equal length covering head and face alike. He invited to meet me at dinner, the first night after my arrival, the Captain of a French barque which was lying at anchor in the river, a pleasant, excitable little Frenchman, who entertained us much by his volubility. During the evening the conversation turned on the delicate question of French *versus* English courage, and he told us a story, which we were not slow to perceive was autobiographic.

"*Attendez donc un peu.* Hear me," he said. "I will tell you a leetle history of a Frenchman who was afraid of noting; no, not of the great Devil himself. There was once, not long ago, a fire immense at Penang; and this leetle Frenchman, he lived there with his old wife, and they have eighteen children. *Mon Dieu!* she was a powerful woman. *Mais helas!*"—raising his hand—"the *bon Dieu,* He have take her! Well, well, hear me. The fire was hot; *sacr-r-r-é-é-é-é nom!*—excuse me, gentlemans; it was as hot as a thousand devils, and it have burn twenty shops, thirty shops, and the Counsellor President, what you call Governor-General, he is there, and all the officers of *artillerie,* and many brave Englishmans, and they all do their possible to extinguish the fire. But stay; the leetle Frenchman he see on a platform, right over the hottest part of the fire, five large jars of water, that would contain perhaps fifty gallons each, and an old beam goes to reach this platform. *Pr-r-r-rou!* the leetle Frenchman is on the beam, and he runs over, although the under part is burning, and quickly he empties all the jars. Ah, he was out of breath, and the people all say, 'Retire yourself! quick, quick! retire yourself!' and he runs; and just as he pass over the beam, cr-r-r-ack! it is broken. But he save himself on his feet, and *les officiers* say, '*Sacré!* it is a brave leetle man!' And is it not enough? But no. The Chinamen they say in English—for many China boy there know English, Sare, quite well—they say, 'Run, run, quick, for here are barrels of gunpowder in the cellar!' And the Counsellor-General he say, 'A willing man here!' But all keep quite silent. Then the leetle Frenchman he spring up and say, 'I will go,' and the President Counsellor shake him, Sare, by the hand, and say, 'Come, my brave!' And the President Counsellor he go down on the floor on his chin, and the leetle Frenchman he take his hands, and down he go into the cellar, and hand up one, two, tree barrel of the powder, and all shout, and say, 'Well done!' After some time comes a letter, Number 504 of the Council, with fine words, and say, 'Here is a Government ship; the leetle Frenchman shall command her.' But he is very independent and has a hot head. He cannot bow to the subordination, and he keep his own ship. He write to Government and say, 'No, no!'"

We rose, glass in hand, and saluted the leetle Frenchman as a "brave," and drank to his health, and to the undaunted valour of all Frenchmen.

I heard afterwards that this man, Captain Martin by name, had on one occasion been attacked in his bed by forty Malays. He received a cut on the head, another on the shoulder, a wound in the back, a stab on the elbow, and two big gashes in the thigh; but, in spite of all, he got hold of a big stick, killed three of the Malays, took two of them prisoner, and put the rest of the party to flight. Then, fearing lest they should return and, in his helpless condition, torture and murder him, he opened a barrel of gunpowder, put it between his knees, and sat smoking cigars till morning, fully determined that, if they did return, he would blow them, with himself, into the air.

When I met him, he commanded and owned the barque "Onega," from Penang to Calcutta, and had put into the port of Chittagong for a cargo of rice. With all my heart I wished him success and "*bon voyage!*"

I was two days coasting along shore in a native boat going from Chittagong to Noacolly, without much consciousness of my surroundings, owing to the disastrous effect which sea-travelling usually has upon me; but at last we hauled up into a creek in the Island of Sidhi, at the mouth of the river Meghna, to wait for the bore, or tidal wave, which is very dangerous to the unwary traveller.

I went on shore at once with my two dogs, Eshkee and Grabby, and found to my surprise that the ground was covered with short crisp turf, and a shrub which looked like English holly, but which I afterwards found to be the *Dilwaria ilicifolia* of tidal swamps; but the effect was delightfully English and home-like, and gave me a pleasant impression of my new district.

We waited till the tide turned, and the bore swept by, an impetuous wave some four feet high, and following in its foamy wake, we soon reached Noacolly. I reported my arrival to the magistrate, and assumed charge of my new duties on the 19th of January.

I soon found that there was plenty to be done, the whole of the district police being still on the old footing, the reforms and alterations of the past year having been apparently unheeded in this small sleepy hollow.

I had seen many dull Indian stations, but for steady and persistent dulness Noacolly surpassed them all. The English society consisted of the civil surgeon and his wife, and the magistrate, who was unmarried. The only available residence for me was a small thatched bungalow, in close proximity to the station cemetery and facing a large tank, which was reported by the natives to be haunted; truly a dreary abode.

My police clerk, an educated Bengali, whose duty it was to copy my official letters, proved to be a cultured individual. His colloquial English was also characterised by much originality of expression. He one day inquired of me if Her Majesty Queen Victoria were comely in appearance; and on my gravely rejoining that she was indeed beautiful, he replied, "Yes, Sir, I understand; a moonbeam of pretty."

"Hardly so beautiful as that, Baboo."

"Sir, in the pictures she is a notorious beauty, with a bob in her nose."

"A what, Baboo?" I demanded.

"A bob, Sir, a ring. I have read in Milton, and also I have read the fine Shackspear."

At this I could not refrain from smiling, which the Baboo took somewhat amiss, taking his departure with the remark, "Sir, your laf make my inward soul ashamed."

My fellow-countrymen were not only few in number, but most unsociable in disposition, and I saw so little of them, that I at length began even to think in the native tongue.

The magistrate in charge was of an imperious and most unaccommodating disposition, and I did not desire to see much of him. An occasional planter would show an unkempt head of hair and beard in the station; but I fell back for companionship chiefly on the doctor, and, not many weeks after my arrival, I succeeded in luring him forth with me on a tour of inspection through the district.

Very different now were my surroundings from those of Hazaribagh. Here were no delights of camp life, of riding, or of sport; but the change was pleasant from its very contrast with previous experiences.

We set off, with a small fleet of boats, to navigate the mighty river Meghna, to which the Ganges is but a child. Here at his mouth Father Meghna is twenty miles broad, with islands on his breast as large as English counties, and a great tidal bore which made a daily and ever-varying excitement. Twice in the twenty-four hours the whole volume of the downpouring river was met and opposed by the incoming tide of the Indian Ocean, which rolled it back on itself in a mighty wave, whose roaring foamy crest, some miles in length, varied from three to twelve feet in height, according to the strength and direction of the wind. In deep water, it passed merely as a large rolling billow; but in the shallows, it rushed along, roaring like a crested and devouring monster, before which no small craft could live. While the tide ebbed, the river ran out tranquilly to the sea; but with the advent of the bore, the current changed, and rushed upwards at a rate of at least ten miles an hour.

A curious police case turned on this peculiarity of the river. Two men, from causes which I need not particularise, were bitter enemies. One of them was an agriculturist on the island of Sundeep; the other was leaseholder of the ferry from that island to the mainland. The ferryman lived in a small house near the river's bank, and, with the help of a hired servant, carried people to and from Noacolly. The distance across was over three miles, and the passage was dangerous for those who were unacquainted with the mud-banks, which at low tide lay bare in mid-stream. To this person's house, one afternoon, came his enemy, accompanied by his daughter and a gay party of guests, bound for a wedding-feast at Noacolly. The ferryman saw them coming, and hastily despatched his servant, who ordinarily rowed the ferry-boat, on an errand to a village at some distance. The party arrived, and demanded to be conveyed across the river.

"My servant is away," answered the ferryman, "and I will not serve you or yours. There is the boat; if you can row, take it and go across."

They took it and went. Half-way across the boat stuck in a mud-bank, and remained there with her living freight till the terrible wave overwhelmed them. The ferryman, who had known that the bore was coming, was tried for his life, but was acquitted, as it was shown that, with skilful rowing, there would have been just time to get across; but doubtless he knew that these hapless ones, not knowing the banks, must needs be lost, and he was in his heart a murderer.

I found the boat-travelling a lazy lotus-eating sort of existence, with the pleasant soft south wind rustling through the feathery bamboo foliage on the bank, while the plash of our oars fell in lulling cadence, and the bright reflections from the water danced and quivered on the woven cane roof of the boat. The day slipped by as insensibly as the even course of our boat on the river, or as the gliding ever-changing procession of the green banks we passed; now it was a village, with the women coming down to fetch water, under the spreading shade of the mango trees; then a grove of slender-shafted areca palms, or a glimpse of the golden-green plumes of the cocoa-nut, which here, within sniff of the ocean, throve wonderfully. How soft and tender the hue of the young rice, thrown into relief by a dark background of the indigo plant. Occasionally a fisherman's boat would range up beside ours, and we amused ourselves by inspecting and bargaining for his silvery commodities. Even the vicissitudes of the weather had their own peculiar charm, for it was by no means always fair. Great towering banks of cloud, blue-black with strangled wrath, would rise swiftly up from the horizon against the wind, and, coming nearer and nearer, our eyes would turn with agonies of apprehension to the cook-boat, bravely struggling on in the distance, as we neared the haven where we would moor till the storm was past.

Always late was that ill-fated craft, always behindhand and behind time; and yet each occupant thereof, from "Khansamah Jee," the table-servant, down to the youngest boatman on board, would firmly maintain, like Mr. Micawber of immortal memory, that they had "only fallen back for a spring," and could overhaul the Sahib's boat whenever it might be needful to do so. If I ventured to point out that it would be pleasing to have dinner served somewhere within two hours of the time it was ordered, and suggested that the cook-boat should start ahead of mine, in order that it might prepare for our arrival, my servant invariably answered me by a long tirade against the "manji," or head boatman of the cook-boat. This unfortunate man, he said, was a pig for obstinacy—of low extraction, and ignorant of polite manners, and he alone was the cause of the delay. If I rejoined that I would deal with the "manji," another argument prevailed, for he then fell back upon the impregnable position that it was impossible to start earlier, as his pots required cleaning. This line of argument generally resulted in my defeat.

I had brought with us in tow a small jolly-boat, and, while waiting for dinner, the doctor and I often went for a sail in the cool of the evening. Merrily we spanked along before the fresh salt breeze, the dogs lying contentedly in the bows, as the boat flew along at a tremendous pace, until I brought her up under the lea of some small fishing-boat, lying at anchor and waiting for the ebb, whose dark crew gazed with astonishment at the two Sahibs with white faces and whiter shirts, who lay, pipe in mouth, at the bottom of the strangely-rigged foreign boat.

All the native boats are without keels, and can therefore only sail before the wind, so that our English method of navigation was an astonishment, and, as my old "manji" remarked it was a wonder to him that we could sail at all, as our boat transgressed every principle of boat-building that he had collected during thirty years of experience on the river.

On the back tack we would sometimes find ourselves in a quandary, the strong tide and a contrary wind proving too much for us, so that we had to take to the oars, which was slow work. One evening, even this last resource failed us, for one of the oars snapped short in my hand, and we were left helpless. Tack after tack we made, with no perceptible effect, for what way we gained by the sail we lost by the current. The sun had set, and the swift-falling Eastern darkness was fast closing round us. There was nothing for it but to anchor under a mud-bank and wait for the turn of the tide, not getting back to the big boat and our dinner till after nine o'clock.

The large police-boat in which we travelled was by no means an uncomfortable dwelling-place. It was one of the six or eight Government guard-boats, employed to patrol the river Meghna and its tributaries for the suppression of smuggling, and also to keep open communication between head-quarters and the outlying police-posts. The whole district being covered by a great net-work of small streams, all communicating with the great estuary of the Meghna, a great deal of illicit salt manufacture was carried on, which it was part of my duty to check.

The guard-boats were manned by crews of twelve oarsmen, under command of the steersman, or "manji," as he was called. They resembled a Roman galley, with a thatched cottage occupying the after part of the boat. This cottage was formed by cane mats bound to a bamboo framework, upon the roof whereon sat the "manji," who directed the course of the boat by means of a great oar, shipped rudder-fashion. The interior accommodation consisted of a bed-place, much infested by cockroaches, and a small sitting-room, which held two chairs, a table, and my harmonium.

One morning, while sitting on my bed, I saw a cockroach emerge from the darkness of a sheltering cranny, and proceed to divest himself of his outside covering. He shuffled off his shiny brown coat, and emerged as white as snow. It was curious to see the tender and solicitous way in which he handled his old clothes, and the careful delicacy with which he extracted his antennæ from their old casings.

He looked very naked and forlorn after the operation, and, much as I loathed his race, I could not find it in my heart to scrunch so defenceless a creature. But a worse fate awaited him. To this innocent, white-garbed one, tittuping gaily through the open window, entered a consequential insect, known as the ichneumon fly, very brave in bright steely-blue armour, looking as if burnished afresh for the occasion. Round my apartment she went, poking into dark corners, entering the depths of my harmonium, and taking a careful survey of each crevice in the floor. A very detective among the insect tribe, this fellow! I thought my new-born friend was doomed; Steely-blue, however, seemed not to notice him, but poked about until, behind my waste-paper basket, she saw something move, plunged for it, and there found a big bloated cockroach, old in villainy. Doubtless she tapped him on the shoulder with a "Come on, my boy; you're wanted!" for a more crest-fallen and despairing aspect no culprit ever presented than this cockroach, when led forth from behind the basket. The little blue knight conducted her captive daintily by one of his antennæ, the cockroach following in a dazed and stupid manner. Having brought him out into the light, away tripped Steely-blue to look for a lock-up, or place of safe keeping, the delinquent meantime, strange to say, making no attempt to escape, but remaining quietly in the place and attitude in which he was left. Back came Steely-blue again, seizing an antennæ, and walking to a crevice in the floor, down which she went backwards, dragging the helpless victim, twice her own size, after her. The "manji" told me afterwards that, in that dark recess, Steely-blue performs a magic incantation, which renders the cockroach torpid, and enables her to lay an egg in its body. Having thus provided board and lodging for her progeny, she gaily flits away in search of other victims. This, however, I cannot vouch for. All I know is that, after an interval, Steely-blue reappeared and flew away. My new-born friend, meanwhile, foolishly endeavoured to crawl into a cranny by the open window, and being extremely weak after his metamorphosis, fell into the river, and was swiftly carried out of sight.

After inspecting some of the outlying police stations, we reached Dhunnia Munnia, where we received an invitation from a European landowner to visit him and have some sport.

This landowner was a Frenchman, whose father had occupied for many years the post of chief clerk to the magistrate of the Noacolly district, and in that capacity had managed—who shall say how?—to amass a very large fortune, owning before his death some thousands of acres of land in that part of the country. His sons were educated in France, and the gentleman we were about to visit was the least favoured of his three sons. The elder brothers had been left the bulk of the property, while the youngest came in merely for five or six villages, which afforded him a rental of about six hundred pounds a year. He was unmarried, and possessed by the fixed idea that to kill tigers and hunt wild pigs was the *summum bonum* of existence. He had no desire to see Europe again, but lived a lonely life on his own estate, keeping six elephants, and possessing the best battery of English guns that money could buy.

Accordingly, on the 6th of March, we moored our boat to the sandy "chur," an alluvial island in the middle of the river, where a family of the best-bred Bengal tigers were said to reside, subsisting for the most part on wild pig, with which the island abounded, or varying their diet by an occasional foray into the mainland. A bullock had been purchased for four rupees, and the poor animal was tethered in a likely place among the long grass which covered the chur, growing in many places to a height of over ten feet.

The next morning our scouts reported that the bullock had been killed during the night and the carcass dragged away. Word was sent to our host, and his elephants were soon descried swimming across the river. The mahouts, or elephant drivers, managed the passage very cleverly, standing on the backs of the great beasts as they swam, and shifting and balancing themselves with their every movement.

The elephant swims with the whole of his body under water save just the tip of his trunk, through which he breathes, and which is elevated two or three inches above the surface. The mahouts, therefore, standing on the backs of the animals, had the appearance of walking or wading through shallow water, although the arm of the river they crossed was both wide and rapid. Elephants swim slowly, but they are practically untirable, and can swim for hours without fatigue. One instance came to my knowledge, where two elephants with their mahouts were caught by the tidal wave in crossing the Meghna. Surprised in mid-stream, one mahout was swept away and drowned, but the other managed to cling to the rope round his animal's neck, and, with the two elephants under his charge, remained for seven hours in the water without touching bottom, the tide having swept them up the estuary, and the current preventing them making much way.

The mahout guides his elephant through the water by the pressure of his feet and toes, or by touching his head with a stick. As our host's elephants swam to us at Dhunnia Munnia one of the great beasts turned over on his side, with a swirl and a splash, the mahout nimbly changing his position, and standing on the upturned flank. This, they said, was the animal's play; but it seemed dangerous sport for its rider, in a deep rapid river abounding in alligators.

When the elephants had safely crossed, and their howdahs, which had been brought over by boat, were properly adjusted on their backs, we mounted and proceeded to beat the "chur."

On reaching the place where the decoy-bullock had been tethered the previous night, the traces of the kill were manifest, and we had no difficulty in following the trail through the long grass till we came on its carcass, already half eaten by the tiger, but still showing plainly the crushing effect of the death-blow. The neck of the animal had been broken and the head twisted round, jaw-bone and shoulder-blade both having been smashed by the terrible onslaught. There were plenty of footprints, or "pugs," as they call the spoor of tiger, round the carcass, and the head mahout pronounced him to be a royal tiger, that is to say, one of the largest size and best breed for pluck and endurance. We went on beating through the tall "sunn" grass, which seemed capable of hiding any quantity of game in its dense cover. Each man stood up on his howdah with rifle at the "ready."

Suddenly, one of the elephants cocked his ears and trumpeted, with the clear metallic clang which denotes danger.

"The tiger is afoot," shouted our host; "there spoke Súndri, my best elephant. She never trumpets for nothing."

The doctor, who was in front, fired, and a tremendous roar showed that his ball had told.

"Push on, push on, follow up!" shouted the Frenchman. But the more haste the worse speed, for we over-went our tiger, and paused in a small nullah, looking vainly for his pug in its sandy bed. After a short consultation, we determined to beat along the nullah, an elephant on each bank and one in the bed of the watercourse. This last post fell to me, and, as I rode along the nullah, scrutinizing the grass on either side with the closest vigilance, I leant forward for a moment, to give some directions to the mahout, when the words were frozen on my lips by the expression of the man's face and his attitude, as he lay huddled up on the neck and behind the ears of his elephant, pointing, without saying a word, to the side of the nullah.

I turned sharply, and there on the high bank close by, and on a level with my face, I saw the tiger. At this point, the sides of the stream were precipitous, and the animal's head was literally not five yards from my own. Life was in the balance. The beast was glaring silently at me, with a ferocity of expression that curdled my blood, and I felt that the least movement on my part would cause him to spring. As I looked, I saw the corners of his mouth curl in fierce snarl, the sure precursor of action; and, swiftly dropping my gun, I fired at a venture, the mahout at the same time urging the elephant forward at full speed. No sound followed the report of my gun, and when we turned, and all met at the spot, we found the tiger lying quite dead, the ball in its brain. As my host remarked, "He was so close, my dear fellow, that you could not very well have missed him."

We had some pleasant days' sport together; but duty soon recalled me to Noacolly, where my police reported to me that the house of a lonely old usurer had been broken into and a total clearance made of all his possessions.

I proceeded at once to the spot, but could learn little from the old man, who seemed thoroughly dazed and heartbroken by his losses, and the night following he committed suicide by hanging himself to a tree at the back of his house.

Somewhat depressed by this untoward ending to my inquiry, I returned to Noacolly, where I was soon prostrated by my first attack of Indian fever, brought on by exposure in this marshy and malarious district. My illness was not rendered lighter by a letter which I received from the magistrate, informing me that I was accused of having tortured the wretched old man till he died, with a view to extorting money from him. The accusation, which was contained in an anonymous letter, went on to say that, having thus caused the man's death, I directed my subordinates to hang the body on a tree and report the case as one of suicide. I replied to the magistrate that I was *anxious for the most complete and searching inquiry to be* made, but I was too weak and ill at the time to trace out personally my slanderer, and I heard no more of the matter.

I had often read tales of ghouls and vampires, pseudo-dead men who walked among the living, sucking their blood to maintain their grisly existence; and the following true record would almost justify the belief in such monsters. I was informed that a wealthy zemindar, named Luckhi Churn, who resided at Mynda, on the road to Luckhipúr police station, was commonly reputed to be a vampire. He was said to pay men to let him suck their blood, opening a vein, and imbibing the fluid through a small reed, with the belief that by so doing he improved his own health. After some inquiry, I found a man who professed to have been thus operated upon. He showed me a small scar on his arm, from which, he assured me, the zemindar had sucked his blood till he was quite weak, in consideration of a present of four rupees. No fewer than two persons were said to have died from their love of rupees and the zemindar's unnatural appetite, and the records of the criminal court bore witness to the fact of his having twice been charged with having thus caused death.

The first time he was committed for trial at the sessions on a charge of murder, but was acquitted for lack of evidence. On the second occasion the magistrate inquired into the case, but dismissed it as not proven; but the zemindar was reported to have spent money lavishly in suborning the witnesses. Probably he found his taste too expensive for modern times, as he was not brought up again to my knowledge. The truth of the charge against him was, however, fully believed by the people at large.

With the hot weather, in April, a terrible epidemic of cholera smote the district, and there was scarcely a native house but had its dying or dead inmates. In one house in the bazaar there dwelt a native pleader of the magistrate's court, who retired to rest at night with six living members of his family. In the morning he alone was alive, the rest had all died of cholera. In a single night he had lost his wife and their two children, his mother, and his sister. The men of my police fell into a state of abject terror, and I had great difficulty in keeping any heart in them. One constable, a lad of nineteen, died in my arms while I was speaking to him, telling him to hope : even as I spoke, his breathing became hurried, his muscles twitched and his body was agitated, as if striving to keep the spirit within its fleshy bounds, and then, suddenly, a great and solemn change hushed the poor frame to stillness. He was gone ; died of exhaustion, after fighting through the acute stage of the malady. The scourge continued to claim its daily tale of victims, in spite of all our efforts to check it, until the rains set in, when, with the first heavy showers in May, it abated as rapidly as it had come. It had been a trying time, and I gladly betook myself to my boats, for a little much-needed rest after the pressure and anxiety were over.

I was bound first of all for the island of Sundeep, where my police were in trouble with some smugglers. A search had been made in one of the villages, by my policemen, in order to seize a depôt of illicit salt which had been stored there for export. The smugglers had resisted the seizure, and in the struggle a poor little child had been trampled to death.

The relatives placed the child's body on a bier, and bore it along, followed by a long procession of mourners, to the magistrate's court-house at Noacolly, weeping, wailing, tearing their garments, and calling for vengeance on the bloodthirsty policemen who had murdered the innocent child.

Poor policemen ! Many and unjust were the accusations brought against them ; above all, in these first days of their organisation. The hand of every criminal, or would-be criminal, was against them ; the thief, the usurer, the oppressor of his neighbour, the receiver of stolen goods, besides darker miscreants, who lived by violence and murder—all united against the common foe. No accusation was too vile, no motive too base to be imputed to those who ventured to do the thankless work of upholding law and order. Anonymous letters usually conveyed the sting ; but often, as in the present instance, the attack was boldly made, and would be supported by any requisite number of witnesses.

The weather was very hot, and I slept on deck in a swing-cot slung from the mast. This cot was made of coarse tent-cloth stretched over a frame of bamboo, made with side-pieces which, when raised, sheltered and concealed the occupant. It was invented by a friend of mine in Hazaribagh, who was a mighty hunter, and devised this ambush, so that he might be slung up in a trece when watching for tiger or bear. It was very restful lying thus, listening to the plash of the oars and the monotonous chant of the twelve rowers.

> Goom ! goom ! goom ! alatoon goom !
> Lal kirani Sahib bhag marata.
> Sahib bagh mara mararey.

Which might be translated,

> Pull away lads, cheerily oh !
> The red-haired English gentleman killed a tiger ;
> Oh, he killed a tiger very handsomely !

I am not red-haired. I believe the pre-historic Sahib thus commemorated was a Mr. Simpson, formerly magistrate of the district, and who was known throughout Bengal as "Red Simmy," to distinguish him from a brother civilian of the same name, who was called "Black Sim."

Far away behind us on the river followed the cook-boat, with Ramtuhul, my khitmutgar, sitting disconsolate on the roof, speculating anxiously on the wrath to come when the cook-boat should arrive late with the dinner cold !

Most refreshing was it, in the fiery heat of noon, to slice the top off a cocoa-nut and drink the tumblerful of cool acidulated water which it contained.

The river navigation was no easy matter for the inexperienced traveller. In addition to the tidal wave, which I have already mentioned, the district was subject to cyclonic storms of incredible violence, fortunately lasting for a very short time, but which often caused much destruction. These storms were heralded by the appearance above the horizon of clouds known to the native boatmen by the name of 'lady's eyebrows,' so called from their being curved in a narrow black arched wisp, and these most surely foretold the approach of a tornado.

The native "manjis," who manage the boats, know all the storm-signals and mud banks and detours of the mighty stream, so that an accident rarely occurs. If, however, the storm comes on too rapidly to allow the boat to gain the shelter of the banks, there ensues a hard struggle for life.

On one occasion I was thus caught in mid-stream, and a most unpleasant experience it was. The "manji" lost his head at the approach of danger, and fell on his knees, knocking his head against the deck, and invoking "Allah" with loud cries. The boat, having no keel, rocked and rolled like a pudding-basin on the waves—and such waves! almost like mid-ocean, owing to the force of the wind and the width of the river. I had to take the helm myself, and "huroosh" the men on, or we should have assuredly gone down.

On arriving at Sundeep, I made a careful inquiry, but could find no evidence to justify the charge of murder against the police, as the child had evidently been accidentally crushed to death; so in June I returned to Noacolly, and made my report to the magistrate, feeling much better for the change of air and scene.

One morning, as I was sitting at breakfast, a great yellow dog rushed in at the open door, and made a lunge at me. Fortunately, my faithful bull-terrier Grabby, who had been lying dozing at my feet, flew at the intruder and diverted the attack, giving me time to get my gun, which stood ready loaded close at hand with which I shot him. I carefully inspected Grabby, but could find no mark of bite or scratch upon him; but my other dog, Eshkee, must have met the strange dog before he came to my room, as in about a month's time she showed signs of rabies. The first symptoms appeared while I was once more out on a tour in the boats, when Eshkee, usually the meekest of quadrupeds, suddenly fell upon her friend and companion Grabby, with obvious desire to devour him. Again and again she repeated the unprovoked onslaught, to Grabby's intense dismay, looking miserably ashamed of herself, after the frenzy had subsided, but apparently unable to control her canicidal impulses. As the days went on the attacks grew worse, and she flew at one of the boatmen, and even pursued my bearer, Munbodh, causing him to climb the mast in a swift agony of apprehension. She was still always amenable to my voice, and I tied her up, hoping that it was not really madness; but no rope would hold her. Slowly and patiently she gnawed it quite through, although we used a half-inch rope for the purpose. Twice in one night she thus released herself, and a scene of dire confusion ensued on board of my small craft, the boatmen jumping head-foremost into the water, while I had to go out in my night-shirt, with bare legs, in order to secure her. Once she took my hand into her mouth, as if to bite it, but dropped it when I reproached her. In a day or two the biting and tearing humour left her, and she grew very weak, and at last died licking my hand.

Poor dear doggie! my bonnie, faithful, affectionate companion! Grabby seemed to share my anxiety, and be conscious that there was something amiss. In the last days he, for the first and only time, deserted his nightly position at the foot of my bed, going out to where Eshkee was tied up, and lying gravely watching her, in a mystified and sympathetic manner. He missed his familiar friend, and we were both very lonely for a time after her death.

Government had issued an order to the magistrates throughout Bengal, that all starving and ownerless curs should be destroyed by the police, to avoid infection by rabies. A great fuss was made about this at the time by the native press, and some stress was laid upon the inhumanity of their English rulers; but in point of fact the Bengalis as a race are not kind to dumb beasts. They drive their bullocks and horses with large sores on their backs, in which maggots breed and at which crows may peck. They overload their small donkeys until the poor creatures' hind legs are bent crosswise; it is customary with them to carry bundles of live fowls head-downward; and if a bird with valuable plumage be caught in a snare, it is a common thing to pluck out a feather, and with it poke out the creature's eyes, in order that its fluttering may not injure the lustre of the feathers. And yet this order of Government made a great stir among these merciful folk, and many were the complaints of English cruelty in destroying poor harmless dogs.

One morning, a fine lively python, measuring fourteen feet long, was brought to me for sale; but snakes were too numerous in the neighbourhood for one to have any wish to augment their number by purchase. I shall never forget the shock I received one morning when, on pushing open the door of my bathroom, which was ajar, a cold heavy snake fell from above on to my naked shoulders; the beast had coiled himself on the top of the half-open door, and my push brought him down with a run. He was as much astonished as myself, and glided off quickly, while I retired hastily to call my bearer, and arm myself with a stick. We killed him afterwards among the water-pots in the bathroom; he was a veritable cobra, with the spectacle-marked hood, but a young one, not measuring quite three feet long.

Deaths from snake-bite were very frequent in the district, and the natives affirmed that some of the water-snakes were more deadly than the cobra. Printed instructions were issued by Government, and distributed at all the police stations, giving directions for treatment, and bottles of ammonia were also provided to be used as antidote in such cases.

My neighbour and official superior, the magistrate of Noacolly did not improve on further acquaintance. I found him to be a most discourteous and ungentle man, even from the first day of my arrival in the district. The bungalow which had been allotted to me stood in the same garden, or compound, as the Government Circuit-house, occupied at that time by the magistrate, but not belonging to him, and the road to my bungalow ran through this garden, passing very close to the Circuit-house. The great man happened to be walking in the grounds when my stores and heavy baggage arrived in bullock-carts, and he peremptorily ordered the drivers to go back, saying that no carts should pass that way, and that, if I wanted my boxes, my servants could carry them in on their heads. The cases were some of them very heavy, and, as this was the only road leading to my house, I naturally took a different view; and, judging that the public road was intended for public use, I sallied forth to reassure my servants, who were somewhat daunted by this magisterial prohibition; and, if necessary, to see the goods brought in myself.

The magistrate had left a "chaprasi," charged to stop the road, and this underling, "dressed in a little brief authority," allowed himself to be exceedingly impertinent to me, and attempted to lay forcible hands on my carts. Him, therefore, I promptly dismissed, with a harmless kick *à posteriori*, and triumphantly bore in my convoy. The next morning the magistrate summoned me before him judicially as a culprit, and fined me fifty rupees for assault. I, on my side, reported the whole matter to the higher powers, and subsequently had much satisfaction when an official reprimand arrived, remitting the whole of my fine, and charging the magistrate with irregularity and ill-will in the performance of his functions. Thus the matter ended; but there never was any cordiality between us, and I had to be careful not to give him an opportunity against me, which he would have been sure to take advantage of.

In the month of July the rainy season was at its height, and the great river came out in flood, submerging the district for many miles round. My boats had no need then to follow the creeks and canals which intersected the country, but could boldly row over the rice-fields, as I visited the different villages and police stations, which were always built on rising ground.

The ordinary boat of the district, called "khunda," was simply a large canoe made from the hollowed-out trunk of a tree. Some of these canoes were surprisingly large, holding from ten to twelve people, but they were necessarily narrow, and therefore somewhat crank, although the people of the country were perfectly safe and at home in them. These boats were made from trees growing in the forest beyond British limits, on the frontiers of the adjacent district of Chittagong.

I occupied my spare time at Noacolly in compiling a "Police Officer's Manual," in the vernacular, being a *résumé*, in brief and easy form, of the law relating to and regulating the ordinary duties of the police. This manual was accepted, and afterwards published, with the sanction of my own department, for general use in Bengal.

I also had the tardy satisfaction of receiving a complimentary letter from Government, thanking me for my exertions in Hazaribagh; and this letter was shortly afterwards followed by orders transferring me from Noacolly to the charge of the larger and more important district of Chittagong.

I commenced with joy to pack up my belongings. I had nothing to regret in leaving Noacolly, save the use of a very fine library, the munificent gift of a neighbouring planter to the little station-school, where I had browsed happily upon many authors not included in my previous school or college curriculum. Here for the first time I met with Steele and Addison, Rabelais and Sir Thomas Browne, Charles Lamb and De Quincey, greatest master of English prose. Here also I found and laid to heart the four great maxims of the philosopher Epicurus, viz., " (1) The pleasure which produces no pain is to be embraced; (2) the pain which produces no pleasure is to be avoided; (3) that pleasure is to be avoided which prevents greater pleasure or produces a greater pain; (4) that pain is to be endured which averts a greater pain or secures a greater pleasure." Fortified by this antique philosophy, I definitively abandoned the drinking of beer!

CHAPTER VII

CHITTAGONG

1864–65

I ARRIVED safely off Chittagong on the 15th of October, 1864, after an uneventful journey down the big river Meghna and along the sea-coast beyond. We waited, just before leaving the river, at a place called Bamni, until the "bore" boomed past, and then pushed out to sea, coasting along until the mouth of the river Karna-phuli was reached, a short distance up which stream lay the port of Chittagong.

Karna-phuli, being translated, means an "ear-flower" or ear-ring. Tradition has it that a wife of a Mahomedan governor of the place dropped a valuable ear-ring in the river, and was drowned in attempting to recover it. This, however, was long ago, before the English "raj," when the Moghul dynasty held Chittagong as the extreme northern outpost of the empire. The aboriginal name of the river is the Kynsa-khyoung.

We rowed up to Chittagong with the rising tide. Before us, in the clear morning light, lay innumerable groups of small low-lying hills, which were backed by more lofty ranges in the distance, all well wooded but scarcely rising to the dignity of mountains.

I was travelling for the last time in one of my cumbrous cottage-like Noacolly police-boats, and, as the flowing tide swept us up stream, the rowers sang some improvised stanzas of farewell, each verse ending with a vigorous chorus of "Goom alatoon goom" ("Pull, altogether, pull!").

As we approached the town and port of Chittagong, the tall masts of European-rigged vessels rose outlined against the sky. These were one or two English and American barques loading with rice, as also sundry brigs, rigged English fashion, but owned and sailed by native residents of the port.

The inhabitants of Chittagong had been ship-owners and ship-builders for many a long year, ever since their first settlement at the place as a colony of sea-going pirates, who were the scourge and terror of the Bay of Bengal; and I could see here and there along the shore, as we passed along, the ship-building yards and slips, showing that the old seafaring traditions of the place still lived.

The town lay chiefly along the river's bank, on the northern shore. The houses of the natives were uniformly constructed of mats tied to a timber framework, which was raised on an earthen platform some three feet high, each house being surrounded by its own small grove of fruit trees, among which the graceful foliage of the cocoanut-palm was prominent.

Behind the native town rose numerous small grassy hills, each topped by a white bungalow. The European population, consisting of Government officials, planters, and rice-merchants, all dwelt on these hills, the low-lying lands being liable to floods, and, consequently, unhealthy. The district of Chittagong, indeed, was by no means a favourite station among officials, although extremely picturesque in scenery, and possessing a comparatively cool climate, as it was undoubtedly at that time a very hot-bed of malarious fever.

The hills and sea-board of Chittagong, until the rise and consolidation of British power, were formerly the battle-ground upon which several races struggled for supremacy. Indigenous hill-tribes, Burmese, Portuguese, and Mahomedans, all preceded us as masters of the country, and each had left behind traces of their rule.

From the first, I conceived a great liking for my new district, and by the end of the year I had comfortably settled down in the saddle, with reins well in hand, so far as concerned the police work of the district. Socially, as well as officially, I found the change from Noacolly to Chittagong delightful. To be rid of my Noacolly magistrate alone was a weight of many tons lifted from my soul; he, from the first, had done his utmost to make life unpleasant to me, whereas at Chittagong I was received by both Commissioner and magistrate in the most friendly manner, while I was invited by the chaplain of the station to share his house, until such time as I could find a convenient dwelling of my own.

The parson's house, like those of all the other European residents, was set on a hill, from whence one commanded a charming view of the river, and of the adjacent country. Far away to the south stretched a broad green plain, interspersed with mango and palm groves, through which wound the silver reaches of the Karna-phuli ; while to the east rose range after range of blue hills, said to be inhabited by wild and savage tribes, of whom I learnt much more later on. To the west and south-west lay the great Indian Ocean, whence daily, at sunset, came a refreshing breeze, which often wafted with it up the river some white-winged ship, full of English faces, to remind one of the old country so far away.

Shortly before my arrival, the district had suffered from a fearful hurricane, which had rolled in upon the coast an enormous storm-wave, destroying the crops, and rendering the land salt and unfit for cultivation. Its chief force, however, had expended itself about Calcutta, and we read of roofs whirled into the air ; of great ships, a thousand and fifteen hundred tons burden, being carried bodily into the middle of rice-fields, or sunk at their moorings, while the very crows were dashed to death against the walls of houses. Now, however, all was calm and peaceful ; the cold weather was setting in, and with pleasant anticipations, I commenced preparations for the annual tour of inspection, when I hoped to see for myself what my new district was like.

The first piece of official work I was called upon to do was the preparation, at the Commissioner's request, of a scheme for the fortification and defence of the post and station of Chittagong. This I duly, and with much thought, prepared and submitted ; and it was, I doubt not, with equal care, read, docketed, and pigeon-holed, as many thousands of other schemes annually are. At any rate, I heard no more of it, and ten years afterwards the port was as defenceless as it was on my arrival there.

I had still, in some mysterious manner, been allowed to remain an officer in Her Majesty's 104th Regiment. My application for permission to join the Staff Corps had at least the effect of producing a cessation of my Colonel's mandates to join; but I now received an official letter from the officer commanding the regiment, informing me that, unless I passed the examination in drill and other subjects, prescribed by regulation, my name, which stood first on the list for promotion to the rank of Captain, would be passed over, and I should be superseded by a junior officer.

A threat of this description, which might be viewed with equanimity later in life, assumes portentous dimensions when one is beginning the race; and I accordingly at once, and with urgency, applied for leave of absence, to proceed to Calcutta and appear before the examining board at Fort William. I had no fears about passing, as I had never allowed my knowledge of drill or military duties to become rusty, having always before my eyes the contingency of a compulsory return to regimental duty. Pending the receipt of a reply to my application, I determined to visit the northern part of my district.

My friend the chaplain had been called upon to celebrate a marriage at Comillah, the next district beyond Noacolly, he being the nearest available clergyman; so we bore each other company as far as the river Fenny, the northern boundary of the Chittagong district, where I bade him farewell, and returned by easy stages along the coast, visiting the different police stations along the road, and acquiring all the information I could as to people and places.

I had been specially enjoined to pay a visit to Sita-khúnd, the fountain of the goddess Sita, a holy place much resorted to by pilgrims, and where the goddess was said to manifest herself not unfrequently to devout worshippers. This sacred spot was situated about mid-way in the Nizampore hills, a coast range which ran parallel to the sea for a considerable distance. The road to the shrine ascended by easy sloping terraces, which had been cut with some skill and considerable labour in the hill-side. I rode up these, accompanied by two of my servants, one carrying a gun, the other my sketch-book, in lazy Indian fashion.

At the foot of the ascent we passed a sacred stone, thickly daubed with vermilion, on which was carved the effigy of Hanumán, the monkey-god. The dwelling of the Mahunt, or chief priest, was situated about half-way up the mountain. He was, in fact, the proprietor of the shrine, and made a very handsome income from the offerings of the faithful.

Here were numerous time-worn temples, their roofs overgrown with moss and waving grasses. Within each of these stood a "phallus," the emblem of creative power as embodied in Brahma, being an upright black stone, strewn with the white flowers of the chumeli, and scarlet madun blossoms.

The Mahunt did not deign to receive my salutations. His servant was busily employed in the verandah of the priestly residence, scouring his pastor's dinner-service of brazen platters and silver cups, and he informed me that His Holiness was engaged in worship, and could not be disturbed. A stream of cool clear water was carried in front of the house, in troughs formed by lengths of the betel palm, split in half, and supported on rough trestles of unhewn logs. The spring had been diverted from its course far up the hill to do service here.

The remainder of the ascent being practicable only on foot I abandoned my pony, and commenced mounting flight after flight of brick stairs which led up the mountain-side, a thousand in number, with landings here and there where the wayfarer might stay awhile to take breath, and look out on the beautiful landscape which lay beneath and around.

Glittering in the morning sun shone the sea, with some native fishing-boats floating idly on the calm water; inland a broad expanse of forest land, broken here and there by clearings and cornfields, and dotted with sparsely-scattered homesteads and moving specks of men and cattle. The bright green of the young springing rice-crops was flecked now and again by some silver pool catching the light like an upturned eye. From the densely-wooded valley below came the sound of a woodman's axe, with the occasional crow of a jungle-cock, and once I heard a barking-deer call. Across the valley to the right rose an almost perpendicular hill, its whole side one tangle of long creepers and dense undergrowth, save just at the centre, and here a gap showed a pathway which led across the face of the cliff. As I gazed at this gap, a striped hyæna passed slowly along a faintly-outlined track, quite unconscious that he was observed.

Up, up, up we went, climbing the apparently endless succession of well-worn steps, slippery in places where some mountain-rill ran bubbling hastily across the path, to plunge into the black gulf of the gorge below. Sometimes our way lay under overhanging crags, bald and grey, but plumy at their base with grass and fern, until at last the brick stairway ended abruptly, and the road ran along comparatively level ground, through tall grass ten feet high, which formed an archway overhead, until we stopped before a low vaulted building, of dark and gloomy aspect, whence issued forth strange sounds of groaning and hissing, while at the same moment a hot blast struck our faces as from the throat of a furnace. It was the fountain of Sita!

My men now urgently besought me not to enter this fearful place, averring that, as we were unaccompanied by a priest, the consequences might be disastrous. However, as I told them, I certainly had not toiled up so long an ascent merely to go back again, and I intended to see whatever was to be seen; so, without more ado, I entered the low arched doorway, and they followed me in great trepidation. Before us lay a gloomy inner chamber, in which a red glow fitfully came and went. It certainly was an uncanny place, and, to a superstitious mind, full of terror. We entered the inner room, and saw before us an opening in the floor of perhaps twenty feet square, where was a black pool of water, out of which leaped and danced lambent tongues of flame. The upspringing of these bright yellow flames from the water was accompanied by the groaning, bubbling, and roaring sounds which had previously disquieted my attendants.

As we stood gazing at the mysterious spectacle, the sounds suddenly increased with an ominous and volcanic intensity, while at the same moment a violent clamour broke out in another part of the building, a noise of great gongs throbbing and booming. On this my men fled for their lives.

I pursued my investigations to the adjoining room, where I found a priest who was busily engaged in banging a great frame hung with bronze bells. In answer to my interrogatories, he informed me that this was certainly the most sacred place in Lower Bengal, but confessed that the deity appeared only on rare occasions, and was never visible to anyone save the holy Mahunt himself, who was specially favoured. I took another look at the pool. The lambent flames reminded me of the tongues of fire which descended on the Apostles at Pentecost. They were doubtless caused by inflammable gases rising through the water; but I could not understand how these gaseous emanations were ignited, as the flames appeared and disappeared intermittently, and there was no steam-vapour. My men exhibited an altogether remarkable alacrity in going down the mountain.

After concluding my official inspection of the different police stations along the road I returned to the parsonage at Chittagong, which had now been shut up uninhabited for more than a week, and found that the place had been taken possession of by an army of fleas. I entered the dining-room unsuspiciously, and after a short interval, found the lower part of my white trousers become quite black with the creatures swarming upon them. It required unlimited sweeping and much sprinkling of tobacco-water before I could re-occupy my old quarters.

The proverb says, "Know a man by his books," and it seems to me that a glance at the daily correspondence of an Indian official is an equally true index of his avocations. Here, as a sample, is a list of the letters which I found awaiting me on my return:—1. Letter from the head partner of my agency firm in Calcutta, offering hospitality should I visit the City of Palaces. 2. From the sub-editor of a Calcutta daily paper, sending a remittance for articles contributed. 3. From the private secretary of the Inspector-General of Police, asking how I liked my new district. 4. From Police-Inspector Rozario, reporting a large illicit salt manufacture at the mouth of the Pheni river. 5. Anonymous letter, accusing one of my police officers of taking a bribe. 6. Police report of the burning of a planter's bungalow by incendiaries. 7. Letter from the Inspector-General as to the equipment of the police with boots. 8. From the same, authorising the purchase of the police yacht "Foam." 9. From the music-shop at Calcutta, sending some violoncello strings and music. 10. From the Babu at the Inspector-General's office, forwarding one hundred rupees, accruing from the sale of the "Constable's Manual." 11. From a German merchant resident at Calcutta, asking for information as to the prospects of tea-culture in the Chittagong district. Beside these, about thirty English and vernacular missives relating to police work, and the ever-welcome English mail.

The Commissioner of the Division, who resided at Chittagong, was a good violinist, and there were besides in the station two other fiddlers, one, the Assistant Magistrate, and the other, Assistant to the Commissioner. This last was a worthy half-caste gentleman, a lineal descendant of the Portuguese pirates, with a very black face, surrounded by a fringe of very fine white whisker. All that was needed to complete the quartett was a bass viol; and I was incited, nay, commanded, by my official superior, to undertake this instrument. I therefore procured a violoncello from Calcutta, and for many days devoted every spare moment to ploughing my weary way through the rudiments, until at last I attained sufficient efficiency to attend the musical *séances* as an enthusiastic but somewhat inefficient member of the quartett.

"Remember, Lewin," said the Commissioner, "if you come to a passage you can't play, don't get confused, but just sway away upon G"; and not only in those quartetts, but also in after life, I have remembered my friend's counsel, and been content to "sway away on G."

In December, I got my leave for a month, and went to Calcutta to pass my examination for the captaincy. I was specially anxious to reach Calcutta quickly, as I had received a letter from my old Shahjehanpore friend and comrade J——, informing me that he was returning from furlough in England, and would arrive in Calcutta just about the same time as I hoped to be there. Curiously enough, it so fell out that the small coasting steamer in which I travelled passed the great P. & O. steamer which had my friend on board as we entered the Hooghly. The large ocean steamer was waiting for the tide to rise, and there was my old comrade waving a salutation from the quarter-deck. We landed about the same time, and together repaired to the Club, where we shared the same room. How glad we were to meet again, and what yarns we spun together until unearthly hours in the morning! Poor fellow! Fortunate, perhaps, it was for us both, that no shadow of his after fate, and my unhappy connection with it, dimmed our happy intercourse.

I read hard in Calcutta for a fortnight at such book-lore as was required for the examination, and then I went before the examining board, and, after due sifting, was eventually declared to be a fit and proper person to command a company in one of Her Majesty's regiments. This end accomplished, I returned with all speed to my duties at Chittagong. My friend J—— obtained the appointment of Personal Assistant to the Inspector-General of Police, a position of confidence and considerable responsibility, but for which his high character and great abilities rendered him peculiarly fit.

In the spring of 1865 I started on my second journey in the Chittagong district, determined, as far as possible, to see men and things with my own eyes, and not through the dirty spectacles of the native officials who hang on to the skirts of every English officer in India; so, leaving behind me clerks, servants, clothes and "square" meals, I shouldered my rifle, and, with a suit of grey flannel and a pair of soft yellow bootees, I set forth on foot one fresh early morning in January on my tour of inspection. I was accompanied by a Mugh interpreter named Sadu, and his boy Apo, the latter carrying my revolver and hunting-knife.

An interpreter was necessary, for as yet I was only able to speak Hindustani and Bengali, while to the south of Chittagong one soon passed beyond the limits of these tongues and entered the zone of Burmese-speaking people, not to mention the hill-dwellers on the borders of civilization, who are "salvage" men speaking unknown tongues.

My baggage consisted of the clothes I stood up in, and besides, only a white lawn shirt, a crimson silk waist-cloth, a tooth-brush, a towel, a piece of soap, and a comb, which, made up into one small bundle, was easily carried by Sadu.

With these slight *impedimenta*, I now passed a most delightful time in the jungle; for the secret of true happiness, either in life or in travelling, is not to burthen oneself with unnecessary luggage. Now and again I would come upon a police station, and then great would be the consternation, bustle, and skurry, at the unexpected advent of the strange new "sahib," whose intentions and disposition were as yet alike unknown quantities, and who, by thus dropping, as it were, from the clouds upon the peaceful constable, evinced uncomfortable vigilance; or we would pass the night in a Mugh village, by some clear swift-flowing jungle stream, where I clothed myself in the full white lawn shirt and crimson waist-cloth (a costume quite *de rigueur*, and worn as full dress by the best-bred men in that part of the country), and sitting on the solid black plank floor of a Mugh house, would endeavour to converse with, and reciprocate the civilities of, my hospitable hosts. Again, I would find myself floating on a river in a boat made of basket-work, the very corracle of our British ancestors, while round me closed a mighty primæval forest, the enormous trees, thickly hung with orchids, veiled with grey moss, and strangled by snake-like creepers, meeting overhead in leafy canopy and matted with the spring growth of the cane. Here, in the heart of the land, was a great dismal swamp, and hither herds of wild elephants resorted in the cold weather, coming down from their hill fastnesses to enjoy the luxury of a mud bath—a wild weird place, worthy in its savage grandeur to be the haunt of the mammoth or iguanodon. Another day I can recall the march through the jungle, where the sun was shut out by the outspread arms of forest giants; there was little undergrowth, only long swaying creepers, with here and there the exquisite bloom of some rare orchid, while the ground was thickly covered in places with monkey-cups, the husks of monster acorns. There was a silence, a great stillness, no sound of any beast or bird, nothing but the cracking of the dead sticks under the feet of our party, moving along in Indian file through the woodland.

We often did twenty miles in the day's march, Sadu carrying my double gun and Apo the bundle. There was apparently little game in the district; the only birds I met with were some Muthúra pheasants, beautiful birds with scarlet wattles and fine blue-black plumage, which I shot among the low jungle near the coast.

I visited and was hospitably received by all sorts and conditions of men. One tribe, however, the Kúmi, were unattractive and I declined to remain a night in their village, being disgusted by the sight of a half-skinned dog which was hung up in process of preparation for the pot, and which, I was informed by Sadu, had been killed for my dinner; I therefore pleaded a pressing engagement and took to the jungles once more. These Kúmis were nearly naked, the men wearing only a breech-cloth of the scantiest description, and in their ears flat discs of brass, the excessive weight of which dragged down the lobes, making holes of the bigness of a crown-piece.

Another and more pleasing tribe was the Tsak, or Chakma, and in their village I halted a couple of days. I was housed in the guest-house, a building which was apparently used as a sort of club by the males of the village, wherein they congregated to smoke and chat when the day's work was done. They were *the jolliest folk imaginable, always laughing and merry.* Immense was the interest excited by my breech-loading gun, and when I fired off the six chambers of my revolver in rapid succession, the applause and satisfaction knew no limits. It was at once proposed that I should become a public benefactor by killing an e'ephant, for the flesh of an elephant, they said, would supply the whole village with food for months. I had never seen a wild elephant, and, with the courage bred by ignorance of danger, I rashly assented.

Accordingly in the evening I sallied forth on the adventure, accompanied by Apo, who carried my gun, and by a Tsak, a cunning hunter, named Hla-pwa-thu (by interpretation, "he who issues forth beautiful"), and to whom, I was informed, fear was unknown. Scouts had been sent out the day before to get news of a herd and to make preparations. A small bamboo platform had been constructed, some twelve feet high, commanding a view of a small pool to which the elephants resorted at night to bathe.

I felt somewhat doubtful as to the result of my expedition, this being my first attempt at this kind of game, and it was not without misgivings that I took my seat on the frail structure where I was to lie in ambush. It was ten o'clock at night, and very cold; the sma'l platform, at a height of twelve feet from the ground, creaked and shook as I seated myself, followed by my two attendants, and settled down, miles away from all things and people civilized, in an unknown forest, waiting for behemoth to come to bathe.

We sat thus for some hours, and very uncomfortable hours they were; Apo, of course, promptly went to sleep, and I would willingly have followed his example, but had the cramp so badly that I could not manage it.

Suddenly, the unpronounceable one quietly laid his hand on my arm and pointed to something in the darkness. Yes! there they were. My first wild elephants! dimly discernible in the dusk and gloom of the star-light. There were five of them, and I felt vaguely glad that there were no more: first came a big tusker, then two smaller elephants, and lastly a female with a young one. I waited breathlessly, until I got what I thought was a fair aim at the ear of the tusker, and then I fired. Bang! Off crashed four of the elephants like a tornado through the jungle, while the tusker remained standing as if stunned. At that moment, the wretch Apo, who had awakened at the noise of the gun, cried out "He's hit! he's hit!" and thereupon, his attention being directed to us by this outcry, the diabolical tusker rushed straight at our frail platform. I saw his great trunk rear itself up in the air, and then, crash! everything went into chaos. I and the guns, with Apo and the unpronounceable one, were scattered to the four winds. We fell, fortunately, among thick high grass, which grew close and rank immediately behind the spot where we had made our ambush, and to this circumstance we probably owed our lives. We lay in the grass as we fell, without moving an eyelash, and the tusker, after venting his wrath by demolishing the platform, departed "grommeling." I was badly bruised by the fall, and one of the guns was broken; Apo had cut his head, and the fearless hunter confessed that on this occasion only his heart had turned to water; and so, for that time at least, our hunting ended, and I returned to my duties at Chittagong.

English capital at this period poured into the Chittagong district in the shape of tea investments. Large tracts of waste jungle-land were offered for sale by Government on very easy terms, and tea-gardens sprang into existence on every side. This sudden influx of European energy into the district could not take place without considerable friction with the natives, who claimed rights of pasturage, wood-cutting, and the like, in the waste lands, the fee simple of which had been disposed of by Government, and ill-feeling was thus engendered between the natives and planters, which manifested itself chiefly in that most vindictive and troublesome of crimes, incendiarism. It was so easily done, caused so much injury, and was so difficult of detection, that many cases occurred; and I can vouch by personal experience that no form of police investigation is so troublesome and difficult as an inquiry into a case of arson.

I was asked about this time, whether I wished to be removed to a better or a more healthy district, Chittagong having an unenviable reputation for fever, but I replied in the negative. I had hitherto had good health, my work interested me, and there was also, I thought, probable openings in the Chittagong district not to be found elsewhere; the far-away blue hills of the south-west frontier seemed to beckon me, and my appetite for jungle adventure, and the free wild life of the wilderness, had been whetted by my late trip to the south.

I had found that at least one-half of my district was peopled by men and women of a like nature to myself, I mean those of Burmese origin and the hill tribes; they were pleasanter to deal with, more manly, more easy to understand, than the cringing, cowardly, lying, litigious Bengalis, who formed the population of almost any other district in Lower Bengal that I could hope to get. The Burman, or Mugh, was a fellow-creature, without caste prejudices, with a noble religion, a man with whom I could eat, drink, and make fellowship; the Chittagong Bengali was like a fox with a cross of the cat—not a man and a brother for me by any means. But although I had no desire to be transferred from Chittagong to any other district, I would gladly have exchanged my police appointment for some other work affording more scope for energy, more outlook for ambition. The police department, I found, was a *cul-de-sac*—once a policeman, always a policeman; and I applied to Colonel Phayre, the Chief Commissioner of British Burmah, seeking employment in the Burmese Commission, not, however, with much hope of success, as an appointment in India at that time was rarely to be obtained save through the usual channels of patronage and promotion.

In June of this year I had my first experience of the local fever and ague which had gained for the Chittagong district so unenviable a notoriety, and having been prostrated for two days, was advised by the doctor to try change of air. I therefore determined to visit Cox's Bazaar, the head-quarters of the southern sub-division, situated on the coast about a hundred miles south. I wondered vaguely who Mr. Cox might have been, who had given his name to the place; but my head being very dizzy, from large and repeated doses of quinine, I postponed the consideration of this to a future occasion.

In the small police yacht, which was at my disposal, I found great solace and contentment. She was yawl rigged, with two large comfortable cabins, pulling six sweeps a side, for river-work. In this boat, the "Foam," I made arrangements for my trip, and, leaving Chittagong on the 11th of June, sailed and rowed along by devious inland channels, striking behind islands, and circumventing mighty Father Neptune by all means in our power until, on the 17th of the same month, we arrived at the Bazaar of Cox.

Mr. Cox, I now ascertained, was a primæval magistrate, who had founded the settlement many years before, in the reign of Warren Hastings. It was a quaint timber town, quite different in appearance from the mat and mud structures of Bengal. The houses were all built solidly, with a platform and framework of massive teak beams—the floors of stout planks, and the roofs of carved wood-work with a palm-leaf thatch.

In dress, habits, and religion the inhabitants were as unlike Bengalis as the houses were unlike Bengali dwellings. A light-hearted race were the Mughs of Cox's Bazaar, taking life cheerfully. They had no idea of hard work, or labour of any sort, save fishing and trading in ships, and passed their time when on land sauntering about, clad in bright-coloured silks, smoking small rolls of tobacco, with a flower in the ear and a smile on the lip. Feastings innumerable went on, consisting of saucers of fish, with highly-seasoned vegetable condiments, and a back-ground of rice; this, with flirting, praying, and the attendance of dramatic performances, made up their daily round.

The men probably worked hard when away from home on the sea, whether as fishermen or traders; but certainly when on shore they did nothing more than what I have stated.

Their women seemed to enjoy perfect freedom of action. They went unveiled, and conversed freely with friends and acquaintances with much propriety, buying, selling, and guiding household affairs. The elders among them were treated with great respect. The younger ones carried dainty umbrellas, and were curious in the arrangement of the single rich silken petticoat which was the universal feminine wear. Their glossy black hair, fastened in a knot behind, was adorned with sprays of orchid and other gay-coloured blossoms.

Even in the measurement of time they were original and peculiar. The night was divided into, first, children's bed-time, from eight to ten; then old folks' bed-time, from ten to eleven; and lastly, young folks' bed-time, from eleven to twelve. During this last hour the young people were left free from the restraint of the presence of their elders, and this was, *par excellence*, the time for courting.

The night after my arrival at Cox's Bazaar, I was invited to attend a Burmese "poi," or dramatic representation, given by a troop of strolling actors. It was scarcely dark when I left the "Foam," moored in the creek, and proceeded to the theatre, which was simply a large tent or awning, pitched on a grassy sward on the outskirts of the town.

On reaching the spot, I took possession of the chair which had been respectfully placed in a good position for the "Sahib's" accommodation, and looked around. It was a curious scene. The whole area was closely packed with spectators, men, women, and children, all sitting on the ground, all smoking long rolls of fresh tobacco, and all intensely interested in the drama, which was in course of performance when I arrived.

The pole supporting the centre of the awning was wreathed with garlands of green leaves and flowers. The stage occupied one entire side of the area, and being simply a stretch of grass, was, of course, on a level with the spectators. The proscenium was marked off by a long row of strange-looking masks hanging pendant from a suspended bamboo; there were grotesque human faces, masks of devils, grinning and glaring, heads of bears and horses, and even detached arms and legs were hung here and there. The whole row was kept in wavy, jerking motion by a man who sat on one side puffing a cigar, and gently pulling a string, one end of which was attached to the bamboo from which the masks were suspended, and the other to his toe. The slow movement of his foot gave the masks a fantastic jiggity-jig, that lent a weird life to the long line of heads that glared upon the audience.

The orchestra was on the left of the stage, and consisted mainly of drums. These were placed in a large circle, a regular family of tom-toms, from the big bummer, used to emphasize a male chorus, down to the smallest tenor drums, upon which love-songs were accompanied. One active performer marshalled the whole of this battalion, and in his concentrated activity brought to mind the local proverb, " On the day of the wedding the mother-in-law is like a pea in a brass plate " ; so our *chef d'orchestre* sprang hither and thither at his drums, never resting a moment.

In the centre of this charmed circle sat a *virtuoso,* who had a divided responsibility. Sometimes he performed upon a clapper of white wood, with which he intercalated passages of asperity and rage ; at others he devoted himself in a dreamy manner to the evoking of wails from an instrument that had affinities with both clarionet and trumpet, and which I felt convinced was the " shawm " of Biblical memory. There were besides two flute players.

When I took my seat, the stage was in possession of the *basso profundo,* who, in the character of a Chinese monarch, accompanied by six of his courtiers (all smoking cigars), walked in the gardens of his palace, and lamented the sad, sad infatuation of his daughter, the Princess A-hla, for a penniless scamp, whose name and attributes I failed to arrive at. The courtiers intoned between whiles a chorus of sympathetic condolence, taking furtive pulls at their cigars to keep them alight. The monarch himself stooped to light his weed at one of the footlights, which were cotton wicks burning in small earthen saucers of cocoanut oil, when the good-looking scamp entered with much humility, and in dumb-show entreated the forgiveness of the irate monarch. Here occurred a grand opportunity for orchestral display, in which the shawm specially distinguished itself. A *duo* followed, which culminated in the angry parent tearing the flower from the scamp's ear and chasing him off the stage.

The next scene disclosed the beautiful princess, who with two female attendants had fled from the paternal roof, and was now supposed to have lost her way in a forest peopled by ogres of the most carnivorous description. The lament of the princess, who was an extremely pretty girl, was quite pathetic, and when she sank down on the grass, overcome with fatigue and anguish, the audience was carried away with sympathy. Now, of course, the lover entered on the scene, accompanied by a faithful henchman, who was evidently the comic man of the piece, judging by the sallies with which he convulsed the audience, and I have no doubt that the play came to a happy conclusion at some period before dawn; but as the leisurely proceedings which I have narrated had already occupied some two hours in performance, and it was "old folks' bed-time," I sought the refuge of my mosquito-curtains on board the "Foam."

While at Cox's Bazaar I received a visit from a wealthy Mugh merchant, a resident of the place, named Chyn-hla-phaw, who carried on a considerable trade between Calcutta and Burmah. He had a fair colloquial knowledge of Hindostani, acquired during his trading operations, and I seized the opportunity to discuss with him the subject of Buddhism, the national religion of Burmah, as well as of the Burmese inhabitants of British territory, who are known to us under the generic name of Mughs. He was a pithy man, full of apothegms such as, "The prison is shut night and day, yet it is always full," or "The pleasure of doing good is the only one that never wears out." I have found, indeed, more true and sincere religious feeling among Buddhists than among any other Eastern people.

The contrast between Buddhism and Hinduism is wonderfully clear and sharp-edged, and I wondered whether it is from the character of the people that a religion takes its colour, or if the faith moulds its votaries. As I talked with my friend Chyn-hla-phaw, a saying of Carlyle's recurred to my mind: "Hast thou considered that thought is stronger than artillery parks, and models the world, like soft clay? also how the beginning of all thought worth the name, is Love, and the wise head never yet was without the generous heart."

The religion of the Brahmans is a gloomy one; how can it indeed be otherwise, when the large majority of the Hindu race is trodden under foot by the governing caste of priests. The Brahmans have a finger in everything; in marriage feasts, at funerals, in all fasts and festivals, the priest must be fed and feed, no matter what the cost. The ritual, too, is grotesque and melancholy, while the comparatively low intellectual position and seclusion of the female sex must tend to sadden still further the lives of millions.

Among the Buddhists no such religious tyranny exists. The priesthood is open to all; indeed, at some period in life almost every man becomes a priest, it may be only for a week, it may be for long years, as the profession can be entered into or left at will. The present King of Burmah, for instance, wore the yellow robe of the priesthood before he was called to the throne. If a young man is disappointed in love, he assumes the garb of the priest, and carries the alms-bowl, shaves his head, and learns long prayers. The repentant robber finds refuge in the temple, and may there purify himself by a life of self-abnegation. Every morning the "phoon-gyee," clad in his yellow robe, and carrying his alms-bowl, solemnly walks through the streets. He speaks to no one, looks neither to the right nor left; but the bowl is none the less speedily filled with his day's food, and were it not so he would have to remain hungry. It is considered an act of high merit to minister to the men who have turned their backs upon the world, and abjured its pleasures in order to attain deliverance from desire, and the "phoon-gyee's" bowl is never left empty.

Benevolence is esteemed the greatest of virtues, and to do no harm to any living creature is the cardinal maxim of Buddhism. "Receive your thoughts as guests but your desires as children."

One dogma is held alike by both Buddhist and Hindu, the doctrine of the transmigration of souls. Both alike thus seek the solution of that most difficult problem of humanity—the reason for the great difference in our respective lots; why one to honour and another to dishonour; why one to health and happiness and another to sickness and misery. The Brahman has adroitly turned the great question into an engine of sacerdotal oppression, declaring that none could hope to attain deliverance save by a strict observance of ceremonial law.

Buddhism is a revolt against this tyranny. Buddha formulated the great principle of universal benevolence and equality, and taught that future happiness, together with ultimate deliverance, was to be obtained, not by slaying animals in sacrifice, or feeding multitudes of Brahmans, but by the practice of individual charity, truth, honesty, and purity. If a man does well in this body, he will have another existence of a higher grade; riches, happiness, and long life will then be his portion in this world; and if he continue in well-doing through a series of existences, he will rise in the scale of individual souls to a superhuman state of felicity, attaining in rare instances even to absorption into the Divine Essence—a loss of individuality, it is true, but an indescribable and incomparable gain in bliss. This crowning state is called Nirvana.

I submitted to Chyn-hla-phaw that the population of the world was continually increasing in numbers, and asked him what was his theory as to the new souls—whence did they come. He accounted for it by saying that there was a world of inferior spirits, who were subject to temptation and fall even as human beings were, and that to the wrong-doers among these was assigned an earthly probation. We held long converse together, and parted with mutual esteem; and thus began a friendship which I am glad to say continued undiminished as long as I remained in India.

I took the "Foam" out to sea next evening. It was beautifully calm, with a soft breeze from the south, and very dark. The sea in places shone bright with phosphorescent light, like latent moonshine stored in ocean. The wind was favourable; I had finished my official inspection of Cox's Bazaar, I had bathed on the white sands, and eaten of the oysters for which the place was famous, and now gave the word to Abdúl Manjee, who had the helm, to put her head towards Chittagong.

I got back to Chittagong on the 27th of June. We came up the river on the flood, and on arriving abreast of the jetty,

I gave the order to "let go." The chain rattled and rumbled out of the hawse-hole, and then, from the shadow of the great black wooden jetty, my boat shot out, manned by four policemen in blue shirts and scarlet turbans, with my fat, oily Bengali Court Inspector weighing down the stern. He brought a large budget of letters—there is no rest for the official; so I mounted my grey pacing pony, which was waiting for me at the stairs, and swiftly ambled through the town up to my small bungalow on the hill-top, with its walls of matting brightly varnished, and wood framework all painted sea-green, which I called home.

I had to rise early every morning at Chittagong, in order to attend parade and superintend the drilling of my men. I do not know why, but early rising had always been a trial to me from my school-days down to my late campaigning in the Mutiny. I liked it none the better now that I had no commanding officer to ordain when I should get out of bed; but I had to get up none the less for that. I have always wondered at the smug self-complacency of the early-riser. Why should a person arrogate virtue to himself simply because his capacity for sleep is limited, the simple fact being that some sleep fast while others sleep slowly. I am a slow sleeper; and, indeed, have always regarded my abandonment of military life proper as materially adding to my length of days, by enabling me to take such periods of repose as are demanded by exhausted nature. In the primary geological formations no trace of man's existence has been discovered, and, in like manner, the earlier hours of the morning are an eocene period unfit for the sustentation of humanity.

Rising thus somewhat unwillingly, one fine clear morning at six o'clock, I solaced myself by the view of the blue distant hills, with fleecy cloud lines floating here and there on their summits; they seemed to lay a spell upon me and to beckon me towards them. The hill country for the most part lay beyond the limits of the Chittagong district, and therefore outside my legitimate sphere of action. There was an English officer in charge of this undefined hill territory, and I had occasionally met him on his visits to Chittagong; but he seemed strangely unaware of his opportunities, speaking of the hills as hateful, and seeming to know little and care less about their inhabitants. His head-quarters were situated at Chandragúna, a day's journey up the river, just at the junction of the hills with the plains. All the hill country to the south of the river Karna-phúli was practically unknown, and much of it had never been visited by Europeans. I collected with avidity all the stories I could hear of the wild tribes, the Kúkis, Shendús, Mrúngs, and others, who dwelt on our borders and traded in our frontier marts, and who occasionally made forays into British territory for the purpose of taking heads and obtaining slaves. I found, however, that little reliable information was obtainable; the only people who visited the unknown country being the wood-cutters, who banded themselves together each year in the cold weather, and went up the river to fell the larger and more valuable timber in the forests of the interior. They were acquainted only with the tribes who were nominally under British control; while of the Kúkis, Lúshais, Shendús, and other independent tribes they spoke with bated breath, recounting fables evidently unworthy of credence, stories of men with tails and villages built in trees—a host of improbabilities.

What little I did hear, however, more and more fed the longing which had seized me to go and see for myself. I had a long talk with the Commissioner on the subject, and he, after hearing all I had to say, was disposed to back me in making an expedition to the hills; and, having thus assured myself of his support, I submitted a formal application to the head of my own department, setting forth my intention of travelling in the hills during the approaching cold season, and asking for a small grant of money to buy presents and defray the expenses of the journey.

The Commissioner of the Division was a very good friend to me in private, beside supporting me officially. He was in many ways a remarkable man, and in our talks and walks together I learned much from him. He was a true Liberal in politics.

"Do not be misled," said he, "by the so-called aristocracy of Conservatism. A Liberal is just as ready as the bluest Conservative to give his life for Queen or country; he does not simply by being a Liberal desire the downfall of the Bench of Bishops, or a communism of property. The true Liberal, in fact, has but one cardinal dogma; he believes in the perfectibility of the human race. The advocacy of mere outward equality is a bar to all true progress, but liberty full and absolute there must be for each one to rise according to individual merit. I recognise in my manhood no inferiority to the manhood of another. I give place to the Lieutenant-Governor of Bengal, for he is now my official superior; but I may be one day myself the Governor of a province. A Peer of the United Kingdom has the better of me in many things, and I grudge him not his advantages, for the road is open to all. There is George Campbell of our Indian Civil Service, his uncle raised himself from being a small Scottish lawyer to be Lord Chancellor and Peer of the realm. Liberty, and the right of each one to do his best, that is the true creed of a Liberal."

Thanks to the good offices of this kind friend, the Inspector-General of Police authorised me to expend a certain sum in the purchase of presents for the wild folk; and I was given to understand, demi-officially, that I might go into the hills for ten days or so, but that no official sanction could be accorded to my expedition. In other words, if I went at all it was strictly at my own risk.

I was glad, however, to obtain permission on any terms, and accordingly at once commenced my preparations for the journey. I laid in a stock of scarlet broadcloth, glass beads of divers colours, brass rings, bracelets of lac and tinsel very beautiful to behold, not forgetting sundry cases of strong liquor. I was told by the Bengali wood-cutters, to whom I have before alluded, that the hill-men were great drinkers, and hard-headed to boot; so I took with me some bottles of spirits of wine, which I hoped would floor the strongest head among them. I also borrowed a couple of elephants to carry my baggage, and ordered for my own convenience a folding bed, consisting of a stretcher of canvas, with a framework for mosquito curtains; a camp-chair of iron and canvas, with a small folding table, and the necessary cooking pots and pans, completed my equipment. The whole was divisible into coolie loads, as I was informed that after leaving the plains and entering the hilly country beyond I should have to abandon my elephants.

We had a farewell music party at the Commissioner's the night before my departure, when we played Weber's "Der Freyschutz," arranged as a quartett; and at early dawn of the following morning I started on my expedition into the unknown country towards which I felt myself so irresistibly impelled.

CHAPTER VIII

THE SHENDUS

1865–66

I HAD pondered long and deeply over my plans, and had determined to strike south-east. To the north and north-east of Chittagong lay an uninteresting country, the greater portion being "regulation districts" of the province of Bengal, and the remainder, ruled by the Tipra Rajah, was for the most part scrub-jungle, sparsely inhabited, with broad plains overgrown with high "sunn" grass. To the east, I might have followed the course of the river Karnaphuli, which had its source far away in the Lushai hills; but on the border was stationed the Superintendent of Hill Tribes, who would probably ask what was my business in his jurisdiction. After a careful study of such maps as were available, I had arrived at the conclusion that by going some distance southwards and then striking east I should get across to Burmah, perhaps, if I went far enough, to China. It seemed clear, at least, that by this route I should strike the head-waters of rivers running into Burmah, and so attain to an unknown country where no European had hitherto penetrated. These cogitations, however, I kept carefully locked within my own breast, knowing full well that exploration or discovery formed no part of the duty of the "perfect policeman." All I wanted was to get loose in the hills, after which, "vogue la galère"—we should see what we should see.

It was on the 14th of November, 1865, that I set forth on my expedition. I was accompanied by two native servants, besides an escort of six policemen, under the command of a staunch old Punjabi sergeant named Fyzúllah Khan, who had attached himself to my fortunes, following me from Hazaribagh. We had two elephants to carry the baggage, which was severely limited in quantity. I trusted for food to the supplies of the country which we were about to traverse; the bulkiest part of the baggage was the two bales of presents for the hill people, and these being the sinews of war were specially looked after, and packed carefully before anything else on the back of the largest elephant.

I marched south, following the line of my police stations, in order to have the advantage of good roads as far as possible before plunging into the forest, and on the 20th of November I reached Manikpur, the last village at which I should camp in the plains. By this time we had done six days of steady marching, and the whole party was consequently in good walking case. Little by little I had discovered and left behind all superfluous articles of clothing or equipment which my escort had brought with them, and my party was now absolutely in the lightest marching order; this was the more necessary as at Manikpur we had to abandon the elephants, our baggage being conveyed, after that, either on the backs of coolies or in boats, as circumstances might direct. I had discarded my small tent at the outset, leaving it behind on the second day's march as superfluous, and I now still further reduced my outfit, confining my table equipage to one iron pot, a frying-pan, and two tin plates, with a knife and fork.

On leaving Manikpur and entering the hills the scenery became wilder and more beautiful, and I experienced a growing sensation of delight at having at last cast loose from civilized man. How joyful was the thought that a few days more of travel would place me beyond reach even of the post, and that consequently, by no possibility could I be recalled from my journey.

Our route lay by a narrow hill-stream, along which we poled our way in dug-out canoes, until, on the 29th of November, I reached a village of the Mrúng tribe, and there halted to gain information and arrange for a change of transport.

The worthy Roaja, or village head-man, politely offered me the hospitality of his house; but I preferred being independent, and camped on the banks of the small stream below. The weather was cloudless and beautiful, so that I had no need of shelter, and my escort being some of them bigoted Hindus, objected to occupying quarters in a Mrúng village, alleging that by so doing they would be defiled. So I encamped on a sand-bank beside the small stream up which we had come, and which sped by on its bright rapid course to the plains, the water tumbling and foaming, fringed at the brink with plumy fern and wet moss sparkling like emeralds, and bottomed with sun-flecked stones that looked purple and golden in the dancing light. A little lower down the stream lay a labyrinth of great gray boulders and hummocks of rock, which must have been rolled down from the hills above on angry days of flood and fury. Here I established myself, spreading my mat and rugs under a tree, while the faithful Toby, my Mugh cook, occupied himself not far off in preparing my dinner.

Poor Toby! his feelings were sorely outraged by the uncivilized proceedings of the last few days, for, be it known, he had been to Calcutta, and had even served as a scullion at Government House, so that he flattered himself he really did know the correct manner in which things should be done. Now the present wild and barbarous mode of travelling was quite beyond his experience. In the first place, he had been limited to two pots; this was a misfortune, but, as I pointed out to him, it offered great opportunities of distinction, and would enable him to show (as I believed) that he could do more with two pots than any other cook with a whole *batterie de cuisine.* Mollified by this compliment, he retired pacified for the moment, but shortly afterwards returned with expostulation written in every lineament.

"Sahib! am I expected to cook *this* animal for your dinner?"

He held in his hand a fine fat frog which, together with some rice and vegetables, had been sent by the Roaja for our consumption. I had to compound with Toby by requesting that the frog might be cooked for me, in the correct way, by one of the hill-men.

I ate this frog along with young fern-tops and some plantain shoots, by way of vegetables, and found it by no means unpalatable. The Roaja promised me a gecko-steak the next day, a gecko being a large sort of lizard; but of this I said nothing to Toby.

My cook's proper patronymic was Tobé-dhun, but I called him Toby for short, in English fashion. In like manner my sergeant's name, Fyz-úllah Khan, was abbreviated, first to Fyzullah, and finally to Fuzlah.

In the afternoon the worthy Roaja came to pay me a ceremonious visit, accompanied by certain elders of his village, and for their delectation I at once produced a bottle of spirits of wine, which was duly handed round, in improvised cups formed by cutting off joints of a small bamboo, and was pronounced a powerfully good liquor.

The drinking of spirits of wine possessed one advantage for me, that, being colourless, I was able to help myself freely from a black bottle full of pure water, and so drink fair with my guests and yet keep my head clear.

It was of importance for me to propitiate this Mrúng Roaja, as my next march lay across the hills, the stream offering no further water-way. Now, in order to cross the hills, it was necessary to have a guide, and also to get eight or ten coolies to carry the baggage. I therefore smoothed down the Roaja to the utmost extent of my ability, discovering indeed, finally, that he and I were actually related to each other. It happened in this wise.

"Respected Roaja, may I inquire your name?"

"My friendly name (may your journey be prosperous!) is Twekam Tongloyn."

"This is most strange! Have any of your tribe ever crossed the great black water?"

"No; why does the Sahib ask this question?"

"Because my name is the same as yours, and we must, therefore, be of the same clan."

Incredulity on the part of the Roaja; the elders looked puzzled.

"What may be the friendly name of the Sahib?"

With dignity. "My name is Urbut Tongloyn (Herbert Tom Lewin)."

Sensation. We exchange pipes in token of the bond between us. More spirits of wine.

This strange and wonderful coincidence gave rise to a long ethnological discussion, in which Roaja Twekam-Tom-Lewin favoured me with the following piece of old-world history.

"God made the trees and the waters, the animals and the creeping things first of all. He made them very well, for he was a great artificer. In one thing only he made a mistake, for in first moulding the alligator he forgot the legs, and the result was a great snake. Now this snake conceived it to be a grievous wrong, in that he had been made without legs, and he determined, therefore, to vex God as much as lay in his power; so he lay in the jungle and watched. Long and carefully he watched, until he saw that God was about to complete his work by making a man and a woman. He fashioned them from fine clay from the river's bank; but it was a long and difficult job, and the work could not be completed within the space of one sun. So every night, when God slept, the snake crept forth from the jungle and destroyed all the work which had been done during the day. On the morrow, when God woke up, he was very angry; but so it happened again, for God must sleep, and whenever he did so, the snake acted maliciously as before.

"God was now much puzzled. At last, after great consideration, he determined to construct a guardian who should watch while he slept; and so he set to work and made a dog, and at night when the snake came as before, to do evil, the dog barked and frightened it away; for God made the dog to sleep with only one eye. So now God was able to complete the man and the woman. He finished the man first, and the woman, who was last made, narrowly escaped destruction, for the dog was busy eating a bone and only just barked in time. This is the reason why the women are of a timid disposition to this day. The snake, however, still keeps up its enmity, and it is while God sleeps that men die; the snake carries them off, and although the dogs still bark and howl, the snake has got used to their noise, and is not frightened any more." "It is a pity," added the Roaja, naïvely, "that God sleeps so much; for, otherwise, we should live much longer."

The next morning I paid my return visit to Twekam Roaja in his village, where I was received with all honour. A clean cane mat was spread for me on the platform in front of the Roaja's house, and here I was regaled with small cups of a spirit which the villagers distilled themselves from rice. After an interval I was conducted into the house, where a rough but not unpalatable meal of burnt pig and rice had been prepared by the Roaja's wife, which she and her daughter served to me upon small wooden platters, with plaintain-leaves by way of table-cloth. I noticed, in the privacy of family life to which I was then admitted, the women laid aside the breast-cloth usually worn, performing the household work with only one small petticoat round their loins.

After dinner we adjourned to the outer platform once more, and the villagers entertained me with a dance, which was performed on the smooth open space in front of the Roaja's house. The music was made by a kind of reed-band. Each performer held a gourd, into which was fitted a long reed stopped with one hole, and each player emitted his single note when his turn came, as in the Russian horn-bands. Little boys blew on the tenor reeds, while full-grown men gave out the deeper notes, which required more breath and power, the gourds acting as reservoirs to contain the wind. At intervals a low sonorous note was interpolated by a gong, the whole uniting in a slow and plaintive but not inharmonious concert.

The dance was performed by young men only, dressed up for the occasion, with feathers in their hair, and holding spears and axes; the performance throughout was conducted with silent gravity, and was of interminable length. The time was marked by bending the knees in cadence. Occasionally the dancers would pause and execute small oscillatory movements, bending their bodies from side to side, after which the solemn circling recommenced. It was not a cheerful or hilarious performance by any means. Smoking and conversation went on unchecked among the spectators, and once or twice small cups of spirit, and some leaves of dried tobacco for smoking, were handed round by the women. I noticed that some of the small naked children who squatted round the circle of dancers held lizards in leash as play-things, and while we sat smoking on the platform, a tame "bim-raj," or king-crow, came fluttering from the house and settled on the Roaja's head, saluting him with great affection. A kindly, natural people on the whole, my intercourse with whom strengthened my feelings of jubilation at having for a time escaped from the plains and the dwellers therein. I had no difficulty now in arranging with the Roaja as to my starting next day. He offered to act as guide himself, and promised the services of his villagers to carry the baggage.

Accordingly, we set off the next morning, and from early dawn until sundown we traversed unknown distances, sometimes following a wild elephant track along the ridge of a hill, at others cutting a path through the close-growing stems of bamboo jungle, or painfully pushing along through acres of lofty grass, eight and ten feet high, giving one a sensation as of a bewildered ant in a hay-field.

Once we had to descend the perpendicular face of a precipice, notching holes for our feet, and using the long hanging creepers as guide-ropes. The danger here was to those who went first, for my Bengali policemen, being unused to this sort of travel, and being, moreover, thoroughly uneasy and frightened at the descent, moved so clumsily that great stones were dislodged, and fell rattling down on the heads of the foregoers. Clinging like a lizard to the cliff, one could not get out of the way; so, when a stone fell, there was nothing for it but to duck one's head, hunch one's shoulders, and take the blow as best could be. One thing was made plain to me by that day's march—the Bengali escort was useless, and I decided to send them back to Chittagong as soon as an opportunity of doing so presented itself.

I was very tired after my first real hill-march, and, what with the fatigue, exposure, and unusual diet combined, I felt rather feverish. Among all my discomforts, I found consolation in the thought that I had, at any rate, accomplished my desire. There we were at last, far away from civilization, on the banks of a new river, which the Roaja informed me was the Rigray Khyoung, or, as the Bengalis called it, the Sungú River, which flowed to the sea through the territory of a potentate styled the Bohmong. Now, as Roaja Twekam owed allegiance to this chief, he was somewhat uneasy in his mind lest his having guided me across the hills should be taken amiss.

But, as the Bohmong was a tributary of the British Government, I did not anticipate that he could actively resent the Roaja's action, or oppose my advance through his territory, although I learned that he viewed with great disfavour the entry of any European into his country.

One comfort was that, by crossing the hills on foot as I had done, we struck the Sungú River a couple of day's journey above the Bohmong's residence, so that, before he could receive tidings of my incursion, I hoped to be away and beyond his jurisdiction.

On the 2nd of December, 1865, I bade farewell to my friendly namesake, the Roaja. I pledged him in a loving-cup, and cheered his heart by promises of support in the event of the Bohmong annoying him; and, animated by a reminder of our relationship, he took his departure, with a yard of scarlet broad-cloth, two pairs of bracelets, and two shillings for himself, while a shilling each and a glass of spirits of wine per head made his men equally happy.

Our camp was beautifully situated on a bend in the higher waters of the Sungú. The river lay spread out before us in a dark, mirror-like sheet, streaked here and there by delicate silvery wind-flaws, like lines of frost-work on the water. The banks rose steeply with over-hanging rocks, plumy with fern and bamboo, and backed by giant trees festooned with creepers and orchids. From the turn of the river below, the breeze bore to our ears the roar of the water as it broke into foamy rapids.

My men dispersed themselves along the shore, seeking to add to our scanty provender by tickling fish under the stones, just like boys after trout in England, producing, however, only ugly creatures something like eels, without scales, and of a mottled brown and black colour, with white bellies.

The faithful Toby viewed this novel description of fish with a mournful shake of the head, as who should say, "Alas! what evil fate brings such comestibles to the pot of a well-ordered cook!"

I sent Fuzlah with an interpreter to the nearest village down stream, to arrange for boats and obtain information, while I smoked a reflective pipe, speculating how soon we should get beyond British territory, and what manner of country and people I should find behind the range of hills which lay to the east. On thinking matters over I wished I had brought with me a better assortment of presents · money, I found, was of comparatively little value; but gaudy-coloured ear-rings, in shape of a truncated cone to thrust through the lobe of the ear, were the universal hill wear, and small hand-mirrors and wooden cheroot-holders would be greatly prized. However, one has always to buy one's experience. I began to suspect that I had acted wisely in bringing my violin. At the Mrúng village I had given great satisfaction by joining in their concert, and I promised myself the delight and admiration of future music parties; for, although my performance was extremely elementary, the instrument was novel, and much appreciated by the hill-folk. Fuzlah and the interpreter returned after an hour, bringing with them some canoes which they had hired at a Kúmi village below the rapids, at the reasonable rate of two-pence per diem, and I practised for some time how to sit balancing oneself in the stern of a dug-out, and at the same time steer with the paddle.

Fuzlah reported that we had struck the Sungú too high, and that it was now necessary for us to descend the stream, a day's journey, to where a small tributary, the Ramakri Khyoung, entered the main river; ascending this small stream we should find a hill path which led across the water-parting to the river Koladan, whose waters flow down to Akyab in the Arrakan province of British Burmah.

Next day, therefore, we started early, reaching Ramakri Khyoung a little before sundown, after a hard day's paddling, in which I took my share. We had to shoot the rapids at the commencement of the day's journey, and this experience was certainly most vividly enjoyable—like a gallop on a fiery and spirited horse.

The boat slipped quietly along at first through the glassy stretches of the upper water, the speed of the current gradually increasing until the water seemed to crinkle longitudinally, and in front we could hear a rushing, roaring sound, which increased in volume as we sped along. The swift, strong stream now became filled with threatening rocks, breaking and fretting the river into creamy foam; not always, however, showing themselves on the surface, but sometimes lying dangerously hidden beneath the water, their presence only to be recognised by the practised eye of the steersman, who tells of the hidden danger by the colour and humpiness of the water. Like a swift bird the canoe flies on, now entering a narrow gorge filled with tumbling turbulent billows, foam-crested, roaring, through which winds a narrow yellow water-path; one felt the mad sweep of the current bearing us on irresistibly to unforeseen events. The men paddled and yelled like demons, and the steersman played his part right manfully. With sudden swift turn of the wrist he sends the boat twirling under the over-hanging trees of the bank, where in a swift-running side-eddy he avoids the thunderous swoop of mid-river fury, then, calling on the paddler at the bow, the canoe is headed out into the mad tumble of the final flurry. Bang! she jumps on the shoulder of a dark hidden rock, plunging off again immediately at an angle of nearly forty-five degrees, down an inclined plane of water, and taking in a good prow full, passes swiftly into the calm water below the rapid. Here all give vent to their pent-up feelings by screeches of victory; and we turn to watch the progress of the boats which follow.

It was a glorious time—a new sensation—the poetry of motion; one flew, as it were, on bird's wings amid the mighty rush and roar of the torrent; each moment was a climax; and I should indeed have felt proud had I been able to sit at the stern and take her through; nay, more, I determined that some day I would make the venture. Mind and body alike were aroused to the greatest activity, accuracy of judgment and quick decision being absolutely necessary, every moment bringing forth fresh and unlooked-for difficulties which had to be met and surmounted at peril of one's life. The excitement, while it lasted, was intense; and our after gleeful gratulation proportionately keen.

The villagers from whom we had hired the canoes, and who also furnished the steersmen, took up a position of vantage on the bank, and watched the "ashiang" (master), as they called me, handle a paddle for the first time, joining in the cheers as each canoe successfully accomplished the passage.

I was more vexed than I can tell at my inability to speak

the tongue of these people. I had, it is true, learned sufficient to give a few orders, but when it came to a real palaver I had to trust to an interpreter; and this was very galling to me. It was detestable and unendurable to be, as it were, minus ears and tongue, and I determined to mend the situation as quickly as was humanly possible.

Before starting up the Ramakri Khyoung I decided to send back my escort of Bengali constables, who, I found, were quite useless for hill-travelling; they grumbled at carrying even the smallest portion of their own baggage; they were acquainted neither with the people nor the language; and they had no powers of endurance. I found them prostrated by a slight attack of fever, or by any of the pains and aches incidental on real hard work, and, moreover, in case of actual danger, I firmly believed they would run away. So I resolved to dispense with their further attendance, and at the same time I took advantage of their departure to communicate with the Commissioner of Chittagong. I sent them back by boat, entrusting to them a full report of all that I had done and what I intended to do, as far as my intentions could be formulated, or as far as I thought expedient. I had left with me Sergeant Fuzlah, true as steel, and the faithful Toby, who clave unto me, although I offered him a passage back with the escort. I also retained two Mugh interpreters from Cox's Bazaar, whom I had hired for the journey.

We suffered many things on our march across the hills from the Sungú to the Pee Khyoung, an affluent of the Koladan River; sometimes we waded knee-deep in water, sometimes myriads of leeches feasted on our blood, making their way to the flesh through the thickest and closest coverings; or we pushed our way painfully through thickets of enormous sting-ing-nettles, whose sting was proportionate to their size; but still ever onwards, until we reached a village on the other side of the water-parting, and I drank at last of the water of another country.

I halted here only for one night, as the inhabitants were very timid, and the place so poor as with difficulty to provide food for my small party. The villagers seemed weighed down with mistrust and suspicion of their kind; they lived in constant dread of attack by hostile neighbours, and with a view to defence they had constructed a strange and quite original stronghold in a lofty tree. Here, at a height of perhaps sixty feet from the ground, in a strong fork of the tree, they had built a bullet-proof house, of thick rough-hewn logs, loopholed in the sides and floor, which might contain some twenty people. Access to this fortalice was only to be gained in Robinson Crusoe fashion, by a series of ladders, which were afterwards drawn up. It was houses such as this, I suppose, that gave rise to the tales I had heard in Chittagong, of hill-tribes who, like monkeys, lived habitually in trees.

On the 7th of December we safely reached Dalakmay, a village on the Koladan, consisting of about fifty houses inhabited by Arracanese British subjects, and at that time the extreme frontier village of Arracan. Here the Roaja, or headman of the village, was suspicious of my intentions, and declined an interview. He furnished me, however, with food, on payment considerably above value, and, to ascertain what manner of man I was, sent to interview me a Burmese doctor, by name Khilu, who had a great local reputation for wisdom. I did my best to reassure the doctor, telling him where I came from, and that my object was merely to go up the river and see the country. On his part, Mr. Khilu begged respectfully to assure me, that if I did go up the river I should never come down again, as my head would be cut off and set on a pole by the Shendús, whom he described as a predatory and powerful tribe living beyond British limits, who feared neither man nor devil, and who, by perpetual forays to obtain slaves, kept the whole frontier in perpetual terror. To this I smiled and responded nothing, save to beg the good offices of Khilu in getting a boat.

At Dalakmay also I found strongholds prepared, in which the inhabitants could find shelter in the event of an attack by the dreaded Shendús; these refuges, however, were of a different fashion from the tree-fort of the Pee Khyoung. Broad rafts were made by tying large bundles of bamboos together, and on this basement, comfortable houses of mat were built, so that in troublous times they had merely to push off into the stream, which here ran broad and deep, and they were secure from their enemies; for the Shendús, being mountain men, could neither swim nor manage a boat.

I learned that not far from Dalakmay was a range of hills called Kyouk-pandong, the summit of which formed a large level plateau, where existed the ruins of a large city, relics of some bygone dynasty. Dr. Khilu assured me that he had himself seen the ruins of temples there, surrounded by fruit-trees such as only grow near the habitations of men; but, he added, "No-one lives there now, save the ogres (rakas) and spirits of the woods (nats) The great king lived there longer than long ago."

The plateau was said to be ten or twelve miles long, and was situated at an altitude of four thousand feet. What an admirable site for a European sanatorium! This, however, was no district of mine, and I had no leisure for archæological research. My object was to reach the Blue Mountain, marked as such on the Government maps, in a territory described as "unsurveyed and unknown," but inhabited by a race called Shendús.

The worthy villagers of Dalakmay, perceiving my anxiety to get on, naturally made an opportunity of my necessity, fleecing me handsomely for food and boat-hire before I was permitted to depart. At length, after much diplomacy, it was arranged that Khilu the Wise should convoy me up stream to the village of Yuong, a Kúmi chief of influence, after which it was expressly covenanted that my blood was to be on my own head, and that no blame was to attach to the village of Dalakmay or its head-man, no matter how untoward my fate.

The appearance of Dr. Khilu, as he entered my boat the morning of our departure to afford me support and guidance, was truly imposing. Clad in a skirted vest of black satin, with a waist-cloth of dark purple silk, shot with black, his grizzled top-knot encircled by a rope of the finest white muslin, he presented a striking contrast to my own weather-beaten and travel-stained appearance. From his neck depended a silver chain, from which hung tweezers and other toilet implements, while under his arm he bore a straight Burmese sword richly ornamented, and so we set forth together in a dug-out, with much majesty.

As we rowed along he entertained me with various short ensamples of his professional skill. For instance, he had extracted from the stomach of one man the skin of a buffalo, which had caused great suffering, and must eventually have caused the death of the patient. I asked how it got there, and was gravely assured that an opposition " medicine man " had caused its entry with evil intent.

" My wisdom, however, was superior to his," Dr. Khilu remarked with self-complacency. " I quickly procured its ejection. I have, indeed, frequently extracted even worms from the brain."

He knew very little, I found, beyond his charms and incantations, or at any rate would communicate nothing of importance; he may perhaps have had some knowledge of simples, and certainly possessed a good modicum of assurance and native cunning.

We reached Yuong's village at midday, and were well received by him. I shortly stated my wishes, and he, on his side, requested that I would remain a day or so at his village, in order that the omens might be consulted. To this I readily consented, as the place and the people were alike a new book for me, and intensely interesting.

Yuong belonged to the Kúmi tribe. The tribal name, Kúmi is derived from " Kú," a hand, and " mi," a man; meaning, probably, the handy men—men neat and adroit with their hands, not to say light-fingered. But this name of Kúmi has been transmogrified by the Arracanese (who speak an old form of Burmese, probably the original form) into Khwé-mi, *i.e.*, " dog-men," in allusion to the tribal custom of wearing a narrow breech-cloth, worn round the waist and tucked between the legs, leaving a long pendent queue like a dog's tail; or it might also have had reference to the habit of eating dog, which is prevalent among them. I questioned my host Yuong as to the flavour of dog, and he pronounced it a most delicate dish. " The dog," he said, " must be young and of one colour, if possible black; parti-coloured dogs are tough, as a rule. The animal should be taken for killing when just weaned from the mother, then nourish him well for a fortnight on rice and butter, and he will be in prime condition. On the day of the feast let him eat as much boiled rice and curd as he is able, and, as he swallows the last mouthful, kill him cleverly by a blow with a club behind the ears; the rice he has newly eaten forms an admirable stuffing."

Yuong much desired to prepare for me a mess of dog after the foregoing fashion; but although I affected omnivorousness, and lectured Toby roundly upon his lack of adventure in regard to new viands, yet one must draw the line somewhere, and I drew it at dog. The village of Yuong was situated on the banks of the Koladan, the houses all being built of bamboo and thatched with palm-leaf. The floor of the chief's house was raised some eight feet from the ground, having an open gallery or verandah in front facing the river. Trophies of deer's horns hung on the main posts, and some dark blue home-spun cloth, in process of manufacture, was fixed in a small hand-loom at the end of the verandah. The woman who had been weaving stepped aside to give me passage as I went up the ladder; water was wanted in the house and she was going to fetch it from the river, carrying on her back, suspended by a grass band over her forehead, a large cane basket, containing six enormous bamboo tubes, which served as water-pails. Another woman, just at the door, was washing some brass plates, while underneath the platform, on the ground below, the pigs grumphed and disputed for the scraps of food which fell, with the dirty water, through the open-work of the bamboo flooring.

On entering the house I was conducted to a seat of honour on a mat at the further end of the apartment, and some rice-spirit was produced, the Burmese name of which was "arak," from which comes the English arrack and the old rack-punch of the time of the Regency. The house consisted of one great hall or common room, with the chief's sleeping-place, raised bed-fashion, in a warm corner near the fire. The hearths, of which there were two, one at either end of the big hall, were made of earth trodden down into a square frame of rough logs; over the furthest hearth, by an iron hook, hung a mighty crock, in which something was simmering; it might, I thought, be—dog!

The walls were of bamboo matting set double, with a space

of four inches between the inner and outer wall, giving coolness in summer and warmth in winter. Over the hearth by the chief's sleeping-place, was suspended a large trophy of horns and skulls. I looked to see if among them were any human skulls; but there were only spoils of the chase—horns of guyal, bison and deer, skulls of bear and wild boar. In the corner, by the bed's head, stood two old flint muskets and a sheaf of spears. Yuong was at first somewhat reserved; but, after hearing all I had to say, he consented to send me on my way as far as the village of Teynwey, the chief of the Kyaws, who, he said, was on friendly terms with many Shendú chiefs, and could, if he chose, assist me materially. He, Yuong, knew nothing of the Shendús. I found afterwards that this last statement was untrue.

After arranging with Yuong I returned to my boat at the water's edge to sleep, but, before retiring for the night, I smoked a pipe with Khilu, who favoured me with more curious information as to his medical practice. The Kúmis, he said were an ignorant and barbarous people, unacquainted with the first principles of healing, and their medicine men quite unable to deal with devils or any of the higher branches of the art. To sores or wounds they applied poultices of pounded rice or warm earth; for headaches the temples of the sufferer were cauterised with a red-hot knife, or bitten until the blood flowed; while for colic or indigestion their remedy was abstinence from food, and the application of a hot "dao" (a broad knife) over a wet cloth to the ailing part.

"All cases of epidemic disease," said Dr. Khilu, "as your honour doubtless knows, are demoniacal; and for these the Kúmis' only remedy is flight. They abandon their sick to die in the villages, and take to the hills, camping out and changing their locality day by day. Should a neighbouring village be attacked, it is placed in rigorous quarantine, no intercourse between its inhabitants and the outer world being allowed, on pain of death. The uninfected villages are thoroughly purified. This," continued Khilu, "has been taught them by me."

Lying old man! the custom of quarantine has existed for ages among all hill races.

"Yes. It is effected by an exorcism of a powerful nature. A monkey is caught, and killed at the entrance to the village by dashing it on the ground, so as to avoid spilling its blood. The threshold of each house is then swept with the dead monkey's tail, after which some of its blood, mingled with dust, is smeared on the lintel of each door. This is generally effective."

On the 14th of December I reached the village of the Kyaw chief Teynwey. This village was strongly fortified, being in close proximity to the Shendú country, a sort of *terrain neutre*, the fusing point, as it were, between our tribes and the independent clans. The news of my coming had preceded me; for Teynwey himself, with a numerous following, came to the river's bank to receive me on landing. Teynwey was an elderly man, perhaps sixty years old; he was attired in the peculiar fine home-spun plaid cloth which is manufactured only by the Shendú women, and is specially reserved for the apparel of chiefs. In the turban which was twisted round his grey top-knot he wore an aigrette or plume, of the fine long-shafted tail-feathers of the "bim-raj," or king-crow. Both his dress and physiognomy bespoke him of different race to Yuong, although I found there were many Kúmis permanently domiciled in the Kyaw village.

I was received with much apparent kindliness, and Teynwey conducted me with some formality up to his village, where a separate house was assigned for me and my followers.

This village I found especially interesting, being the firs really fortified place I had met with in my hill travels. I contained fifty-four houses, and was situated on the top a hill about five hundred feet high, looking down on the river, which flowed below in a narrow and somewhat rocky channel. The place was unapproachable on three sides, owing to the steepness of the hill scarp, and was besides surrounded by a strong stockade of unhewn logs, having a frieze or topping of bamboo spikes some feet in length; round the stockade, at intervals, were look-out places and stations for firing. The sole entrance was by a steep winding path leading to triple doors of strong hewn timber plank three inches thick. It was altogether a formi lable defensive position, the only weak point being, that the houses, built of bamboo thatched with palm-leaves, could easily be set on fire by rockets or fire-tipped arrows. I soon ensconced myself in my temporary abode, to the door of which Teynwey himself conducted me, there taking his leave. I was evidently regarded with much curiosity, a European being, I found, an unknown animal in those parts.

Yuong brought to see me a Shendú chief, the head of a small village community in the vicinity, and I need hardly say that I regarded him with the keenest interest, as being the first man I had seen of the nation I had struggled so many days to arrive at. He was accompanied by four Shendú women, and could speak no language save his own. He wore the distinctive Shendú head-dress, the turban being wound into a lofty horn-like projection over the forehead. I inquired the origin of this singular head-dress, and was informed as follows:

"In the ancient days, in times of old, the squirrel and the horned owl had a dispute, and the squirrel lost his temper and bit the owl on the head, so that he became all bloody and assumed a frightful aspect. The squirrel became so terrified at this that he fled for his life, and the owl devoured all the young squirrels. Now one of our chiefs observed this incident, and pondered thereon; then came to him God's messenger, the tiger, and told him that what he had seen was an instruction. So since that time the Shendú tribes wear their hair high on the forehead, like the horns of the owl; and when they go to war they bind scarlet cloth on their turbans, so that, like the owl, they may take heads."

The Shendú women were quite different in appearance to those of other tribes. The hill women I had hitherto seen were remarkable for the scantiness of their clothing, it being rare to see a skirt lower than the knee; but these Shendú women covered their bosoms with a decent chemise and wore long petticoats of clean home-spun, while over their shoulders hung handsome robes of the Shendú plaid. Their hair, also, was neatly done in bands on either side of the face, and knotted behind. Altogether the impression left on my mind was that they were a higher race than the ordinary hill people. Their features, I especially noted, were not of the pronounced Mongolian type that characterised all other hill races that I had seen; these Shendú women, indeed, as far as features went, might have been Portuguese half-castes from Chittagong.

I presented the chief's wife with a friendly offering, in the shape of some gay-coloured beads and a small pocket mirror. She accepted my present with a gracious smile, and returned the civility by drawing from her breast a small gourd, which she solemnly handed to me. I inquired what was to be done with this; was I to keep it? Yuong explained that this was an act of great favour; the gourd contained the lees, or tobacco-water, from the bottom of the small hookah which each woman smoked, and this water was considered a great preservative of the teeth and gums. It was expected that I should take some of the filthy stuff into my mouth, and retain the same for some time, returning the gourd to its owner with due acknowledgments. Truly, a most unpleasant custom. It was my ardent wish, however, to reach the Shendú country, and I could not, therefore, stick at trifles; so, with inward loathings and a smiling face, I conformed to the requirements of politeness.

On handing the old Shendú a cup of spirits, he would not be persuaded to touch it until the women who accompanied him had first partaken, and they also required polite pressing before they would taste the liquor. These were all small signs, but still I noted them as not unimportant indices of the character and status of the people whose acquaintance I sought. There was to be a grand feast and solemn council in the evening, when I was expected to set forth the objects of my journey, and when the future action of Teynwey would be decided. At about 8 P.M., therefore, I adjourned to the chief's house. I had not far to go, as the small house which had been assigned for my reception was in close proximity to Teynwey's premises. The feast I found had already commenced, with its usual concomitants of dancing and drinking. The music was rude but forcible; there were any number of drums, and an instrument resembling a guitar, which was thrummed with a sort of "plectrum" of bamboo, fastened to the thumb of the player. The instrument had frets, so that there was some attempt to produce tune, but rhythm was of course the great feature of the music.

The dance was performed by men only, about twenty in

number, who marched slowly round in a circle in measured processional time. The leader held in his hand a brazen-hilted "dao," adorned with a flowing tuft of goat's hair dyed scarlet; the other dancers also bore weapons of various descriptions. The dance thus proceeded: one step, a pause; two more steps, all the dancers sank down on their hams, rising again in time to the music; another step, then cut a caper, and so on, *da capo.* At the urgent request of Teynwey, who had been informed of my eminent musical ability, I put in an *ad libitum* accompaniment with voice and fiddle.

After a short time passed thus, Teynwey led me to an adjoining room, where the solemn business of drinking was being accomplished. Here was a double row of enormous earthen pots filled with "khoung" a sort of sweet, slightly-intoxicating beer, made from millet-seed, which is the universal beverage on all festive occasions in the hills. Beside each pot sat a drinker, who imbibed the fluid through a reed as we should take sherry cobbler. Here, on a fine mat spread near an open window, we seated ourselves, pipes were lit and the palaver commenced. During the afternoon it appeared that sundry experiments in divination had been tried, by the inspection of the entrails of the animals killed for the feast, and by the breaking of eggs, at which Dr. Khilu had assisted on my behalf, and the omens were reported to be very favourable.

Teynwey therefore informed me that he would assist me to the utmost of his power, and it was arranged that, after due sacrifice to the spirits and solemn oath of friendship and alliance between me and the Kyaws had been made, an embassy should be despatched to Kheynúng, the nearest Shendú chief of importance, asking him to come and escort me to his village. I tried hard to induce Teynwey to allow me to accompany the embassy to Kheynúng, without further delay; but this, he assured me, was impracticable, as my entry into the Shendú country without permission would be deemed an act of hostility. At any rate, neither guide nor coolies would be forthcoming, so I had no choice but to await the course of events.

That night I got no rest, for the village was the head-quarters of biting creatures, who made night hideous; so early the next morning I beat a hurried retreat to the river's bank, where the villagers speedily ran up a small bamboo hut for me, and another for my followers.

In the afternoon Teynwey, Yuong, and a number of other persons of consideration, came down from the village to the river-side where I now dwelt, and together we swore a solemn oath of friendship. The ceremony was performed in this wise. A young "guyal" heifer was thrown down, and its neck firmly fastened to a stake which was firmly driven into the ground, the two ends of the cord by which the animal was bound were held, one by me and the other by Teynwey and his followers. The Kúmi chief Yuong, who was a clever man and cunning in divination, officiated as high-priest, keenly and critically watched by the opposition practitioner Dr. Khilu.

Yuong took in one hand the brazen-hilted "dao" decorated with scarlet goat's hair, and in the other held a brass cup containing arrack. From the cup he took a mouthful of liquor and blew it out in spray over the sacrifice, then another mouthful over me, and a third over Teynwey and his company; then raising high his right hand he invoked the spirits of the air and water, at the same time plucking out some of the prostrate animal's hair and scattering it to the wind. After these preliminaries, with two or three vigorous strokes of the "dao" he severed the animal's head from its body, and taking some of the warm blood on his forefinger, smeared it on my forehead and on my bare feet, as also to Teynwey and the others who had taken part in the sacrifice, invoking at the same time the wrath of the spirits on the head of him who should be untrue or unfaithful in the affair to which we had set our hands.

The slaughtered animal was quickly skinned, dismembered, and its flesh divided among the participants, to be cooked and eaten at their pleasure. Not content with this, Teynwey cut up the liver into small pieces, and each one of us had perforce to eat a bit—raw. This being done I retreated to my shanty, and took a sip of brandy, the raw flesh having nauseated me, and then sat down to solace myself with a little music on the fiddle.

The messengers to Kheynúng were to depart that same day; but still, make what despatch they would, I found I should have to wait a fortnight at least for their return. Accordingly, I resigned myself to the inevitable delay, and made up my mind, meanwhile, to explore the country in the vicinity. I took sweet counsel with my fiddle, and decided that, so long as I eventually obtained access to the Shendú country, the fortnight's inaction, although irksome and tedious, was not of any real consequence. Teynwey and his people seemed simple and sincere, while the solemn function just gone through was, I thought, a guarantee of the chief's good faith. Thus I mused as I bowed *arpeggios* on the violin, singing "The blue hills' secret shall yet, shall yet be mine," when suddenly I received a blow which knocked me into the air, and I fell over on my side in a sickening agony of pain.

I had been sitting cross-legged on a shawl, with my back turned to the low door of the hut, occupied with my fiddling, when a bullet entered, and striking me a little below the hip, passed down the whole length of my thigh, coming out just above the knee. The gun had been fired by one of the hill-guides who had brought me across the hills to the Koladan, and who instantly decamped into the jungle. Whether the shot was accidental, or whether the chiefs had determined to prevent my going any farther, is doubtful. My servant Toby saw the man strolling by the door of my hut, and stooping down to look in, but merely thought he was attracted by the music; then the report of the gun was heard, and the man bolted.

I was in great pain, and thought my last hour had come. Fuzlah and Toby hurried up lamenting, and with some assistance carried me down to Yuong's boat, which lay moored at the water's edge, and having procured rowers by offers of liberal payment, the canoe was soon bearing me rapidly down the river on the way to Akyab. I confess I thought I had not an hour to live, for I had seen the wound, and it seemed to me impossible that the ball could have traversed the whole length of my thigh without severing some artery, in which case I must inevitably bleed to death.

I remember vividly how I lay at the bottom of the small dug-out canoe, in a pool of my own fast-flowing blood, filled with bitter anger at such an unforeseen and impotent termination to my journey. It was very hard, I thought, to die thus; and so all things slipped away and I became unconscious, I suppose, from loss of blood.

When I again opened my eyes, I cannot tell how long after, I was much astonished to find myself still in the flesh. I was very weak, and the atrocious pain in my leg reminded me of what had happened; but the bleeding had stopped, and the disappointment in my heart was the worst pain of the two. It seemed so ignominious to be beaten in this way. However, there was no help for it, and I lay, still uncertain of my life, with the good Toby weeping at my head, and Sergeant Fuzlah, forward in the boat, urging the rowers to greater exertion. I know not how the time passed, it seemed all a tangled, feverish dream; but three days had somehow elapsed, when I heard a friendly English voice hailing my canoe, and Fuzlah responding. It turned out to be Major M——, the Superintendent of Police at Akyab, who was out on duty on the lower reaches of the river Koladan, and who learned, with infinite surprise, that a wounded and unknown fellow-countryman was in the small boat coming from the head-waters of the river.

I had eaten nothing for three days, save a little rice, and I was very weak, and unable to explain my appearance; but I began now to hope that I might live, taking comfort from the mere sight of an English face, and the sound of an English voice. In a few hours we reached Akyab, where I was lifted out of the boat, and carefully and kindly conveyed to Major M——'s house. Here the doctor came, and put me to infinite torture by probing my wound; he shook his head and pronounced my escape to be wonderful. No bones, it appeared, had been broken, and the small arteries, which had been cut by the passage of the bullet, had staunched themselves by contracting during the time I had lain still in the canoe. He said that a more lengthy flesh-wound was seldom seen; probed me again; considered it remarkable that the knee had escaped fracture; pointed out to Major M—— how the track of the ball had followed certain anatomical conditions existing in the limb; and then bade me be of good cheer, as the case was most interesting, and in a few days I should have strong food.

And so it passed. I got well with astonishing rapidity, becoming endowed with an appetite of superhuman voracity, and in a short time could hobble, or rather hop, about on one leg, well on the way to convalescence.

Meanwhile, Sir Arthur Phayre, Chief Commissioner and Father of the Province, arrived at Akyab on a tour of inspection, and, having listened to my story with kindly interest, asked whether I felt inclined to renew the attempt to gain admission to the Shendú country. It is needless to say that I jumped at the opportunity, and it was speedily arranged that I and Major M—— should go forth together, and make another effort to explore the unknown country. This time we were to move under the ægis of Government; that is to say, my previous proceedings were duly reported to the Government of Bengal, and on the recommendation of Sir Arthur Phayre, the sanction of the Lieutenant-Governor was accorded to this fresh attempt. I also received letters from my friend the Commissioner of Chittagong, who said very kind and flattering things in respect of my doings, and urged me on to fresh exertion. The new expedition, therefore, set forth under the most favourable auspices. I had been wounded on the 15th of December, 1865, and reached Akyab at midday on the 20th; on the 5th of January, 1866, although my wound was still open, and my leg somewhat stiff, I had yet sufficiently recovered to make a fresh start.

Sir Arthur Phayre, who took a great interest in the expedition, himself accompanied us for the first two hundred miles, and we reached Dalakmay on the 12th of January. Here he bade us farewell, and Major M—— and I continued our journey towards the Shendú country. The Chief Commissioner entirely concurred in my view, that the injury inflicted on me had been accidental, or at any rate that Teynwey and his people had no part in it; treachery, if treachery there were, came from the Bohmong, the Chittagong potentate, whose subject the man was who had fired the shot. Our present expedition, therefore, was entirely a friendly one, and we took with us only a very small escort.

By the 18th of January we reached once more the village of Teynwey, whence I had not long before taken so hurried a departure. The old chief received me with astonishment, stroking and feeling my body with much solicitude, being clearly of opinion that, if I was not dead, I ought to be. My wound, in truth, had healed with wonderful rapidity; and this speedy convalescence was attributable mainly to the simple abstinent life which I had led for so many weeks previous to the accident. No bread, no beer, no butter, no flesh save an occasional chicken, a dish of rice, and sometimes fish, with constant exercise in the open air, was evidently uninflammatory diet; but still I felt deeply thankful that matters had turned out so fortunately, and that there I was once more at Teynwey's, sitting with Major M——, discussing the chances *pro* and *con.* of our journey, as we smoked a pipe together after a frugal meal of eggs and rice.

The river flowed below, dark green, with eddying ripples, and beyond rose the hills, tier upon tier, thickly clothed with jungle. The small dug-out canoes in which we had travelled up stream lay moored on the sandy shore, and there was the faithful Toby searching in the stern of the boat which he had occupied, to find a pod or two of red pepper wherewith to flavour his dinner-pot.

We found at Teynwey's that my messengers had returned from the Shendú country, bringing with them the son of the chief Kheynúng, by name Aylong, who had been sent by his father to interview me, in response to my previous friendly messages. After considerable haggling with Aylong as to the number of red cloths, brass vessels, and strings of beads which should be paid to Kheynúng by way of "footing," on our part all was at length satisfactorily arranged, and the indispensable, final ceremony of the oath was gone through, in which Major M—— joined. The following morning we resumed our onward journey, bound for the village of Kheynúng, a Shendú chief who ruled over a village containing perhaps, a hundred houses, and through whose mediation we hoped to proceed still farther on our voyage of discovery.

A curious trait now became noticeable in the Shendú character. The men, six in number, who composed Aylong's party, evinced a horror of water; not only did they avoid ablution, and drink as little as possible of the element, but no amount of persuasion would induce them to set foot in a boat. Major M—— and I therefore went by water in our canoes, while the Shendús plunged into the apparently pathless jungle, to reappear, however, towards sundown, at our first camping-ground, many miles up the river.

I became great friends with the young chief Aylong and his friend and henchman Yitchee; they were never weary of examining me and my belongings; my clothes, my writing materials, my pipe, my arms, and my general comportment, were all subjects of the closest interest and observation to them. The difference in the colour of our respective skins seemed much to exercise their minds. Aylong would take my hand and nurse it, stroking it and saying, *Apah, apah-tloh,* "It is good, it is fair;" or would pass the rough and sun-burned article to Yitchee, who in his turn would examine it with much curiosity. We were evidently the first white men they had seen.

My tobacco being exhausted, Aylong gave me some from his own pouch. This was a most welcome gift, tobacco being pretty much the same all the world over.

Our first day's journey lay up the Koladan River, until we reached the Sulla Khyoung a smaller stream, which ran into the big river from the east. We ascended this tributary for some distance, until sundown, when we camped at a place where the Shendús told us we should have to leave the boats and commence to march by land. Our coolies, men from Teynwey's village, quickly ran up rough shelter huts of split bamboo and plantain leaves for themselves, while Major M—— and I slept in our canoes.

The following morning early, we hauled up the boats and concealed them in the underwood by the side of the stream, which was here somewhat deep, to avoid their being stolen or meddled with by other wayfarers, and by sunrise we set out on our journey.

The forest through which we took our way was dark and gloomy, the trees were very lofty, with comparatively little undergrowth. There was no living thing to be seen, not even a bird or a monkey; no sound broke the deep melancholy stillness of the woodland, save occasionally the far-off note of the bell-bird, a chime like that of a deep sweet bell in the recesses of the forest, or the heavy thud of some large acorn-like fruit tumbling to the ground.

The party was headed by Yitchee, who led us through the apparently pathless labyrinth of the forest with undeviating accuracy; it seemed almost as if he moved by instinct, and yet now and again some mark or other slight indication would show that he was pursuing a predetermined path. His guidance must have been rendered more difficult by the frequent wild elephant tracks which meandered everywhere through the forest, and, judging by the marks and droppings, these animals must have been very numerous.

We marched perhaps fifteen miles in a north-easterly direction, as far as I could judge by the sun, and by the moss, which always grows thickest on the north side of the trees, and then we halted, camping in the forest for the night. The next morning the march was resumed. Hour after hour we tramped along, now in sun, now in shade, until, about two in the afternoon, we suddenly espied three strange Shendús coming from the opposite direction; one of these carried a spear, while the other two men were armed with flint-lock muskets bearing the English Tower-mark. They also carried powder-horns made from the horns of the guyal or hill bison, beautifully inlaid and ornamented with silver and ivory. These strangers halted, and entered into conversation with Aylong, inquiring who we were and whither we were going. They were informed that we were bound on a friendly visit to the village of the chief Kheynúng, Aylong's father; and they, on their side, gave us to understand that they were the scouts or advance guard of a large party of Shendús, under another chief, and that we could not be allowed to proceed without his orders.

This unforeseen incident occasioned much parleying, until at last it was arranged that Aylong, with two of his men, should go forward to the hostile chief, and if possible come to terms with him. On this our hill coolies began to chatter and put down their loads, being evidently uneasy in their minds. After a short interval Yitchee, Aylong's henchman, returned, and told us that the advancing party numbered some four hundred men, and that, as ill-luck would have it, they were out on the war-path; he thought there might be difficulties, and being himself unarmed, he asked me to lend him a weapon of some sort. I accordingly handed him my silver-hilted sword, a relic of the Indian Mutiny, retaining for my own protection a Ghurkha hunting-knife and a revolver. I never saw my sword again for the space of two years, when it was faithfully returned by Yitchee through the Akyab authorities.

Old Teynwey himself, who had accompanied us, seemed somewhat alarmed, and, pulling me by the sleeve, made signs that we had better retreat. On looking back, I saw that the coolies had taken up their loads again, and were running off as fast as they could in the direction we had lately come. Having come thus far, Major M—— and I could not make up our minds to go back again without good reason, and we signified as much to Teynwey. Presently we heard the Shendús calling for Aylong in the jungle—so he apparently had fled!

At this juncture Yitchee cautiously approached, and invited me by signs to accompany him into the jungle, and on my shaking my head and pointing to my companions, he leaped quickly away and disappeared in the forest.

Old Teynwey, who stuck by us to the last very manfully, now entered into earnest expostulation with the strangers; he spoke quickly and with vehemence, and once he took the hand of one who seemed to be the leader, and lifted it to his forehead with a motion of entreaty. The strangers, however, preserved a grim and taciturn demeanour, eyeing us fixedly and replying to Teynwey only in monosyllables. After a little while Teynwey ceased entreating, and without another word turned and quietly retreated after his coolies, who had long ago disappeared on the back-track, carrying with them all our possessions—food, raiment, ammunition, presents, &c.

Matters now began to look really unpleasant. Here we were, alone in an unknown forest, confronted by five unfriendly strangers, who had at their backs, in the dim recesses of the forest, four hundred more of the same kidney. We were six in number: there were Major M—— and myself, M——'s two orderlies, and Sergeant Fuzlah, all well armed, and the faithful Toby, my cook, who valiantly carried in his right hand a large toasting-fork.

We now began to see men moving in the jungles round us, and four of the Shendús went quietly behind a tree, where the observant Sergeant Fuzlah followed them, and reported that they had primed their guns from the long powder-horns they wore at their waists.

Major M—— and I consulted together hurriedly; we were alone, without an interpreter, and consequently without any means of communicating with these people and explaining to them the friendliness of our intentions or the enormity of their conduct. Their object was evidently to capture us, alive if possible, dead if it must be, but in any case to plunder us of all we had; and yet it seemed almost impossible to give up our enterprise when we were on the very threshold of success. It was heart-breaking.

As we were thus conversing, I saw one of the Shendús from behind a tree deliberately raise his piece and cover my companion M——. Sergeant Fuzlah, with admirable promptitude, raised his rifle and covered that particular Shendú, who thereupon lowered his gun, and scratched his head in an attitude of embarrassment. At the same time a hideous old grey-bearded Shendú, who, with smiles and gestures (reminding one of the old nursery rhyme respecting Mrs. Bond and her ducks, "Dilly, dilly, dilly, come and be killed"), had been inspecting the rifle of one of M——'s orderlies, with a quick jerk attempted to wrest it away. There was no longer the faintest doubt as to their intentions, and I said to my friend M——, "Fate is against us, my boy. We shall be surrounded and disarmed if we stay here much longer."

M—— gave the order to make ready, and with levelled guns, but without firing, we slowly retreated. Seeing our threatening attitude, the Shendús at once took cover, and whether it was that they feared to expose themselves, or whether they had orders to take us alive, I know not, but no shot was fired. We, on our side, had no desire to commence hostilities or to waste our ammunition, so we slowly retired, presenting a firm front with levelled guns.

"Sahib," said Fuzlah, "they are outflanking us." And so it was, for on our right and left we saw through the trees the figures of Shendús swiftly running.

A little further on, the jungle grew more dense, and we availed ourself of this cover to run also, as fast as we could. I soon found, however, that my leg pained me a good deal, and I began to doubt my powers of continued flight.

Yet a little further, and we came to the baskets containing our baggage, which had been abandoned by the coolies in their flight. There, alas! I saw on the ground my cherished meerschaum, my beloved fiddle, and my diary full of sketches and notes of travel. Alack, alack! no time had we to stay, but the provident Fuzlah stooped as we passed and carried off my long "choga," or dressing-gown, which lay along the ground.

A short distance further, and the sound of shots reached our ears in front. Our enemies had over-run us in their eagerness and were attacking the coolies, content, I suppose, with the certainty of taking us afterwards. We held a hurried council of war. Personally, I was obliged to confess that I could go no farther, as my leg began to feel like lead and was very painful; accordingly, we turned off sharp to the right, and within a hundred yards we found a hollow surrounded and covered with dense undergrowth. Into this we all crept, crouching like hunted beasts, with the determination at least to sell our lives as dearly as possible.

Major M—— had throughout the journey been accompanied by a small pet dog belonging to his wife, who was away in England, and this small animal now proved a source of great danger. Dropping shots were heard occasionally, in the distance, but all else was silent, and we began to hope that we had been overlooked, when suddenly the sound of voices was heard in the wood; the Shendús were calling to each other, and evidently searching for us. We looked at one another, and preserved a deathly silence. I could hear my own heart beating. One felt that in a few moments the end, whether by lead or cold steel, would arrive.

There was a rustling in the bushes above us, and we grasped our weapons. M——'s cursed little dog gave a low growl. I had my knife out at once to cut her throat, but M——, who was very soft about the little beast, huddled her up into the breast of his coat and silenced her there. By the mercy of God we were not discovered; the searchers passed on, the shots ceased, the shouting died away, and as the day darkened to its close a mighty forest stillness fell on all. Slowly, like a great peace, night came on, and we still possessed our lives.

Now and again we could hear the wild elephants trumpeting as they came down to their feeding-grounds, and once the air was stirred by the deep roar of a tiger. Soon the moon began to rise, and we agreed that it would be well to follow the path, if we could find it, and return to the boats under the shelter of night. Cautiously we emerged from our hiding-place, and in Indian file took our way in the direction whence only that morning we had come. What a long time ago it seemed.

The jungle seemed to grow denser and darker, and the path came to an end; but still we struggled on, hoping against hope. Thorns tore our flesh or held us fast; great creepers twined in a tangle round our limbs and detained us; at times our passage was barred by some close thicket through which we had to force our way, now creeping, now pushing, now falling; caught by the hair and strangled by the neck; yet still we struggled on. At one place M——'s hat was knocked off his head by a branch, and in the darkness we could not find it again. What a long interminable nightmare it was; but still we toiled on, on. Even if we were off the path, still every step we took removed us, as we hoped, from the neighbourhood of the marauders who had caused our disaster.

At last, bruised and worn out, we came to a stand from sheer exhaustion. In front of us rose a lofty hill, and we felt unfit to face the ascent; so climbing a short distance up the slope, to get above the malaria of the low-lying jungle, we lay down, all six of us, on the the ground, and I soon fell into a dreamless slumber with my head upon a stone. My last recollection was that my good Fuzlah carefully tucked round me the old "choga," which he had rescued from the baggage and had carried all through the night wrapped round his waist.

When the morning dawned I woke with a start, and for the moment I hardly realised where I was; but soon came the bitter remembrance that we had failed in our enterprise, and were fugitives in the great trackless wilderness that surrounded us.

We arose, braced ourselves up and buckled ourselves in.

My leg felt very stiff and numb, but I hoped that the warmth of exercise might mend this. Major M—— lamented the loss of his hat during the wanderings of the night, and tried to improvise a head-covering with some leaves. We were hungry, but there was nothing to eat; thirsty were we but there was no water. The question now was what course to pursue; to descend into the valley filled with our pursuers seemed suicidal, for they doubtless were making diligent search for the prize which had escaped their grasp. We determined, then, to ascend the hill-range which lay in front of us, and, if possible, strike the river Koladan, which, according to our calculations, lay on the other side; there, we thought, it would be easy to construct a raft and float down to Teynwey's village.

Accordingly we set our faces at that hill, and ascending, soon found ourselves entangled in a dense jungle of bamboo, through which we had to cut a way, taking it by turn to lead and hew a path through the tough stems with my "kukri," which here proved of great service. The sun rose higher and higher, and M——, being without a hat, suffered terribly from the heat. I was filled with anxiety lest he should be prostrated with sunstroke, which would have been a fearful addition to our troubles. However, we made a sort of sombrero for him of plantain leaves, which was better than the bough with which he had previously tried to shield his head, and then, encouraging each other with the hope that we should soon see the Koladan, we pushed on bravely.

For five mortal hours we toiled up that hill, until at length, parched and breathless, we gained the summit. I saw Fuzlah, who was leading, sit down wearily, and then I too, on reaching the top, sank down in dismay, for before us lay, not the hoped-for valley of the Koladan, but another hill, and beyond that more hills, but no sign of a river. We had evidently mistaken the lie of the country, and matters began to look very serious. We had no food, but that could be endured for some time yet, and at the worst we could fall back on M——'s dog, which still faithfully followed his master's wanderings. What we could not do without, was—drink; it was impossible to preserve reason or life without water, and no drop had passed our lips for twenty-four hours.

As I sat there, all parched and aching with thirst, what visions crossed my mind! I recalled the long reaches of the Koladan, with the morning breeze, cool and perfume-laden, wooing the placid dark-green water until it dimpled into smiles. I thought of India, that thirsty land, and realised the devotion with which all Easterns regard water; how their many religions all unite in the necessity for ablution, how their poetry sparkles with crystal fountains, how the digging of a well gives a title to salvation, and how appalling to dying men was the mockery of the mirage, the Fata Morgana of the desert. Ah! what would I not then have given for one small cup of water!

I was roused from my reverie by Toby, who came dragging *after him the succulent stem of a wild plantain tree, and by* mashing and squeezing the pulpy fibre of this we managed to obtain a small quantity of fluid, which, together with some of the fruit, we divided among us.

From where we sat on the hill-top we had a grand view of the Shendú country; range upon range of hills rose up blue in the distance, while here and there to the south we could discern the Sulla Khyoung, which we had quitted so hopefully two days before, winding like a silver thread in the valley below.

We had neither strength to breast the ranges which lay in front of us, nor resources wherewith to bribe the tribes to the east; water alone was what we now wanted, water at any cost. We resolved, then, to retrace our steps and make for the Sulla Khyoung, keeping a good look out to avoid the Shendús; so once more we turned on the backward track. We had gone but a little distance, when I heard a loud crashing noise in front.

"What is it?" I asked.

One of M——'s orderlies replied, "A tiger, Sahib; here he was lying, and I nearly stepped on him. I think he must have been asleep."

Bah! what is a tiger! The valley below into which we were going was full of human tigers.

"Push on, cautiously, for your lives."

I could walk better now that our path lay down-hill; but my wound not being yet quite closed, the leg began to drag and felt rather numb. I did not, therefore, lead the advance, but followed behind Major M——, one of whose orderlies went in front.

Suddenly I saw M—— and the orderly go down on their faces as if they were shot; I crouched down also, as did the rest of the party, and then, cautiously crawling forward on my belly, and peer'ng through the grass, I saw three Shendús who barred the path. One of them was sitting in the fork of a tree with his gun over his knee; the two othe s stood beneath. They were evidently on the watch.

We all crouched hiding in the long grass, and looked at each other. What was to be done? We could wa t until darkness came on, and then surprise the picquet. It might be done silently, and we were two to one; but from the lowland we heard the sound of many voices Our way was closed here, for the time at any rate; so we again turned back, and painfully re-ascended the hill until we reached a shady thicket, where we concealed ourselves. Soon he voices in the valley grew louder; there was laughing and cheering, then the sounds grew fainter and died away; the enemy were probably returning to their homes.

After nightfall we cautiously descended; the hostile picquet was gone, although under the tree where we had seen the man sitting there still smouldered the embe s of their watch-fire. A little further on, and we reached a stream which ran right athwart our course, and in which I buried my whole face, drinking deeply. Here we halted for at least an hour, quenching the thirst that had consumed us; and by the time we moved on again it was very dark, and a thick fog came up the valley, confusing us greatly as to the bearings which we had taken in the morning. We pushed on, however, in what we thought to be the direction of the Sul'a Khyoung. The ground seemed to fall lower and lower, the trees to grow larger, and the jungle darker and more gloomy, as we proceeded.

It was growing late, we were chilled to the bone, and very hungry, and at last agreed to halt in a small hollow, shut in on every side, so that we could make a fire to warm ourselves without much risk of discovery, a fire which might also serve to scare away the beasts which we could hear from time to time

N 2

moving in the jungle around us I was very young in woodcraft then, and our sole chance of making a fire lay in four wax matches which I fortunately had in my pocket. We collected a small heap of sticks and leaves, but they were damp from the mist, and three out of the four precious matches were expended in vain. How carefully we coaxed and manœuvred with the last one; fortunately, this time we were successful, and at length a cheerful small flame brightened the dark hollow where we had sheltered ourselves.

The question for consideration now was, how long could we hold out without food in our wanderings? And it was then and there determined that, *faute de mieux* we would eat the dog the next night. Even poor M—— himself, in spite of his affection for the "wee beastie," gave way before the necessities of the case, and agreed to sacrifice his favourite.

Our native followers began to grow very despondent, with the exception of Fuzlah who, throughout our difficulties presented a front of cheerful but dogged determination. As true as steel was Sergeant Fuzlah, and yet with a soft heart for those he loved. Poor Toby wept copiously, bitterly declaring that he was born with a blackened forehead, that his fate was evil, and that he should never, never see his home again. He still bore as his weapon of offence and defence the stout kitchen-fork to which I have before alluded.

Our fire began to grow low from want of dry fuel, and at last it went out and all was dark. No sound then broke the chill stillness of the night, except the patter of the dew-drops falling thick from the leafy canopy above us, and an occasional scream from a wild elephant away in the forest.

When the morning came we girded up our loins, and a somewhat hot discussion arose as to the proper direction to be pursued. Major M—— and all the others were of one mind; they desired to go downwards, following the lie of the land, until they struck the Sulla Khyoung, by following which, M—— reasoned and the remainder concurred, that we must eventually reach the Koladan.

I have never been able to account for my behaviour at this juncture, but I doggedly refused to follow this course, and avouched my firm belief that our safety lay in following a directly contrary direction; and so we parted, they going downward, while I and Fuzlah, who stuck by me, went the other way. Wonderful to relate, I had not gone thirty yards through the jungle, when I stepped out upon a clearly-defined well-trodden pathway, which was evidently the road by which our coolies had fled, and along which our enemies had returned when we heard them passing. This was, indeed, a providential discovery, and hastily despatching Fuzlah to recall M—— and the rest of the party, we were soon progressing along the new-found track.

We had not gone far when a feeble voice called to us from the bushes. It was a servant of M——'s who had fled along with the coolies, and not being able to keep up with them in their headlong flight, had hidden himself away in the jungle, and would probably have died there had we not passed by; for, in addition to his sufferings from hunger and thirst, he had been attacked by fever, and could now hardly drag himself along. We supported the poor wretch between us as best we could. He said that, after he had concealed himself in the jungle, some two hundred armed Shendús had passed by in swift pursuit of the coolies, and that shortly after he had heard cries and musket-shots. The Shendús returned the next day by the same path, but in larger numbers, perhaps four hundred in all; they carried packages, and had some prisoners bound with them, and seemed in high glee, talking and laughing together.

At about one o'clock in the day we reached the Sulla Khyoung, at the place where we had originally disembarked; but to our great discomfiture not a boat was to be seen, all had been removed from the place where we had hidden them. After searching a while we at length discovered one boat, which had floated a little distance down the stream and was stranded on the opposite bank. The stream was here deep, and darkly suggestive of alligators, but there was no time for hesitation, and before long we had secured the small dug-out canoe which was fortunately unharmed. Only one paddle could be found, so we had to make oars for ourselves, of pieces of split bamboo put crosswise in a slit stem of the same useful plant; and at length, with much thankfulness of heart, we seated ourselves in the boat and pushed off.

My previous practice in steering proved now of good service, for none of the party had the least idea of steering with a paddle; but it was not without misgivings that I took my seat in the stern, as I thought of the great rapids in the Koladan, through which I had to guide our somewhat cranky craft.

We found on shore near the landing-place some handfuls of rice, probably spilled from one of our own baskets, and this we munched with a little water, and felt much the better for it; and so we left the shore and paddled away with infinite thankfulness.

Soon we shot out of the Sulla Khyoung into the broad sunlight of the great river, and I could hear the roar of the rapids in the reach below. Mentally I pulled myself together, as it were, commending myself to the good God who had hitherto so mercifully protected us; for I felt so exhausted and weak that, if we came to grief in the rapids, I knew I must go under. After all we had gone through, now came the reaction, and my leg felt cold, numb, and lifeless as a piece of wood. However, I hurooshed my crew and determined to send her at it with a rush.

The roar grew louder, the river became streaked in parallel lines shooting downwards, the banks flew past. The critical moment was approaching; on ahead I could see a howling, tumbling, foamy waste of tossing water. I stood up to take my bearings; right down the centre went a pathway of comparatively green water. I settled down again into my place with a "Pull all, for your lives," and with a firm quick turn of the paddle I sent her head into it.

Whish! over great smooth shoulders of water and dark down sucking eddies that came and went, like a flash we went; the men cheered and paddled like demons, there was a rush and a roar, we took in a little water, and then, more by good luck than good management, we found ourselves floating in comparatively smooth water below, slipping on rapidly to Teynwey's village, where food and friendly faces awaited us; and our souls were filled with a great peace and contentment, for we could at length call our lives our own.

Major M—— and I gripped each other's hand with full hearts as we stepped out of the boat; and thus ended my unsuccessful effort to explore the blue hills of the Shendú country.

CHAPTER IX

THE HILL TRACTS OF CHITTAGONG
1866–67

LOOKING back at the events of those past few weeks, I felt deeply thankful to God for my preservation throughout so many dangers. Death, possibly by torture or slavery, would certainly have been our lot had we been captured by the Shendús; but, in spite of the failure of the expedition, I thought, and still think, that our lack of success was attributable more to ill-luck than to mismanagement.

The Shendús, who acted as our guides, were of a clan which was at feud with the village whence came the party which we met in the forest, and this party was at the time out on a marauding expedition when we unluckily fell in their way. On the part of the Shendús from Kheynúng's, who had sworn friendship with us, I felt sure there was neither collusion nor treachery. I had eaten with them; laughed, drunk, and smoked in their company; we were friends, in fact, and they had more to gain than to lose by our safe conduct. It will also be remembered that, when about to seek safety in flight, Yitchee invited me to accompany him, and he must subsequently have been at considerable trouble to effect the restoration of the valuable sword which I had lent him, and which, had he been dishonest, he would most certainly have retained.

That chapter, however, was closed, and at Akyab I remember how strange everything seemed, after all the excitement and rough adventure of forest life, to find oneself once more safe and sound among English people, putting on clean linen, and sitting at meat like Christian men.

I telegraphed to Chittagong for my police yacht, the "Foam," to be sent round to Akyab, in order that I might return by sea to my district. The open air life I had been living for so many weeks, the constant change of scene, combined with the severe bodily exercise, had prevented my taking much thought hitherto. We had lived *au jour le jour* in truly animal fashion; but now, with my face turned towards Bengal again, I speculated somewhat ruefully as to how the police work of my district had gone on during my long absence, and what my Inspector-General would have to say on the subject.

Akyab is one of the most beautiful and picturesque spots I have ever seen. It is situated in a lovely land-locked bay, the distant shores of which are backed by the blue hills, the fastnesses of the Khyens. The houses of the European residents, built along a sea-shore which stretches in miles of white sand, remind one more of an English watering-place than of an Indian station. The natives of the place are, by a large majority, Buddhist in faith and Burman by race, and I found them a bright cheery people, contrasting favourably with the sullen bigotry of the ordinary Mahomedan, or the caste prejudices of the Hindus of Lower Bengal.

I now regretfully bade adieu to my friend and comrade Major M——, and to other kind and hospitable fellow-countrymen at Akyab; and the 16th of February, 1866, saw me on board the "Foam," coasting along pleasantly enough under easy sail, bound for Chittagong. I lounged on the deck, in the shadow of the great mainsail, gazing at the white coast-line with the blue hills beyond, and listening to Abdul Manji, the yacht's sailing master, a good specimen of the Chittagong Mussulman, who related to me the astonishing adventures which I had, it would seem, encountered, according to the stories current among the natives during my absence.

"Yes, Sahib," said Abdul, "Sherban Ali, the cloth-merchant, who you know lives near the mosque in the Burra Bazaar, told me all your wonderful adventures some time ago. We heard how you had disguised yourself as a Cabul merchant, and, having dyed your face and hands, got access to the King of the Shendús, who, however, discovered you to be an Englishman, and ordered you to be impaled. This, however, could not be true. Inshallah! you blackened the king's face instead, so Sergeant Fuzlah tells me."

I looked forward, and saw Fuzlah smoking a peaceful hookah and yarning away to the boatmen in the bows, while Toby sat by on the broad grin. Abdul continued:

"And we heard how you made your escape from the king's village, and fortified yourself in the valley, holding out for weeks against all his soldiers, and finally making your escape by swimming the river at night. Allah-t-allah! It was wonderful! But, my lord, Fuzlah will not admit that you all had to eat dog. Do the people there live on dog, Sahib? Khair! It is well. Your honour's fortune is great, for the day I left Chittagong the Lord Sahib from Calcutta arrived in a steamer and is waiting to confer a dress of honour upon your Highness."

This was news indeed. The Lord Sahib was, of course, the Lieutenant-Governor of Bengal, who was on tour, and although Abdul's "dress of honour" was all nonsense, still, at this juncture, a personal interview with the head of the Bengal Government might help much to smooth my rugged Inspector-General, and might even bring me into the sunshine of official notice.

I reached Chittagong on the 19th of February, and was received with open arms by my kind friend the Commissioner, who at once despoiled me of my later diaries, which, together with the letters he had previously received from me, he hastily sent off for the perusal of His Honour the Lieutenant-Governor of Bengal, who was lying off the port of Chittagong in a Government vessel.

In the afternoon we visited the Lieutenant-Governor, Sir George Campbell, and I was accorded a very favourable reception; after which I returned, well pleased and much relieved that I had escaped censure in undertaking such an expedition on my own responsibility.

I telegraphed to England to give my home-people tidings of my safe return (a telegram of a few words from Chittagong to England at that time cost £5 8*s*. and was five days in transit); and then settled down again in my little bungalow on the hill-top, and resumed my routine duties as before, enlivened by the evening game of racquets, in which all the station indulged, and by occasional music at the judge's or Commissioner's house.

In the "Calcutta Gazette" for March, 1866, I saw myself promoted to the rank of Captain in Her Majesty's 104th Regiment, and on the same page found my appointment, by the Bengal Government, to officiate as Superintendent of Hill

Tribes in the Chittagong Hill Tracts. This last appointment was entirely due to the kind offices of the Commissioner, who, having been directed to prepare a scheme for the better administration of the hills, had recommended me as the fittest person for the post in question.

In the official letter which conveyed the Government sanction to my appointment, the Lieutenant-Governor expressed some doubts as to whether I had the training necessary to deal properly with the somewhat intricate revenue and land settlement questions that frequently cropped up on the border; but the Commissioner guaranteed my ability, and promised a close supervision of my work, which disposed of the difficulty.

I took charge of my new appointment on the 15th of April, being vested by Government with the full powers of a magistrate in criminal work, besides the necessary authority for the trying of civil and revenue cases, and the Commissioner lent me his own small river steamer to convey me and my belongings to my new district.

Chandraguna, then the head-quarters of the Hill Tracts, is situated eighty miles from Chittagong up the river, just on the borders of the regulation district of Chittagong. The Superintendent's bungalow, provided rent-free by Government, was built on a small hill, overlooking the broad reaches of the river Karna-phuli to the west and south, and backed on the east and north by high jungle-clad hills, grading backward higher and higher to unknown distances. The house was small, containing only a sitting-room and a bed-room, with bath and store-room; the situation was beautiful, and it was my delight to sit and work at a table in the verandah with all this new and lovely scenery spread out before me. The ground outside the verandah was carpeted thick with the mimosa (sensitive plant), while at the corner of the bungalow there grew a fine pomegranate tree, which was, when I arrived, covered with scarlet blossoms. A little lower down the hill was the kutcherry or court-house, where the administration of justice was carried on; and here also, under a police guard, was deposited the Government treasure-chest, in which were kept the revenues of the State. Lower still, on the banks of the river, stood ten or twelve shops, dignified by the name of "The Bazaar," and close by were the mud huts of the police barracks. Here there were quartered some fifty men in reserve, who were employed from time to time to relieve the garrisons of the three frontier guard-posts, which were situated in different parts of the hills, and which were maintained to repel the incursions of the independent frontier tribes.

I soon settled into the saddle and began to catch a good hold on my work, mindful always of the adage, " For him who does things at the proper time, one day is worth three." So I did all things as far as possible by rule. I rose generally at 6 A.M., took a cup of tea with some fruit, and then studied Burmese for an hour; after this I opened my letters and heard and gave orders on all police reports. At 10 A.M. I went to kutcherry, to hear such cases as came on for trial, such as suits for rent or the recovery of debts, divorce cases and family disputes. There seemed to be little vulgar crime in the Hills, but I was much troubled by low Bengali attorneys, who were attracted to the district by the ignorance and simplicity of the hill people, and who set themselves to foment litigation and promote disputes. The hill folk proper, I found, did not have recourse to the English courts if they could possibly avoid it; in the first place, because the majority of them did not understand Bengali, which had been fixed as the court language, and secondly, to avoid the expense of employing an attorney and of paying the Government stamp fees, both of which were required in all cases at that time. I resolved before long that, with the assistance of the Commissioner, things should be altered in regard to legal procedure.

After kutcherry I had to drill my policemen; in this I was ably assisted by my old friend Fuzlah, whose transfer to this district I had been able to arrange along with my own, and who now blossomed forth in all the dignity of a sub-inspector or jemadar, to which grade he had been promoted in recognition of his services during the Shendú expedition. I also had the assistance of another good soldier, named Ruldro Khan, who had served through the Mutiny as a havildar in Rattray's Sikhs, and who afterwards, on entering the police, had attached himself to my fortunes, following me from Noacolly.

Both he and Fuzlah were tried soldiers, thoroughly trained

in drill and discipline; but the rest of the Hill Tract Frontier police were for the most part a poor lot of men, chiefly consisting of Bengalis, quite unfit for any work demanding a stout heart, and who, if it came to fighting, would probably show unanimity in running away. There were, it is true, a sprinkling of Manipuris among them, who, if properly trained made good soldiers, but the value of these men was materially lessened by the rigidity of their caste prejudices.

After inspecting and drilling the men I usually walked through the bazaar, to hear any complaints, after which I paid a visit to the Government elephants, of which there were six attached to the district. There were at that time no roads in the Hill Tracts, and travelling was usually done either by boat or on foot, through the jungles or along the beds of streams, and for this latter work the assistance of elephants was indispensable.

I was pleased to find myself already known to the hill people under the name of Hurbut Tongloyn, my old acquaintance Twekam Tongloyn of the Matamori, with whom I had foregathered on my way to the Koladan, having published abroad his relationship.

I had not been long at work in my new appointment when the rainy season set in, and I then learnt, for the first time, the full delights of the rains in a hill country. Fungi sprang up on my boots in the night; if my books were left untended for a couple of days, they became plentifully garnished with blue mould; while my poor violoncello resolved himself into his elemental parts, all his glue gave way, and I found him lying in his case in pieces. As a set-off, with the advent of the monsoon, fevers and other forms of sickness cleared off, and with a refreshingly lower grade of temperature we quickly attained a comparatively clean bill of health. The Hill Tracts, in truth, were not a healthy abiding place, and although afterwards I got acclimatized, and grew to love the country very much, yet at first I was subject to frequent attacks of lassitude and low spirits, feeling myself perceptibly growing older, and, although I was but seven and twenty, my head was thickly sprinkled with grey hair.

Little by little I made myself theoretically acquainted with my small kingdom, and I now looked forward anxiously to the coming cold weather, when I hoped to travel about, and make the acquaintance of the people of the Hill Tracts.

During the rains all locomotion perforce ceased, the rivers being in flood and the country impassable, and I utilised this quiet time to study Burmese, which was the vernacular of the majority of the hill people. I agreed fully with the local proverb, "No speech, no knowledge," and was rewarded by finding, as the weeks went on, that I could understand and speak the language fairly well.

My charge, the district known as the Chittagong Hill Tracts, is situated between 21° 13′ and 23° 47′ north latitude, and 91° 46′ and 92° 49′ east longitude, containing an area of nearly 7,000 square miles, and a population, as ascertained by the census of 1872, of 63,054 souls. The district is bounded on the north by the independent state of Hill Tipra, on the south by the Akyab district, and on the west by the Regulation district of Chittagong. The eastern boundary was at that time undefined, but might be considered as extending just so far as British influence could make itself felt.

The district itself was divided into three parts: (1) the southern division, subject to the Bohmong, a chief of Burmese extraction; (2) a central tract inhabited chiefly by the Chakma tribe, under the regency of their chief's widow, the Rani Kalindi, the heir, her grandson, being still a minor; and (3) the northern portion, inhabited by Burmese-speaking clans, with a sprinkling of immigrants from the Tipra district, who paid annual tribute to our Government through a Burmese chief known as the Mong Raja. North, south, and west of the district we had no trouble, our boundaries being conterminous either with British districts, or with countries subject to British influence; but to the east were the independent tribes known to us as Kúkis, but more properly to be called by their own generic title of Lushai. They were a numerous and aggressive people, offshoots of the mighty Singpho horde which stretches from Assam, between China and Burmah, as far as the Shan country, near Siam in the south, and of which my old enemies the Shendús were also a branch.

These Lushais were the standing problem which embarrassed all local administration; they continually raided into the Hill

Tracts, attacking and plundering the inhabitants, burning the villages, slaying the men, and carrying off the women and children into slavery. This had gone on for years, until the fear of these inroads had at last established a broad tract of depopulated and deserted country, lying like a zone between us and the Lushais, extending from north to south in a breadth of perhaps fifty miles.

The nearest Lushai chief, named Rutton Poia, had been attacked and his village burnt by a British retaliatory expedition under Major Raban, in 1861. Since then various small raids had been made, which, however, we were unable to bring home to the perpetrators; so that between ourselves and the Lushais a hollow peace might be said to prevail. The situation, in fact, was strained, and hostilities might break out at any moment.

There had been two Superintendents of Hill Tracts before my time. The first one, Captain M——, was known locally as the "pugla Sahib," the mad master; but, mad or not, he had made his mark, and his exploits still lived in the memories of the people. Amongst other things, he once pursued a party of Lushai raiders, and caught them red-handed; they outnumbered his small party as five to one, but he at once attacked and put them to flight, killing two of the raiders with his own hand, and rescuing the captives whom they were carrying away. On another occasion he had himself lowered from the top of a lofty cliff which overhung the foaming rapids of Burkhul, on the Karna-phuli River, and then swam, or rather was hurled down the rapids, emerging safely, to the astonishment of the hill people, about half a mile down stream. These and other feats of personal courage and physical ability had given him great popular reputation, but he had not given satisfaction to his official superiors, and was consequently removed to make room for my predecessor. This gentleman, bred and brought up in the strict school of regulations, law and legal procedure, proved, I believe, too square for the very round hole of the Tracts, and so he also was removed, and I was put in on trial.

Not long after my appointment to the Hills I received a letter from Colonel (now Sir Arthur) Phayre, Chief Commissioner of British Burmah, whom I had met at Akyab, informing me that he had sent in my name to the Government of India for appointment as Superintendent of Hill Tribes on the Koladan. This unsolicited favour was very flattering to me, and I at once wrote thanking him and accepting the appointment. This I did because I preferred Burmah to Bengal, and also because the Burmese appointment would be a permanent one, while my post in the Chittagong Hill Tracts was at that time only temporary. I was not sure, moreover, whether the climate of the Chittagong Hills would suit me; for during the few months I had been there I had felt languid and weak, while my old wound troubled me a good deal, small abcesses having formed near the place of exit of the bullet. The doctors assured me that no bone was injured, and that no splinter had been left behind, so that these unfavourable symptoms could only be ascribed to climatic influence. Eventually, however, the question was settled by the Bengal Government declining to let me go to Burmah, at the same t me appointing me permanently as Deputy Commissioner and Political Agent of the Hill Tracts of Chittagong, on an increased salary. About this time, also, I was admitted as a Captain into the Bengal Staff Corps, and ceased to belong to Her Majesty's 104th Regiment.

My friend J——, with whom I had chummed in old days at Shahjehanpore, still kept up a correspondence with me. He had lately married a sweet young wife, and was holding his old appointment as Personal Assistant to the Inspector-General of Police in Calcutta.

I had not long to wait for my first news of the Lushias, for on the 7th of July it was reported that a band of them had entered British territory, and cut up three villages belonging to the Bohmong, in the hills south of Chandraguna; a detachment of the same party also plundered and burnt another village, nearer to me on the Kaptai, a small affluent of the Karna-phuli. They killed four villagers, and carried off into captivity no less than eighty persons. This raid occurred at a very unusual time, in the height of the rainy season, when the difficulties of hill travelling were greatly increased, and when the Lushais, like other hill folk, should have been employed in cultivation.

I started at once on foot, with a party of police, in pursuit of the marauders, but could find no trace of them, they having made their dash and retired as swiftly and secretly as they had come. The exposure, however, that I underwent, and the anxiety of this fruitless pursuit, the sleeping out in the forest amid heavy rain, combined with scanty food and severe fatigue, brought on a sharp attack of fever, by which I was prostrated for some time.

The difficulty of adequately defending the long line of frontier, consisting as it did of hundreds of miles of pathless forest, weighed upon my mind greatly at this time, and I found myself day and night reflecting upon the problem. There seemed but two alternatives: we might either, at a great cost, send a punitive expedition and destroy the villages of the raiders; or we ought to strengthen our cordon of police posts, and establish an efficient line of defence along the whole frontier. Either of these courses would entail great additional expense on Government, and as the standing paradox was to obtain security without increase of expenditure, I thought it unlikely that either of my alternatives would be acceptable to my superiors.

What other way, then, was open to me? This was the subject of my reflections; this cud I chewed and re-chewed, ruminant. The main point was evidently to obtain some influence over these Lushais. My predecessor, Captain M——, had gained great renown by his lucky surprise of their raiding party, and he was currently reported among them to be invulnerable to shot or steel. Could they be brought to consider this quality as one generic to the race of Hill Superintendents?

Now, in my somewhat miscellaneous reading, I had come across an account of the conjurer Robert Houdin's experiences among the Arabs. The French Government had brought him over to Algiers to undertake a contest with the native marabouts, and he had been completely successful in establishing a reputation as a mighty magician. Among other tricks I remembered one in which he had permitted an Arab to fire a loaded gun at his breast; the gun contained a marked bullet, which was immediately afterwards produced by Houdin from between his teeth.

I was pretty quick with my fingers, and determined, if possible, to reproduce this trick among the Lushais, being quite sure that, if successful, my renown would transcend even that of the famous Captain M——.

It was not long before the wished-for occasion presented itself. At the end of September I went on a visit to the village of Ishan Dewan, one of the headmen of the Chakma tribe, which was situated close to our most advanced police post of Kassalong, a long day's journey from my head-quarters up the Karna-phuli. The main object of my visit was to meet some Lushai messengers who had been sent to me by our old enemy Rutton Poia, and, if it could be managed, I intended to accompany them back across the frontier and pay a visit to the chief in his own village.

The Lushai "karbaris" (literally "men of business") duly arrived, and met me at Kassalong. In their interview with me they stated that Rutton Poia was anxious to maintain the friendly relations at present existing between us, and trusted that his people might be permitted to trade, as heretofore, at our frontier markets. He wished also to assure me that he had had nothing to do with the late raid on the Bohmong's villages. I listened patiently to all they had to say, and then replied that, as the matters they referred to were of the highest importance, it was necessary for me to see their chief personally. Would he meet me at Kassalong? Impossible. Then I would myself go to him. After some demur this was at length agreed to.

Ishan Dewan did all he could to dissuade me from the enterprise, reminding me that it was not so long ago that Rutton Poia had murdered, or caused to be murdered, a sergeant and two of our frontier policemen, who had been sent on a friendly message to his village. I meant going, however, and told Ishan that, although there might be danger to a policeman, there could be none to an official of my exalted position.

I ordered Jemadar Fuzlah, with twenty of my best men, fully armed, to accompany me, and the next morning we started in dug-out canoes on our journey up stream. About six miles from Kassalong we reached the Burkhul rapids, a grand tumble of water; here it was that my predecessor, Captain M——, had been let down from a lofty over-hanging crag, which towered a hundred feet or more above the roaring water, to take his perilous swim. Truly a bold and dare-devil feat!

The Lushai "karbaris," like my old friends the Shendús, would not trust themselves in boats, but went on foot. My boats were paddled by some of Ishan Dewan's Chakmas, who accompanied me much against the grain, being in fear of their lives; I was, however, compelled to employ them to manage the boats, as I found to my astonishment that the hill police were, for the most part, unused to rowing, and quite unable to steer a canoe. We dragged our boats painfully through the rapids, having often to work waist-deep in the water; but above was smooth and easy going, so that we paddled along without further interruption, until towards sunset we reached Utanchatra, where we found the Lushais awaiting our arrival, they having travelled on foot through the forest.

Here we drew our boats on to the great flat rocks which formed the bed and banks of the river, and camped for the night. The Chakma boatmen lighted a fire on a sandy place by the side of the river, and the bright flames irradiated a small zone of the surrounding forest, throwing into denser blackness the depths of wood and stretches of dark water that lay beyond. Our dinner, such as it was, was speedily despatched, and the men, tired with their day's work, were soon stretched sleeping round the fire or in the boats. No sound broke the stillness of the night, save the lapping of the water against the side of my boat where I lay smoking a final pipe, and thinking of the day's journey.

I thought of our start in the grey dawn, when the mist was still floating in white wreaths upon the river; then how, as the sun rose in the heavens, my men warmed to their work and paddled with a will, making the canoe jump again and the hills re-echo with their hill cry, the "hoia." Suddenly all would hush, and a whisper be passed back to the Sahib that a deer was within shot, drinking at the margin of the stream; or of a troop of monkeys to be seen gambolling in the branches of the overhanging trees, some drinking at the water's edge from out the hollows of their tiny hands, while a few hundred yards further off a fine jungle-cock strutted in the morning sun.

Midday, perhaps, was the least pleasant time in the twenty-four hours, for then all creatures were silent, all had withdrawn to the shade and shelter of the forest; only the large black forest-flies were out, settling on one without a sound, and with the softness of a piece of cotton wool, the first sign of their presence being a sting as of a lancet-thrust. Once, with a clack of wings like some aerial machine, the great hornbill passed over our heads, to or from his nest, where doubtless he had left his mate sitting on the eggs, duly plastered up with mud, leaving only room for her beak to receive the nourishment he brought her. The natives will not keep the large bill of this bird in their houses, although they will eat its flesh. The bill they believe to cause discord in families and to promote quarrels between husband and wife.

Then came the evening with its chorus of frogs and the shrill horn of the mosquito, while the sun westering in golden stretches of light made the river a path of glory. As twilight fell, I remember, an old tree we passed on the bank was full of fire-flies, who sent forth a beautiful silvery radiance, making the whole tree beat, as it were, in pulses of light, fading and flashing.

The next morning early we left our boats, and followed a jungle-path leading towards a lofty range of hills some ten or twelve miles distant, on the top of which was situated Rutton Poia's village. Our path for some distance lay over low-lying undulating ground, crossing occasionally a rivulet, or passing through dense forest jungle ; then it rose on a hill spur, winding up over boulder-covered slopes, among huge trees thickly hung with creepers and orchids, until at length it narrowed into a close, rocky defile. Here for a little space we halted, to allow the "karbaris" who guided us to parley with two wild-looking Lushai scouts, who, each armed with an old fire-lock, were posted on the summit of a towering rock which commanded the path. Then we passed on again, until at last the path came out on to a sheer precipice several hundred feet in depth, along the face of which the path was led, by a sort of bamboo ladder resting on wooden piles, driven firmly into crevices in the rock. A very awkward and shaky pathway I found it for my booted feet, and I was heartily glad when I arrived safely at the other side, where we reached a long grassy slope which led to the summit of the hill. On reaching the end of the ascent we were confronted by a crowd of forty or fifty Lushais, armed with guns and spears, and presenting a somewhat truculent and offensive aspect. I took no notice whatever of these persons, recalling the hill proverb :

> If you go into a strange river take in your flags ;
> If you enter a strange village, take the strut out of your walk ;

or better still, as my hill servant quoted :

> In your own village crow and be a cock, but when
> You're in another, you must be a hen.

I sat down on the grass to recover breath after the somewhat stiff pull up the hill, and the "karbaris" went on to communicate to the chief, Rutton Poia, the advent of his unlooked-for visitor.

The Lushais held aloof, regarding us in surly, scowling fashion ; nor would they respond to any friendly overtures on the part of my men. I ordered Fuzlah to see that our retreat was not cut off ; but inwardly I reflected, with some disquietude, how easy it would be to catch us like rats in a trap, by simply breaking down the bamboo ladder not far below. I gazed upon the Lushais with much curiosity, as they were, with the exception of the "karbaris," the first fair sample of the race which had come before me.

They were well-made muscular men, of somewhat dark complexion, and with a surly, forbidding cast of countenance. Their whole clothing consisted of a single long home-spun mantle or sheet of cotton cloth, sometimes white with a blue transverse stripe, or of a dark-blue fabric, the stripe being crimson or yellow. Their straight black hair was bound in a knot upon the nape of the neck. Some of the youngest and best-looking of the braves had small bunches of brilliant-coloured feathers, crimson, blue, and yellow, stuck ear-ring fashion through the lobe of the ear. About half of them carried guns, which, as far as I could make out, were all Tower-marked old flint-lock muskets of King George III.'s time ; some of these had been re-stocked and handsomely painted in red, black, and yellow. Two or three among them, I noticed, wore the handsome guyal powder-horns which I had previously seen among the Shendús ; and some smoked pipes made of

bamboo and lined with copper, similar to one with which Yitchee had presented me.

After a short interval, the "karbaris" returned, and intimated that Rutton Poia would consent to receive me; but that, on account of the fears of the women and children in his village, he was unable to admit my armed escort, who would have to remain outside. This did not admit of argument; so, after a brief consideration, I ordered my men to camp where they were, placing a sentry on the bamboo bridge, and then, taking with me Fuzlah and my hill boy Adupah, who was useful as an interpreter, I set forth to the village, preceded by the "karbaris."

The Lushai village lay before me, a confused mass of houses thickly scattered over the hill-side, and nearly all on different levels. The village was surrounded by a palisade of enormous logs, as thick as the leg of an elephant and ten feet high. The entrance lay through a stockaded passage, thickly studded with downward-pointing bamboo spikes, and defended by two heavy doors of rough-hewn timber, so thick as to be practically fire and bullet proof. On passing through the passage, I found the stockade was lined with men in readiness to repel any attack. Evidently these Lushais were a suspicious race, accustomed to treacherous dealing.

The village itself was built on no fixed principle, each householder having apparently placed his dwelling where it seemed best to himself. There was, however, the semblance of a main street, and down this we solemnly walked, preceded by the "karbaris," towards an isolated building standing in the centre of the village, which, they informed me, was the guest-house, where I was to be lodged. Opposite to this was Rutton Poia's abode, a large barn-like structure, a hundred and fifty feet long by forty broad, raised on a low platform about four feet from the ground. It was thatched with wild-palm leaves, and its entrance adorned with long lines of skulls, buffalo, pig, and deer, over the doorway.

I looked anxiously to see if I could distinguish any human heads among the trophy, but could see none. This I considered a favourable sign, for I had been informed that the heads of the unfortunate policemen who had been killed here, not more than a year ago, were hanging up over the chief's doorway, and I drew a favourable augury from the fact that they had been removed out of regard for my prejudices.

Another hopeful circumstance was that the village was thronged with women and children, all crowding out to look at the strange white man, for I knew that in case of danger the women and children were first of all hidden away. These females were stout-legged and not uncomely, clad in the scantiest of blue skirts round the hips, the upper part of the body being shrouded in the national home-spun sheet. All children under ten were, without any exception, naked.

I was shown up the ladder into the guest-house, a one-roomed dwelling, with walls of bamboo mat, raised on a high platform, to which one mounted by a sloping log cut in steps.

I asked when it would be convenient for the chief to see me, and was informed that the moment had not yet arrived, as Rutton Poia had sent out to summon some of the neighbouring chiefs, but that I was to be formally introduced to the family circle on the following day. This information I extracted from one of the "karbaris," who was affable and fairly communicative, and who had evidently been told off to attend upon me and keep me in a good humour, as he devoted himself exclusively to my service.

Towards sundown some food arrived for us from the chief's house; a rough and barbaric mess of seethed pig's flesh and rice, garnished with greasy capsicums. Some rice and other uncooked food had been sent to my men outside the village, as I ascertained from Fuzlah, whom I sent out to reassure the party and see that the sentries were properly posted.

I was somewhat troubled by the inquisitiveness of the boys and young men of the village, who climbed up perpetually to peep into the guest-house. For hours together eyes glistened through every crack in the walls, giving one an uncomfortable sensation; but as the evening came on they retired, and we were left alone for the night. To prevent surprise I had undertaken to watch until midnight, while Fuzlah and Adupah would share the remainder of the night-watch, keeping guard while I slept.

I had brought with me a soft quilted "rezai" to sleep on,

and, with a rug wrapped round me, and sword and pistol under my head, I lay and thought long and deeply upon my line of action on the morrow.

The position was not altogether a pleasant one, and caused me to cogitate much upon the nature of fear, and to wish that timidity or nervousness could be excised by a surgical operation from the characters of those who did not desire these emotions. I have found through life that, although one can always force one's body to do the right thing at the right time, yet that to eliminate nervousness from the mind is a much more difficult matter. An old Swedish story came into my head as I lay there thinking upon the curious inequalities of disposition which we call cowardice.

When Charles Gustavus, King of Sweden, was besieging Prague, a peasant of most extraordinary and portentous visage demanded admission to the royal service, offering, by way of qualification, to devour a whole hog in His Majesty's presence. The celebrated old General Königsmarck was standing by the King at the time, and he, although a soldier of proved courage, was rather superstitious. Regarding, therefore, this astounding offer of the peasant as something " uncanny," he remarked to the King that the man was probably a sorcerer, and should be burnt.

" Sire ! " said the peasant, highly incensed at such uncalled-for interference, " if Your Majesty will make that old man take off his sword and his spurs, I will eat *him* immediately, before I commence on the hog."

This terrible threat, combined as it was with a preternatural expansion of the hideous peasant's jaws, had such an effect on the old General that he forthwith fled, never stopping until he reached his own quarters, where he continued shut up in a melancholy and desponding frame of mind, brought on by disgust at himself for having given way to panic. It is the unknown and the mysterious which produce the mental tumult which we call fear. *Omne ignotum pro magnifico.*

During the early part of the night the sounds of rough chanting, accompanied monotonously by a drum, reached us from the chief's house ; but soon all was silent, and the village seemed wrapped in slumber, save a guard of two or three Lushais, who lounged smoking by the chief's door. It was a novel position: on a hill-top two thousand feet or more above the sea, everything different from my customary surroundings; climate, scenery, scents and sounds, all different, all new. I had no desire to sleep, and Fuzlah also seemed disinclined for slumber and gladly drew towards the fire at my invitation to have a chat. *He* was of opinion that the Lushais were a murderous-looking lot of scoundrels, and that what we ought to have done was to have brought fifty more of our men and burnt down the whole village. Then we talked of our Shendú adventure, and this led to his own previous life, and he recounted many things of wars and stratagems, when as a comparatively young man he had served as a soldier under the Maharaja of Cashmere, at Gilghit. Insensibly my attention wandered. I had so much to think of in the present that I could not give heed just then to the past; so Fuzlah soon wrapped himself in his rug and went to sleep.

About eleven o'clock a stealthy step came up the ladder, and the "karbari" put his sly head in at the door. Finding my eye upon him, he smiled vaguely and went away again; probably he had come to see that we were doing no mischief.

At midnight I roused Fuzlah and tried to sleep myself. I had, however, seemingly scarcely closed my eyes when I was awakened by an extraordinary noise, something between a bull's bellow and a railway whistle. What was it? We started to our feet, and Fuzlah and I were looking to our arms when Adupah said, "It is only the guyal calling, Sahib! Look, the dawn is just breaking, and they are opening the village gates for the beasts to go out to pasture."

These guyal were beautiful creatures, with broad fronts, sharp wide-spreading horns, and mild, melancholy eyes. They were the indigenous wild cattle of the hills, domesticated by these equally wild Lushais; all day long they were allowed to wander untended, feeding on the leaves and grass in the jungles, but returning always each to his master's house at night, to receive a handful of salt, of which they are immoderately fond. The Lushais make no use of the milk, regarding that fluid, indeed, as an unclean excrement; but they would slaughter a guyal occasionally, on high days and holidays, for the sake of the flesh, which is esteemed a great delicacy among them.

A little after sunrise the "karbari," with two or three other Lushais, came to say that Rutton Poia would receive me; accordingly, accompanying them, I entered the low, dark door of the chief's house. Inside, I found myself in a long, low room, where, although the hour was so early, numbers of men were assembled, sitting along the wall with their backs against the mat, smoking, while down the centre of the room was the inevitable line of huge earthen pots full of hill beer, and at each pot two drinkers sucking up the liquor through reeds.

Making our way through this crowd, who did not incommode themselves by moving out of the way too much, we passed on to the further end of the room, where, in a small partitioned recess with a window looking out over the hills, sat Rutton Poia, with sundry other chiefs.

I looked at the chief with considerable curiosity, and he at me with, I daresay, equal interest. He was a small, dark, athletic man, with a melancholy cast of countenance and large, stern eyes; he wore no ornament or insignia of his rank, save that his mantle was of a finer texture than the ordinary homespun worn by other Lushais. On my coming the chief and those who were with him made no motion of welcome; but the "karbari" showed me a mat, where I and my two attendants seated ourselves. A pause ensued, during which the chiefs sat like so many brown images, each wrapped round in his mantle. Inwardly I fumed greatly at the rough incivility of these barbarians; but I had not come all this distance in order to lose my temper, so I restrained myself and endeavoured to assume a brown-image-like aspect, as like that of the chief as possible.

At length Rutton Poia grunted. The "karbari" translated this sound by saying that the chief wished to know why I had brought a formidable party of armed men to his village. I replied that my men were armed in order to defend themselves from the dangers of the road; but that, having reached Rutton Poia's village, I had now no need of arms, as my presence showed. I requested that the chief would dispose of the contents of a bale which I had brought with me. The said bale was quickly opened and the contents, consisting of scarlet cloth, cotton sheeting, beads, looking-glasses, &c., were carried off by the chief's retainers; but Rutton Poia and the rest of them still sat like brown images.

"I am glad to hear," said I, "that Rutton Poia disclaims all participation in the outrages which have recently been committed in my country to the south; and I have come here in consequence, to confirm the friendship between us."

No reply. Some brass cups containing a strong spirit were handed round.

"The prevention of such occurrences is my duty," I continued; "or, when not preventable, we can punish our enemies and Rutton Poia knows that what I say is true."

This was a side shot at the chief personally, for I knew that he had been himself in command of the party which was so effectually routed by my predecessor, Captain M——. On this, Rutton Poia took a big gulp of spirits, and then addressed a remark to the interpreter. I noticed that he stuttered in speaking, but whether this was through nervousness or habit I could not tell. I hoped he was nervous.

"The chief says that Captain M—— was a magician. Is it true that he had a charm against shot and steel?"

"All Sahibs," I rejoined impressively, "are alike gifted with this power by Government on their taking charge of the Hill Tracts. If you have a gun handy I can easily prove this to you."

On a sign from Rutton Poia a gun was brought; the chiefs communed with each other in low tones, the drinkers left their pots, and a crowd of heads peeped over the partition.

"Now," I said, "charge that gun." The "karbari" carefully put in a measure of powder. "Now a bullet." He was putting in the bullet when I stopped him—"Stay! let me see the bullet." It was handed to me. "Lend me a knife." One of the chiefs produced a knife, and I proceeded to cut a cross on the bullet; then, raising it up so that all could see the mark, I said: "You would all recognise that bullet again?" Murmurs of assent. "Then see, I take that bullet and I place it in the gun, thus; then I ram it home in this manner. Now, prime the gun."

It was a heavy flint-lock musket; the "karbari" carefully primed it. Rutton Poia rose and carefully examined the priming.

"Now," said I, "fire at my chest." The "karbari" hesitated.

"Do as the Sahib tells you," said Rutton Poia.

I covered my eyes and face with my arm, and the "karbari," at a distance of about ten yards, took a careful aim and fired. I staggered for a moment, as if receiving a shock, and then, putting my hand to my mouth, from between my teeth I took the marked bullet.

"Is that the ball that was in the gun?" I asked calmly, handing it to Rutton Poia. The excitement was intense. The chiefs were now all standing, and the bullet was rapidly passed from hand to hand amidst exclamations of astonishment. It was indeed the marked ball!

We resumed our seats. Conversation among the Lushais now became vivid; their immobility had disappeared.

At last one big fellow, Vanlula I think was his name, got up and began to make a speech. I need not further describe the pow-wow which followed; suffice it to say, that by 4 o'clock that afternoon I was on my way back to the boats, having contracted a solemn alliance, offensive and defensive, with Rutton Poia and his allied chiefs, the compact having been duly ratified by the sacrifice of a guyal, with the proper ceremonies, and sealed by infinite potations.

Skilled magicians, I suppose, are never nervous, or it is, at any rate, part of their profession to appear imperturbable; but I confess that, as I lay in my canoe on my way down stream, it was with a shiver of excitement that I recalled the scene at the Lushai village, and thought of the moment when I changed the pewter bullet of the Lushai and substituted for it a waxen ball carefully blackleaded outside, according to Professor Houdin's receipt, which I had prepared before starting, and which was of course mashed to pieces in the gun when rammed home, while I concealed the marked bullet under the base of my thumb. When the "karbari" was about to fire at me, I covered my face with my arm to keep the powder and pieces of wax out of my eyes, the same movement enabling me to pass the bullet into my mouth, whence I was of course able to produce it after the explosion. I went straight down the river, stopping only one day at Chandraguna, and reached Chittagong on the 24th October, 1866, being anxious to report what I had done to the Commissioner.

He was much amused and interested at my adventure, but advised me to hold my tongue about it officially, as Government would certainly not approve of what I had done in contracting engagements to assist a Lushai chief, and my irregular proceedings might incur severe censure if officially reported. I accordingly said no more about the matter; but I determined, none the less, that as long as I remained in the Hills I would loyally perform my part of the compact, and would help Rutton Poia and his clan against their savage neighbours, as far as lay in my power. I must add that they too, on their side, did faithfully observe their engagements, and to the last day of my service in the Hills they remained true to the alliance we had contracted.

I remained a fortnight with my friend the Commissioner in Chittagong, both for the sake of the change of air, as also to consult him about the various reforms which I wished to introduce in the Hill Tracts.

I had previously received a present from the Mong Raja, in the shape of the slave-boy Adupah, who had accompanied me to Rutton Poia's. This lad had been pledged to the Raja, when quite a child, as security for debt. Of course on his conveyance to me all claim on him was at an end, and he became a free agent. I mention his manumission as illustrating the curious custom of debt-slavery which prevails, I believe, among all Turanian races, and which I found in force in the Hill Tracts.

If a man wished to borrow money he deposited as security a son or daughter, whose services were taken as payment of interest for the debt, and the release of whom was dependent on the repayment of the original loan.

I know that these debt-servants were, as a rule, well treated, and the custom being very ancient and universal, required to be tenderly dealt with.

The hill proverb said: "A thorn under the flesh is unendurable, so it is to have a relative in slavery." My predecessor had regarded the custom with abhorrence, as slavery pure and simple; and whenever an instance came within his knowledge he at once released the debtor servant, much to the loss and wonder of the creditor, who vainly explained that the arrangement was made by mutual consent, and that they had no wish to depart from ancient custom. No; they were informed that slavery was contrary to English law, and that their debts could be sued for in court. Most of the creditors preferred letting the debt go; for at that time our courts were not resorted to or esteemed in the Hills. The better class of hill men depended entirely on this custom to supply their household with domestic servants, there being no system of hired service, although the debtor servant system really came to much the same thing in the end. The Mong Raja, for instance, informed me that he had personally suffered great inconvenience; my predecessor, it appears, had released his whole household, so that for some time the house-work had to be done by the Raja's wife and daughters.

The country, in fact, was not ripe for so sudden and great a social change as was here involved. Had our courts really been resorted to by the people at large, the old system would have lapsed of itself; but as a matter of fact I was the only judicial officer in the whole district; the court language also (Bengali), was incomprehensible to the majority of the people, so that to thousands of men and women living far away in nooks and crannies of the hills, English law and justice were practically unknown.

The real rulers of the Hill Tracts were undoubtedly the chiefs, and they, I found, were highly suspicious and jealous of any infringement on their power and prerogatives. My proper place, they considered, was to remain an ornamental representative of Central Government. But this, of course, was not my view.

I liked my work more and more, feeling somehow that I was fit for it, and heartily glad to have got out of the Police into more congenial employment; but I soon found that, with the best intentions for the good of the people, it was impossible to govern actively without raising up enemies on every side. I was not satisfied to see things run in the old grooves, but where

I perceived a fault, an error, or an abuse, I attacked it boldly, and took no rest until the thing was altered. This course, unfortunately, pleased no one: not the people, for they, like sheep, were contented to be shorn, so only that they might tread the accustomed ways, following ancient customs: not the wrong-doers or abusers of power, naturally; for who is it that can endure being put in the wrong? And finally, Government did not like a stirring up of mud; they desired peace, quiet, and economy, and new brooms found no favour in Calcutta.

Petitions and complaints against my administration began to pour in, but I was nobly supported by the Commissioner, who believed in me, and sympathised with my somewhat Utopian schemes; so that at first I had merely the trouble of replying to the allegations of the different petitioners, and showing that they had nothing substantial to complain of. I may, perhaps, briefly state here what was the position in the Hills at the time, and what were the reforms which I desired so ardently to introduce.

First, our relations with the independent frontier tribes, Lushai, Shendú, and others, were very unsatisfactory. We had no direct dealings with them, nor were we able to prevent or punish the periodic raids which they made into British territory for the purpose of obtaining slaves and booty.

It was necessary to make our cordon of police posts thoroughly effective, in order to repel force by force; also, if possible, friendly relations should be entered into with the more powerful of the independent chiefs, as in one instance, I had already done. Sooner or later, I felt sure that Government would have to undertake a punitive expedition against the more aggressive of the tribes. "First the stick and then the sugar-stick," is a golden maxim in dealing with wild races.

Next, there was the status and authority of our own subsidiary chiefs to be considered, those who dwelt in British territory and owned allegiance to the British Government. There were, as I have stated, only three of these chiefs, viz. the Bohmong in the south, the Rani Kalindi in the centre, and the Mong Raja to the north. These chiefs had hitherto exercised paramount authority throughout the hills, keeping all power, profit, and information in their own hands, and, with a view to maintaining their position, they had hitherto opposed all efforts of the Government representative to introduce any change whatever into the administration.

It was plain that, unless I were content to be the merest shadow of authority, I must convince them that my power was greater than theirs. Now the outward symbol, as well as the inward basis of the chief's authority, was the collection of taxes from the inhabitants of the hills. Their chief source of revenue was a poll-tax, so much a head from each adult person. This kind of tax has ever and always been obnoxious to men in general, and in the present instance the system of taxation was rendered still more hateful, its inconveniences being exaggerated by the ignorance of the British Government as to local custom.

The three great chiefs above-named farmed the revenue, each paying a lump sum to Government, and collecting through sub-agents, to whom they leased the right of collection in different villages. Our officials, before the appointment of a separate Superintendent of Hill Tracts, had recognised this system of sub-letting, and accorded to it the legal status of ownership; hence arose another species of slavery, for go where he would each hill man was still the chattel of some petty sub-farmer of revenue, and was bound to pay him head-money and do him service, on pain of being sold up or otherwise punished by order of the courts.

In meddling with this system I felt that I should raise up a cloud of enemies, as who indeed does not who dares to attack a "vested interest"? But still, the system was radically wrong, and there could be no substantial improvement in the well-being of the people until some amendment was made in this.

After long consultation with the Commissioner, we at length decided that the best thing to do was for me to go to Calcutta, and personally lay the whole matter before the Lieutenant-Governor, with whose sanction alone any radical alterations in the existing revenue system could be made.

Accordingly I repaired to Calcutta, and submitted to the head of the Bengal Government my scheme for the administration, fiscal and political, of the Chittagong Hill Tracts; this, although it involved some immediate increase of expenditure, would, I felt sure, promote in the long-run the welfare of the people, and aid in developing the resources of the country.

While in Calcutta I stayed with my friend J——, who, with his young wife, seemed as happy as possible. His marriage, indeed, appeared to have turned out well, although I was puzzled by it at the time, as he had always been a cynic and a scoffer at things matrimonial. We passed a very pleasant time together, recalling old scenes of the Mutiny, when we had served as boys together; and I left him without any foreboding of the heavy trouble so near at hand.

CHAPTER X

THE HILL TRACTS OF CHITTAGONG (*continued*)

1867

"One can do without mankind, but not without a friend."
Hill Proverb.

A GREAT sorrow overshadowed my life, at the beginning of the year 1867—the loss of my dear friend J——, under circumstances so painful to myself that it left a scar, which the many years since passed have failed altogether to obliterate.

Hardly had I returned to the Hills, after my trip to Calcutta, when the news of a fresh Lushai incursion into the Bohmong's territory called me a hundred miles away from my headquarters, and absorbed all my time and attention. Two villages had been attacked, eleven persons killed, and thirty-five carried away into slavery. The enemy, as usual, came and went like a fox to a hen-roost, vanishing before any news of their presence could reach me. There was nothing to be done in the way of retaliation, as I had neither men nor authority; but I established a strong outpost, hoping thus to guard against future outrage in that quarter.

On returning to my quarters at Chandraguna, I found that I had been favoured in my absence by a visit of inspection from one Major B——, Deputy Inspector-General of Police, who had been deputed to overhaul my office, and report on my doings generally. This officer had put up at my house, and having completed his perquisitions, had departed before my return.

I smiled when I heard his name, for J—— and I had often laughed over a ludicrous, but somewhat cruel, practical joke we had played him, in a little love affair of which we had been cognizant; but I thought his visit of inspection very unusual and sudden, as notice is always, in such cases, given beforehand to the officer chiefly concerned.

However, I had nothing to conceal or to fear, and I troubled myself little about the matter. How very different would have been my feelings, had I known then what I learnt afterwards, that poor J—— had written to me, warning me that Major B—— was coming in no friendly spirit, to spy out my doings, and bidding me put my house in order. In my absence Major B—— had possessed himself of this, my private letter, and forwarded it to the Inspector-General, saying it had been enclosed to him with an official return from my office.

But of all this I knew nothing, not even the existence of such a letter, until one morning, a short bitter note came from J——, saying that my carelessness had been the cause of his ruin, and bidding me fare as well as I could with that weight on my conscience. The following day came a telegram to say he was dead, it was feared by his own act.

The shock was terrible. I racked my brain in vain, trying to imagine how I could have been concerned in this tragedy, until the following letter enlightened me.

The Inspector-General has asked me to send you a line about poor J——'s sudden and sad end.

You will probably have received a letter from J—— himself, telling you that his note to you had been placed in the hands of the Inspector-General. In consequence it was arranged that J—— should retire from his appointment as Personal Assistant to the Inspector-General. He was, however, to remain in his quarters until his resignation had been sent in, and his leave, for which he proposed to apply, had appeared in orders.

On the evening of Friday last, J—— put his wife in her carriage and sent her off to a ball, and after reading for an hour or so he went to bed.

When Mrs. J—— returned, about 1 A.M., she found her husband insensible from the effects of a strong dose of chloroform, applied in a sponge-bag to his nose and mouth. Her cries soon brought assistance, and medical aid was speedily available; but it was too late. J—— had taken some chloroform the day before, as he was not feeling well, and was naturally much depressed, but, on the earnest solicitation of his wife, had promised not to resort to it again.

The Inspector-General is satisfied that the return of the note, which has been the origin of all this trouble, was purely accidental.

How could I think it accidental, knowing as I did the bitter grudge B—— had harboured against both J—— and myself for years past, and that he would be glad to have a chance of retaliating on us. I was full of bitterness and soreness of heart, and strove hard to bring it home to him. I laid the whole matter before the Commander-in-Chief, demanding an inquiry; but there was not evidence enough to bring the case to a court-martial, and it was never satisfactorily cleared up, although privately his conduct was condemned by all who knew him. He, too, now is dead.

My poor friend's death haunted me like a shadow by night and by day, waking or sleeping; and I threw myself into my work with renewed and feverish zeal, striving to forget. But of course my health suffered, and I had frequent attacks of fever, with enlargement of the spleen, and but for the kindness and care of my good Commissioner Y—— at Chittagong, who had me nursed and cared for in his own house, and who strove to cheer me and to win me back to my enthusiasm for my work among the hill folk, I do not think I should have pulled through.

They were the simplest, the most kindly folk, these hill people; truthful, and capable of strong attachments; having also a great appreciation of straight and even-handed justice. I found them ground down by ignorant, narrow-minded chiefs; harassed by litigious, lying Bengali usurers, and oppressed by the constant dread of Lushai or Shendú raids.

Many of them were Buddhists, but the rest had a sort of vague natural religion, a belief in spirits of air and water, of hostile demons warring in storm and sickness, but with nothing to guide or help them in their daily lives. They needed schools, they needed religious teaching, they needed simple, upright dealing, and protection for their lives, and their belongings. These needs I set myself to supply, but the obstacles first to be overcome were by no means insignificant.

To begin with, there was the hitherto supreme power of the hereditary chiefs, who indeed paid tribute to our Government, but who stood entirely between us and the people. They were very jealous of their authority, and I quickly recognised that I must either gain their co-operation or set them entirely aside, if I wished to reach the people. The stick or the sugar-stick—for them the choice—but by one or the other, or by both, I intended to rule.

Foremost among these chiefs ranked the Bohmong, who ruled

over the southern half of my district. Buddhist by faith, Burmese by tongue, he oppressed and tyrannized over the people at will; not stopping even at murder, when he thought it necessary in order to gain an object or confirm his power. He acted with impunity, for who should bear witness against so great a one?

Sometimes detailed accounts reached me of some evil deed; but when I tried to call witnesses to prove it, all would deny having any knowledge of the occurrence, and I would hear afterwards that they had been told that, if a word escaped them, they and their families would be rooted out and driven away in a night, while rumour would say it was simply another Lushai raid.

I had no police worth the name to help me in the detection and punishment of crime. The men under me were simply a frontier guard, and of no use whatever even in the simplest inquiry.

I tried first to conciliate the Bohmong and gain his confidence. I visited him, talked with him, consulted and argued with him, but in vain. He eluded my visits as often as he could, and sent me presents, which I declined, pleading our Government prohibition. When I did see him, he smiled and nodded assent to all I said, but he did as little and hid as much as he was able.

I could get no tangible proof of his evil-doing, although it was known throughout the country; and of course I could get no help or countenance from the authorities without proof positive. But I promised myself that I would one day be even with this old fox.

I had a small police post in the Bohmong's village at Bundrabun, where he resided. This post, which served to keep open communication between head-quarters and the southern guard-posts, had been established much against his will. I counted on the police officer in charge of this post to give me reliable information about the Bohmong's doings and designs. I soon found, however, that I learnt nothing of importance, while the chief seemed to direct his plans with a singular knowledge or prescience of my own movements, and even of my intentions.

At length I learnt that my policemen had been suborned, and

that not only my personal movements, but also all letters and despatches to the southern outposts, which passed through Bundrabun, were submitted to the Bohmong, and systematically opened, read, and re-sealed in his presence; the post-bag being carried by the police havildar direct to his house. This, if proved, was a clear offence against the law; and I laid my plans carefully to bring it home to the offender.

Accordingly I one day detained the post-runner until past midday, under pretext of having to send an important dispatch, and then gave him, in his bag among others, a large letter sealed conspicuously and marked urgent, containing orders to my senior jemadar in the south.

It was a long day's journey across country, through the jungle, from my head-quarters at Chandraguna to Bundrabun, and I calculated that the runner would reach the chief's village at nightfall. The bag would be taken from him by the police and brought to the Bohmong for his usual inspection, and, arriving so late, would, in all probability, be left with him for the night.

I kept my own counsel till nearly sundown, when I summoned Fuzlah.

"Fuzlah, take four of the best men and get ready a boat to cross the river."

"Are we to be armed, Sahib?"

"Yes, carbines and twenty rounds of ammunition. Light marching order. Take no food, but eat a good meal before starting. We have to go all night. Be ready in half an hour, and let all shut their mouths."

Fuzlah saluted and left me, and in less than an hour later our little party was safely landed on the other side of the river, and marching in the twilight for Bundrabun.

It was a long and weary march. The path was not very good, and the darkness became oppressive, as the moon had not risen, and our way lay for the most part through dense forest. We stumbled along, splashing through swampy ground, or wading through mud and water, as we crossed the bed of some small stream. Once we made a detour, to avoid a village where the post-runner was usually relieved, and once I halted for an hour to rest.

It was about three o'clock in the morning when we halted on the banks of the Sungu river, on the other side of which, dark and silent, lay the sleeping village of Bundrabun.

"Fuzlah, do you know where the ferryboat is? It should be here."

"No, Sahib. At nightfall it is always hauled up on the land on the other side. Shall I shout and wake the ferryman?"

"Be silent. Not a word above a whisper. One of us must swim for the boat."

Quickly one of the men divested himself of his accoutrements and upper garments, and silently swam away in the darkness.

We waited anxiously. Five minutes, ten minutes—and no boat appeared. I could risk waiting no longer, for the morning star had risen, and the village would soon be stirring. So we all swam across, making several journeys for clothing, arms, and ammunition, which had to be carried on our heads. We had just accomplished our last swim when my first emissary appeared.

"I have been a long time, Sahib, but I could not bring the boat, as the paddles had been removed, and I was searching for them."

"Hush! not a word. Forward!"

We moved on swiftly and silently, with unshod feet, to the police station.

"Go in, Fuzlah, and without noise bring out the havildar. Warn him briefly that I know all, and that his only hope lies in submission and full confession. Order the others to remain quiet in the house."

Secret and summary action was necessary. Firstly, because the havildar was a hill man, and he and his relatives were subjects of the Bohmong; secondly, because unless I carried out my plan swiftly and thoroughly the chief would frustrate all inquiry by causing a timely disappearance of my witnesses.

Fuzlah reappeared shortly, bringing with him the havildar, much agitated. I did not stop to ask questions, but ordered Fuzlah to bring him with us, and at once led the way to a gloomy thicket hard by. Here we paused, and I deliberately drew out my revolver, and, gazing sternly at the havildar, I slowly cocked it and took aim at his head.

The man fell down, caught hold of my feet, begging for mercy, and confessed all he knew. The post-bag was at the Bohmong's, beside his head, with the letters opened. The havildar had himself taken it to the chief, and had been sent away when the Bohmong found the large sealed letter marked urgent. He saw the seal broken before he left. This was enough to act upon.

"Jemadar Fuzlah, fall the men in. Fix bayonets, left turn, quick march!"

Dawn was breaking as we threaded our way through the silent street of the big village towards the chief's house. Heads were popped out here and there, and inquiries made as to who we were and what we wanted.

I led straight for the Bohmong's house, swiftly and silently, then rushed up the ladder, leaving my men at the foot, and so across the entrance platform and into his sleeping-room. The bag was there at his head, the letters open and scattered about beside him. In a moment I had him and the bag both out on the platform, where my men joined me.

It was a strange scene, lit up by the first rays of the morning sun. The platform, with the astonished chief, surrounded by my five policemen with fixed bayonets, myself bare-legged, with pointed revolver, clad in country home-spun, all wet and dripping, muddy and torn, after our night's travel and swim across the river. Below us a surging crowd of muttering villagers, among whom some spears began to show. We had the wall of the house against our backs, so could not be surrounded.

Presently there was a stir and drawing back among the crowd, and the chief's brother arrived, puffing and blowing with the unusual haste he had used, and with a big umbrella held over his head. I briefly but audibly explained to him that it was necessary for me to take away the Bohmong as my prisoner to the guard-house, and that any attempt at a rescue, or violence on the part of the people would cause his death.

The crowd rolled back murmuring, and I conveyed my prize with all speed to the police guard-house. Here, in the face of everybody, I proceeded to try the case as a magistrate, formally recording the evidence, and calling on the chief for his defence.

A great family council was forthwith held, and the Bohmong humbled himself before me, making submission, and promising that, if I would overlook this offence, he would for the future be entirely guided by my advice. But I was inexorable; the majesty of the law must be vindicated.

The culprit then pleaded that he had not himself broken the seal, it was his Dewan who had opened the Government letter. I *took down this statement, which was corroborated by the* chief's brother.

"Fuzlah, arrest the Dewan."

The Dewan, a near relative of the Bohmong's, was therefore arrested, and a quarter of an hour later was on his way down stream to Chittagong, closely guarded, to await there my coming.

After this I relented somewhat, and presently we came to an agreement. The Dewan was to be the scapegoat, the Bohmong consenting to bear witness against his servant and to give him up to me for punishment in the face of his people.

Further, the Bohmong himself being an old man, would resign the administration of affairs into the hands of his brother, and seek the rest and repose he so much needed in a religious life.

After this I took boat to Chittagong, where I had an interview with the Dewan, informing him that his masters had sacrificed him to save themselves, and pointing out that his only hope of my protection lay in his making a full disclosure of all he knew. So I completed my chain of evidence, and the overthrow of my enemy was complete.

Not without cost, however; and, the price I paid for my success was a bad attack of fever and ague, brought on by the fatigue of the night march, the cold swim across the river, with the subsequent excitement, which prevented my drying my wet clothes.

The new Bohmong was loyal to me, as he owed me his kingdom and feared to lose it like his brother if he offended. Thus matters were peaceably settled in the south.

There remained to be dealt with the Rani Kalindi, who ruled over the central portion of the Hill Tracts, and the Mong Raja to the north. The latter potentate had from the first evinced a friendly disposition, and I apprehended no difficulty with him ; but the Rani was an old widow woman, swayed and directed by interested advisers, and her attitude remained persistently hostile during the whole term of my residence in the Hill Tracts.

The first attempt she made was in the Kutcherry, or Law Court, sending up test cases and then appealing against my decisions, first to the Commissioner at Chittagong and afterwards to the High Court at Calcutta.

I was very careful, however, with my work, and when doubtful always postponed decision till I could refer to my friend the Commissioner, so that she failed to catch me tripping in the performance of my official duties.

Next a very harassing mode of attack was adopted, and one much in favour in the East. Anonymous petitions were sent to Calcutta, charging me with all sorts of crimes, and were returned to me by the Bengal Government for any reply or remark I might wish to offer. This was sufficiently annoying, but I had at first no difficulty in refuting groundless accusations.

But constant dropping will, as all know, wear away even a stone, and by persistent complaints an impression was gradually set up that something must be wrong. The continual fire of anonymous letters and petitions had been disregarded, but at length the Lieutenant-Governor received a petition duly signed by seven leading hill men, containing formal charges against me of various sorts of injustice and oppression.

On receipt of this the Lieutenant-Governor wrote to the Commissioner at Chittagong, directing him to proceed at once to my head-quarters, and make a rigorous inquiry into the facts alleged in the petition and into my administration generally.

I confess that I felt deeply hurt and mortified at the time, and betook myself in high dudgeon to Chittagong, there to await the result, and to show by my absence that I had no wish to influence or alarm those who desired to bear witness against me.

The Commissioner repaired to my head-quarters and summoned before him the men whose names were affixed to the petition; but these testified that they had made no complaint and signed no petition, and that the writing of their names was a forgery. Many counter-petitions were put in to the Commissioner, professing the entire contentment of the hill people with my rule, and among these I was glad to hear of one from the new Bohmong, Momphru, who now reigned in his brother's stead, while the Mong Raja, Keo-ja-sync, made a long journey in order personally to request the Commissioner that I might not be removed from the Hills.

The upshot of the matter was that the Commissioner wrote to congratulate me on the result of his inquiry, saying that he should report favourably to Government on the good work I was doing in the Hill Tracts.

Yet another kind message I had from the Lushai chief, Rutton Poia, who sent two karbaris to me with the following curious invitation.—"The chiefs hear that you are at enmity with the great Lord Sahib in Calcutta. If this be the case, they invite you to come into their country. Each of the chiefs will give you a house from each of their villages, and men will flock to you on account of your being proof against bullets. Come to us, brother. You will be a great chief."

Truly a generous offer; and had the inquiry ended otherwise than it did, I do not feel sure that I should not have shaken off the dust of civilization and accepted the offer.

As it was, however, I thanked the chiefs cordially for their kindness, and assured them that there was no enmity between me and the great Lord Sahib, but on the contrary he had graciously been pleased to approve my work and strengthen my hands. I should, however, never forget the goodness of their hearts towards me.

As a result of the inquiry I was promoted to a higher grade, and also received a letter thanking me for my services; and I vainly flattered myself that I had done with the Rani's persecutions. But having failed in her attack on my honour she next directly assailed my life.

I had attended the great Maha-muni fair, a gathering of a religious character, which was ceremoniously observed by the hill people every year. I was tired, over-tired, in fact; and although I went to bed early I could not sleep. I got up after a time to try and light a pipe, but could find no matches, and my servants were all away in their own quarters some distance below my hill-top. The kutcherry, with its treasure-chest, guarded by a sentry, was about two hundred yards distant, and my bungalow was completely isolated. The weary hours dragged on slowly as I lay tossing, trying to compel the sleep that would not come. As I lay in bed I could see through the open doorway, in clear weather, the sky-line of the distant forest and the stars sparkling above; but this night was dull, and the square frame of the door leading from my sleeping-room into the verandah was mistily outlined in grey, as the moon shone fitfully through the clouds.

I had lost count of time as I lay drowsily looking at this grey square, and wondering vaguely what might be the round black knob which seemed to form part of the door-jamb, when the appearance of a second black knob close beside the first roused all my faculties. In an instant I was vividly awake, for I knew that the knobs represented two men silently peering into the darkness of my chamber.

One thinks quickly in moments of extreme danger, and I speedily decided what to do. Fortunately my room was absolutely dark, and they could see nothing of me. Grasping the loaded revolver which I always kept under my pillow at night, I slid noiselessly out of bed, on the side furthest from the window, and watched cautiously.

There was a whispered conference, and the doorway was filled by the dark shapes of four men, their spears glinting in the faint moonlight. They were evidently discussing who should enter first. At last one came in and crept stealthily to the near side of the bed. I heard the thud of his knife striking at my empty place; and then I could stand it no longer, but let drive at him with my pistol, and with a yell jumped for the assassins.

There was a helter-skelter and rush as I discharged my revolver after the cowardly ruffians; then the guard came running up, and my servants appeared, and there was great jabber and confusion. Someone was wounded, for we found two spears thrown aside and followed blood tracks into the dense jungle behind my house; but they got clear off, and I never discovered who had been concerned in the attack. I heard enough to know that it was instigated by the Rani, but not enough to bring the charge home to her.

For some time afterwards I had a sentry in the verandah of the house while I slept, until, by the advice of my friend the Mong Raja, I turned my bedroom into a holy place, where deeds of blood were impossible, by enshrining there a fine image of Buddha with which he presented me. This sacred object I set up on a pedestal, and under its protection I slept for the future in safety.

It was by invitation of the Mong Raja that I had visited the Maha-muni fair, which was a remarkable gathering of its sort, both on religious and social grounds, showing the hill folk in a favourable light. The temple or shrine of Gautama Buddha was built on neutral ground, at a place midway between the hills and plains. At the annual festival thither flocked the hill folk to worship, and crowds of Bengali shopkeepers, with keen eyes to business, came to dispose of such wares as were sure to attract the fancy of the simple natives.

I arrived the day before the gathering and pitched my tent in a mango-grove. The temple hard by was a square, domed, whitewashed building, with a door on each side, opening on to a corridor, which ran round the entire building. In the centre was a dark domed chamber, in which was set up a gigantic gilt image of Gautama, full forty feet high, in a sitting posture. Before the image burned a row of small oil lamps, and close by was a frame of bells; these were jangled by any intending worshipper, to give notice to the image of his presence and devotional intent.

The Bengali traders arrived the night before the festival, and hastily erected small booths of bamboo matting, where early in the morning they spread out their wares. Sweetmeat sellers were there, as at all fairs in all countries; stalls of copper and brass-work; shops for the sale of flaring cloths and bright-coloured kerchiefs of cheap cotton and silk fabric; sham jewellery; pan, betel-nut, and tobacco, and everything likely to please the hill folk, were spread out in tempting abundance.

The pilgrims arrived generally by villages, each community dressed in gala attire and preceded by a drummer. The maidens were clad in home-spun skirts of dark blue bordered with scarlet, and white breast-cloths barred with chocolate and red, also of home manufacture. They wore silver or coral chains round their necks, and orchid blossoms stuck coquettishly in the long hollow, truncated, silver cones which most of them wore through the lobe of the ear. The girls loved flowers, and the young men would rise before dawn and go far into the woods to seek the graceful sprays of white, lilac, or orange-coloured orchid bloom, which was the favourite adornment of their sweethearts.

Each party was in charge of one or two elders of their people; but there were undoubtedly many more young folk than old at the gathering. The girls of each party kept together as they marched, and laughed gaily as they came within sight of the glories of the fair.

Each party on arrival deposited their baskets under some convenient tree, where they intended to take up their abode during the festival; and then proceeded at once to make obeisance before the great image of Gautama in the shrine.

Afterwards came a stroll among the shops. There are no shops in the hills, and the Bengali traders drove a roaring trade. Great was the demand for yellow candles and crackers for the night season, when the fun grew fast and furious. Red thread, strings of beads, cheap fiddles, snowy muslins, and gay kerchiefs, all found a ready sale. A peep-show with views of Delhi and Calcutta afforded infinite delight; while an ourang-outang from the Straits, in a cage, who was exhibited as a wild man of the woods, proved a great commercial success.

Sometimes a purchase would be negotiated requiring a certain discretion and reserve, when the presence of "those impudent lads" was eluded or openly deprecated. Long meshes of black or dark brown hair could be obtained by those whose locks were scanty, and were worn plaited along with the natural hair to augment its quantity. Those who could not afford hair bought thick strands of plaited silk or black mohair for a similar purpose. The wearing of artificial hair seems a well-nigh universal custom. The Chinese lengthen their pig-tails in this manner, while on the borders of Tibet the custom prevails among both men and women. I remember once hearing the remark made by a Tibetan on a passing girl, " She is young ; she does not yet wear deputy-hair."

There seemed great freedom among the young people at the fair, but all within the bounds of decorum. Sweethearts wandered hand in hand, stopping first at the sweetmeat stall, then at the shop where was sold betel and pan. This last was more important a purchase than might be guessed by the uninitiated, for in the hills the presentation of the innocent green pan-leaf with betel-nut and spices inside, accompanied by a certain flower, is a declaration of love. If the spice is placed in one corner, with a peculiar turn of the leaf, it signifies " Come away with me." The addition by the girl of a touch of turmeric outside conveys a negative ; while a piece of charcoal thrust inside the leaf is tantamount to a scornful dismissal.

As the day wore on lovers became bolder, and the mute pleading of the pan-leaf was discarded in favour of voice and flute. The girls once more banded themselves together and sang—

The hills stretch in long ranges,
In long ranges ordered by God.
The cockscomb and the marigold, O maidens, do not sow.
The hills stretch in long ranges,
Ranges driven by God's hand.
The cockscomb and the marigold, even if you sow,
O, maidens do not wear them,
Or your hearts will die away ;
As cockscomb and marigold wither, your hearts will pine away.

Sad and plaintive was the air, but as it died away the young men in chorus shouted back merrily—

A dweller on the mountain is the bumble-bee ;
He lives in a dead bamboo.
All alone lives the bumble-bee ;
A gay young bachelor is he, all alone on the hill side.

All give the " hoia " or hill " Jödel." Then, with preliminary trill, a solo begins, as some melancholy swain would seek to sway his mistress' heart by intoning a more doleful ditty.

A flock of birds I see flying,
But one bird is left alone,
All alone, sitting on a high tree,

A crowd of men I see paddling,
But one man sits alone,
All alone without a companion.

The singer pauses for a while in his song and rends the air with the wailing of his flute. Then readjusting his turban, and putting his hand behind his ear, he again uplifts his voice in yet more touching strains.

From afar I see the waters of the Kynsa river
Flowing white in the valley.
What good have I from gazing at its waters?
Some other will bathe therein.
From afar off gazing I see a lovely maiden;
White and fair is she.
What good have I from gazing at her beauty?
Some other will obtain her love.

Thus song answered song and the day wore on till dusk, when all thronged to the corridor of the temple; and all was heat and confusion as the crowd circled round the shrine bearing each one a lighted taper. All night long from dusk till dawn they made carnival, letting off crackers, and trying to blow out each other's candles.

For three days the charivari continued almost without intermission, till on the morning of the fourth day signs of departure became manifest. One after another the booths closed, as the lucky shopkeeper who had sold all his wares made up his accounts, and made ready for his journey home.

Outside the temple a number of yellow-robed priests showed themselves, each sitting under the shade of an enormous umbrella, stuck in the ground, telling their beads or reading solemnly from some palm-leaf manuscript. To them came the villagers, as each community assembled, to receive a final benediction before leaving the grove.

Beside each reverend father was dug a small hole in the earth, into which each worshipper put an offering in the shape of a silver or copper coin. Over the hole was placed a small tripod formed by pieces of fresh-split bamboo twined round with green leaves and flowers. From the tripod extended a pure white thread, which passed round the shoulders of the whole party seeking a blessing, and terminated in the hands of the priest, who, with shaven crown and yellow robe, stood in the centre of the group.

Slowly the holy man pours water over the tripod as he mutters a formula; slowly he passes the thread round the impatient group; slowly he extends his hands to pronounce the benediction.

"Hasten, my Lord Priest, the boat is waiting," exclaims some saucy young maiden, who is instantly hushed and rebuked by her elders. So in turn each party is blessed and dismissed, and quiet falls upon the shrine for yet another year, while the priests and their acolytes collect together the candle ends and small forgotten pieces of property left by the faithful.

It was a pleasant mirthful gathering, and I reflected much, as I returned to my own quarters, on the loss or gain which civilization brings. These people thought no shame of their human nature, with its loves and passions, and yet in all simplicity preserved their modesty and self-respect. I had often heard of the vicious excesses and drunken debauchery of savage races, and for aught I know this may be the case on the coast of Africa or New Guinea; but here in the Hill Tracts, throughout the three days' carnival, I had not seen one drunken man nor witnessed any discourtesy to a woman. They seemed an honest kindly people, happy in their homes and in their simple Buddhist faith, and I doubted much if they had anything to gain from the introduction of European ideas. The Lushais and Shendús were made of different stuff and needed very different dealing with.

The wily Bengali múktears, or attorneys, were the bane of the Hill Tracts, and I never relaxed in my efforts to banish them from the country. Soon after the fair I had the pleasure of finding good cause for shipping the last three of them out of my district. As a matter of course they petitioned against me, both to the Commissioner and afterwards to Government; and in the report I was called on to make in consequence, I did not spare them. I pointed out how they lived on the ignorance and weakness of the hill folk, stirring up strife and fomenting litigation; how they strove to weaken the authority of Government by inciting to appeals against my orders merely on grounds of legal quibbles and misrepresentations. I also let it be publicly known that, if any hill man thought a decision or order of mine was wrong or unjust, I was content to have it referred to the Commissioner; but that I should consider as a grave offence any trying to get the better of me by legal subterfuge.

I found personal influence the only way of dealing with these simple people. The legal code and the Government were merely names without meaning to them, too vague and too remote to influence their daily life. The man they could see and hear, whom they could please or displease, love or hate, he was for the time being their chief and their king.

The crafty Bengalis took our laws and used them as direct engines for oppression and extortion. If the crop of a hill man failed, or he wished for money to pay for the marriage of his daughter, he would borrow from a Bengali money-lender twenty or thirty rupees. This would be obligingly lent to him at the rate of five per cent. a month, or sixty per cent. a year, The hill men are honest, and would continue to pay this heavy interest until, with much toil, they had collected and were ready to pay off the principal of the debt.

Then what followed? I will give a not uncommon case. The hill man presents his money. "Very good, my friend," says the usurer. "See now, I destroy your bond." So saying, he tears up truly an old bond, but not the hill man's bond. The poor man can neither read nor write, but goes home happy that the debt is paid and he is a free man again.

The Mahajun bides his time, and then appears in court with his bond, and files a suit for debt against the hill man, whom we will call Nilchunder, for money borrowed with compound interest and costs, and a summons is accordingly granted against the said Nilchunder to appear and defend the suit.

On the day appointed for hearing the case, the usurer lies in wait for the arrival of Nilchunder in his boat; then, hastening to greet him with effusion, and with a face and voice full of concern, says, "My dear friend, how truly I grieve that through an error you have had this trouble and this unnecessary journey. There is no need for you to appear. Give me your summons and I will put matters right with the Sahib, while you go and eat and drink at my house."

So the poor fly goes to eat and drink, while the wily spider goes to court, where the case is duly called, and Nilchunder not appearing, a decree *ex parte* is given for the whole amount sued for.

The Mahajun hospitably entertains his victim and speeds his homeward departure, giving no word or sign of his business till the time for appeal has gone by and the decree is made absolute. Then the storm bursts on the head of the luckless hill man, who finds himself loaded with an overwhelming debt, which he has never incurred, and can never hope to discharge; and so he becomes practically the Mahajun's slave for the term of his natural life.

The above is no fancy sketch. I have known even worse cases than this. And I was, indeed, happy when the Government listened to my urgent appeal and sanctioned the following proposals:—

"No middle-man or attorney to be allowed to act in hill cases.

"No stamps to be required in certain cases, thus reducing the price of justice (*i.e.* costs) to a minimum.

"The legal interest recoverable on debt not to exceed 12 per cent. per annum, and a limit of time to be set, beyond which no debt could be recovered."

I felt this was real progress, making the English court of justice not only attainable but attractive; no longer to be regarded by the hill people as a great engine of oppression, but rather as a shield and bulwark between them and injustice or extortion.

The dwellers in the Hill Tracts of Chittagong might roughly be classed under two headings: the Khyoung-tha, or children of the river; and the Toung-tha, or children of the hill.

The former, as their name signifies, lived near the river, and were experts in water-craft. They were for the most part of Arracanese descent and spoke that language, of which Burmese is a modern offshoot. They followed the Buddhist religion and customs.

The Toung-tha shunned and feared the river, and, like the Shendús, could not sail a boat. I consider them to be autochthonous tribes, springing originally from the great Singpho horde, and speaking cognate dialects of the same speech. They were less numerous than the Khyoung-tha, and numbered about 13,000 souls, of whom 5,000 were Bunjogis, Pankhos and Mros, under the Bohmong's protection, and 4,000 Tipras under the Mong Raja. The Khyoung-tha comprised about 36,000 Mughs under the Bohmong, 28,000 Chakmas who acknowledged the Rani Kalindi as chief, and the Mong Raja's clan of perhaps 3,000 people.

The tribute or head-money paid to the chiefs was from four to eight rupees yearly for each family, according to the number of adults. Unmarried men, priests, and widows were exempt from this tax. Every adult was also liable to be called upon to work for the chief gratuitously three days in the year, and an offering of first-fruits was expected from the head of each family.

Each village had its Roaja or head-man, who was chosen, as a rule, by his fellow-villagers as their representative. This Roaja collected the poll-tax, but was himself exempt from paying it; he decided all petty disputes and cases which were not sufficiently important to be taken to the chief; and on him devolved the responsibility of carrying out all executive orders. The title "Roaja" comes from "roa," a village, and "tcha" or "ja," to eat: therefore "roa-ja" would be "the man who eats (or lives by) the village."

Although nominally Buddhists, I found that the Khyoung-tha also observed the nature-worship, which was the religion of the wilder Toung-tha—bowing and making sacrifice to the spirits of wood and stream. But in every village the Buddhist "khiong," or temple, was to be found, built of bamboo and mats in the smaller villages, and of solid planks and teak timber posts in the larger communities. Inside was an image of Gautama, made of alabaster or gilt wood, in front of which were placed the daily offerings of fruit and flowers, the worshippers removing their turbans, knocking their foreheads on the ground, and making reverential genuflections.

On the walls of the temple hung a number of small black boards, these were the tablets on which the village boys are taught to read and write, should the priest be sufficiently instructed himself to impart this knowledge.

Anyone may become a priest; but I did not find that the

profession was a popular one among these simple hill folk. Many a one shaved his head and put on the yellow robe for a time; but permanently to live on alms, to profess celibacy, and forego all merriment and secular gratification, did not suit their temperament, as the Buddhist priest takes his religion very much in earnest.

The raised platform in front of the Khiong is the general place of evening resort, whither the elders of the community repair to smoke together and chat, while on the smooth swept plot of ground below them, the boys play at their favourite game of "konyon." The konyons are large flat disc-like nuts, in colour resembling horse-chestnuts. One nut is set on edge, and to project his konyon catapult fashion with the middle finger of the left hand, and triumphantly to "nick" the adversary, causes unmixed joy to the player's heart.

Every year before the cultivating season commences, the ceremony of "shiang pruhpo" (which corresponds to our confirmation) takes place. The boys of the village on attaining the age of eight or nine years are clad in yellow garments, and, with shaven heads, sit in a circle before the priest. In front of each boy is a small oil-lamp burning, which is kept trimmed and bright by the sponsor, or nearest male relative, who attends, each on his postulant. Reverently the boys join their hands, bow their foreheads to the ground, and make the responses after the holy father, professing their faith. When the ceremony is concluded, they remain for seven days in the temple, dressing and living like priests; during this time they are supposed to be engaged in religious meditation, and indulge in no frivolous pastimes.

Marriages are contracted early, but never before the age of seventeen. The young man chooses a girl he would like to marry, and if his parents concur, an envoy is sent to the girl's family. The ambassador arrives by boat, and calls aloud saluting the inmates of the house, "Oga-tsa! A boat has come to your landing-place. May it be fastened?"

The girl's parents generally have a shrewd notion of what is coming, and if they are favourably inclined the envoy is requested to make fast his boat and enter the house. As he goes in he asks, "Are the supports of the house firm?" If the answer returned is, "The house is old; its supports are weak," he knows that there are difficulties to be overcome. The entrails of a fowl are then examined, and eggs are broken for omens. Dreams are also anxiously looked for by the female relatives of both parties, and are interpreted according to recognised formulæ. An astrologer may be called in, by whose aid the stars are consulted, and a favourable day chosen for the wedding.

Invitations are issued by sending a letter accompanied by a small gift. To send a notification of the ceremony without sending a gift would be regarded as most mean and unworthy.

When the marriage-feast is prepared, pigs and fowls are slaughtered, vegetables and rice are cooked in various ways, and bottles of fiery "arak," or rice spirit, are made ready by the dozen.

On the day appointed the bridegroom arrives at the bride's village, with a numerous following and much noise. The bride's relations bar his entrance with crossed bamboos, and over this barrier he must drink a cup of spirits and pay a forfeit before he is allowed to proceed. Should there be many relatives the way will be thus barred three or four times before he reaches the house of his betrothed.

Then the ceremony is performed. A new-spun cotton thread is wound round the man and girl. A priest mumbles some holy sentences, and, with crossed hands full of cooked rice, administers alternate mouthfuls to bridegroom and bride. In the presence of all their friends and neighbours they take each other for better or for worse, the little finger of the man's right hand being crooked with the woman's left. Then the new husband and wife bow down and make reverence before their elders, knocking their foreheads on the ground. They are then seated side by side, and the nearest relatives knot their garments together, and all present place before them goodwill offerings and presents.

Divorce is uncommon among these people; but in cases of infidelity or incompatibility of temper the chiefs have power to dissolve marriage.

I remember well the first divorce case that came under my notice. It occurred while I was on a visit to the Mong Raja, with whom and with whose family I formed ties of sincere and mutual esteem and friendship.

I was sitting with the Raja on the raised platform in front of his house, drinking tea in the cool of the evening. Suddenly our peaceful silent smoking, was disturbed by a young and very pretty girl, with flowers in her hair and silver ornaments on neck and arms, who rushed up the ladder and threw herself at the Raja's feet in a passion of tears.

After her ascended slowly, one by one, a number of villagers wrapped in their long home-spun mantles, who quietly sat down on the platform to the right and left of the chief. The Raja smoked on silently, until the woman's sobs had grown somewhat less violent, when he remarked quietly, " Weeping is good for women."

A few more puffs of fragrant tobacco, and as the sobbing still continued, he added with solemnity, " Three conditions are to be avoided. First, not to be able to weep ; second, to weep without knowing for why ; third, to weep too much."

The last condition was pronounced with impressive distinctness, and an assenting murmur went round the assembly. The girl raised her head.

" My father ! I cannot live with Tawngey. I *hate* him ! "

" What has he done ? Has he beaten you ? "

" No ; he has not beaten me. That I should not have minded. He suspects me. He watches me, and I will not endure it. I demand to be divorced. Oh, my father, be it on your head ! "

" Tawngey, come forward, thou son of foolishness ! What is this I hear ? "

Tawngey appeared, slinking shamefacedly from the depths of the crowd. First making a lowly obeisance, he sat down before the chief.

" My lord," said Tawngey, " I saw her flirting with——"

" It is false—it is false ! " vehemently cried the girl, dashing away her tears. " I went with the other girls to draw water at the stream, and Adui's sweetheart Pawthee came and began laughing, and so we splashed him with the water. Then this man " (pointing with concentrated scorn at the wretched Tawngey) " this man was spying behind a tree, and he came and dragged me by the arm and abused me before them all. I have never suffered such shame. Release me, O my father! I will not live with him."

Here she again prostrated herself at the Raja's feet. A dead silence ensued, broken only by the girl's sobs. Tawngey looked as though he wished the earth would swallow him, but he said not a word.

Suddenly the Raja spoke again and gave orders. "O you and you" (naming two or three elders among the spectators) "take away these two wicked ones, who disobey the holy law. Strip them of all their clothes, save one cloth only to the woman, and shut them up together in the great empty guest-house. In the morning I will hear them again. Enough! I have spoken."

So the young couple were hustled off, and shut up in a bare empty house, with but one garment between them. The night was very cold, and as I pulled my thick wadded quilt over my shoulders before going to sleep, I admired the shrewd wisdom of the Raja.

In the morning when their clothes were handed in to them, and the door was opened to conduct them before the chief, they quietly slipped away hand in hand, and departed peaceably to their own abode.

All love stories did not end so happily as this one, unfortunately, and a case of murder that came before me disclosed a genuine tragedy.

One Bupia, a young man of the Chakma tribe, loved a girl of his own village whose name was Shoniamala. Her mother was dead, and she lived with her father and brother. This last was named Hiradhan. Bupia loved the girl; they had known each other from childhood, and he followed her everywhere, feeling happiness only in her society, and rendering her the hundred little services which a lover might do—filling her water-bamboos at the stream, helping her at "juming" time, and when she went to gather fire-wood. But he was poor, and could not give the forty rupees which Shoniamala's father demanded for his daughter's hand.

For two years Bupia tried vainly to get together this money; but ill-luck attended his efforts, and at last he asked the girl to elope with him. Poor young things! I will give the deposition made to me by the brother Hiradhan, to show the result of their rashness.

"Last Friday, when I came home from work, my father asked me, saying, 'Where is your sister? She went forth to fetch water from the stream, but has not yet returned, although the time is long since. See also where is that fellow Bupia, who always follows her about. He may know where she is. Or if he is also gone, then he has taken her away.'

"So I went and sought for her by the stream, but she was not there; and I sought for Bupia, but he was not to be found. So I was full of anger, and called together some young men, my friends, and together we went off in search of my sister.

"We went fast but silently through the forest, and in the valley below we saw them. Bupia went first, and my sister followed holding his hand, and they were laughing together and did not hear us. Then I became enraged, and ran at Bupia and cut at him with my 'dao.' He leaped swiftly aside, and the blow fell on my sister, and the blow cut her through the side. She said only, 'Oh brother!' and then fell dead. Then I was frightened and ran away."

It is customary in elopements for the young men of the village to go in pursuit of runaway couples. If they are caught, the girl is asked if she leaves her home voluntarily, and if so, the matter is settled by surety being taken for the payment of the money asked by the father, or less, if it is held to be excessive, If the lover has no means, and is thought to have behaved in an underhand and dishonourable manner, he is sometimes beaten; but the murder committed by Hiradhan was quite beyond custom, and because he was seized by an ungovernable fit of rage. He was hanged for the crime.

Under the new rules the people began to have much more frequent recourse to my court, and all manner of cases came up for decision. In questions of social matters, such as divorce or infringement of local customs, I always referred the cases to a village jury; but when they came under the penal code I had to decide myself.

"Juming" disputes often arose, one village against another, both desiring to "jum" the same tract of jungle, and these cases were very troublesome to deal with. The "juming" season commences about the middle of May, and the air is then darkened by the smoke from the numerous clearings.

This appellation of "juming" is given to the system of cultivation which is universally followed by all hill tribes in India from the Himalayas to the furthest point of Siam. A suitable spot is selected, by choice on the breezy shoulder of some hill; the undergrowth is cut and the smaller trees felled, the large forest trees being left standing, on account of the labour required to cut them down. A spot covered with a growth of bamboo is considered the best, as the bamboo ash is a good fertiliser, and the ground is easily cleared.

When all is cut, the mass is left to dry in the sun, and then heaped up and fired. The villagers stand round the clearing with long bamboo sticks to beat the flames and prevent them spreading to the forest. But if a high wind comes, their efforts are occasionally vain, and then is to be seen that grandest and most awful of all spectacles—a forest fire.

When the firing of the *débris* is successfully accomplished, the larger logs and pieces of wood are dragged to the side to make a fence against the raids of wild animals. Nothing more is done till the rains set in, when cultivation proper begins. As soon as the sky is seen to grow black with clouds, every village is left empty, and young and old, men, women, and children, may be seen climbing up-hill to the jums. Each one carries a dao and a small bamboo basket slung at the hip, which contains a mixture of the seeds of rice, cotton, maize, and cucumber.

Before long comes the muttering of the thunder and the welcome patter of the first drops of rain. A moist coolness strikes upon the skin, and with a sudden swoop the rushing rain-wind flutters leaves and garments, whilst from every lusty throat rings out, clear and light, again and again, the gay "Hoia!" or hill-call.

To work, to work! Welcome is the wetting. It is esteemed a bad omen not to be thoroughly soaked on the day of sowing the seed. This sowing is a simple process. First a hasty dig with the square end of the dao, then a handful of mixed seed is placed in the hole, and the earth thrown over.

When the sowing is completed, house or rather hut-building is the next care. The materials have previously been collected and laid ready, and until the harvest has been garnered each family will live on its jum, weeding the young crops by day, and defending them by night from the beasts that would fain come to feed on the fresh-springing green tops.

The dao is the national weapon, and serves all purposes, both in-doors and out, from peeling fruit and vegetables to building a house or digging a field, with equal ease. It is simply a broad pointless knife, about eighteen inches long, square and flat at the end and narrow at the haft: it has a wooden handle six inches in length, and is worn without a scabbard. The fighting dao is similar in shape, but longer, and usually worn with a sheath. Like the agricultural weapon, it follows a strange obtuse curve, which gives it a somewhat hump-backed appearance. In both the blade is sharpened on one side only, so that two cuts only can be given—one from the right shoulder down to the left foot, the other from the left foot to the right shoulder. In the unskilled hands of a European the weapon is apt to turn round, often inflicting serious wounds on the striker; but used by a hill man, it deals a stroke of wonderful power.

The jum-house is built entirely of bamboo, the hearth being ingeniously and simply formed by binding together four rough logs in a hollow square, which is filled up with earth well beaten down, and smoothed over with clay. On this a fire is at once kindled, and an offering made to the spirit of the place, whose favour and protection are sought for the coming harvest-time, and for the well-being of the cultivators.

The fire is kindled by means of a fire-stick, or piece of bamboo a foot long split in halves. A nick of one-eighth of an inch is cut in the silicious outer cuticle of the bamboo. This cut is deepest in the centre, just piercing through to the inner part of the wood. A slip of the flexible outer covering about two feet long, is fitted to the exact size of the nick, and drawn backwards and forwards rapidly in the groove by the operator with ever-increasing velocity, until smoke shows itself, and a sort of incandescent dust collects inside the fire-stick. This dust is carefully placed among chips and dry moss, and blown upon until it is nursed gently into a flame.

This somewhat tedious method of fire-kindling was nearly discarded before I left the Hills in favour of Swedish matches, and doubtless will soon be a custom of the past.

The seeds in the jum rapidly put forth their fruit and ripen for harvest. First the maize comes to maturity in July; then melons and cucumbers ripen, and finally, in September, rice and cotten are harvested. The rice is at once beaten from the ear on a threshing-floor in the jum, and is then packed in straw, and carried down to be stored in the village granary.

The crop is usually good, but the method is a very wasteful one. Putting aside the loss of trees, which is great, the land once jumed must lie fallow for eight years, in order that the undergrowth may yield the necessary amount of ashes for fertilising. Thus it happens that, when all the land in the vicinity of a village has been exhausted by juming, the whole community has to migrate to a fresh place; and to this necessity may be traceable the impermanence of all hill-dwellings and the restless nature of the people.

Houses on the hills are invariably constructed of bamboo, with centre-posts of unhewn timber. The walls and floors are of bamboo matting; the roof and framework of bamboo stems, and the thatch itself is often composed of bamboo leaves and twigs, although for this purpose the broad leaf of the "krúk patur," a species of dwarf palm, is deemed preferable. The whole structure is tied together by cordage of split cane, not a nail or piece of metal being employed.

It is difficult to over-estimate the importance of the bamboo in the domestic economy of the hills. It is used for pipe-bowls, for fish-traps, for torches, for baskets, for drinking-cups, platters, and pillows, for ladders, for looms, for umbrellas, for a hundred purposes, mats to sit and sleep on, and sticks wherewith to cudgel an adversary. It is the veritable staff of life to the hill man; and one tribe, the Riang Tipras, have gone further still, for "thereof he maketh him a god, and falleth down and worshippeth it."

CHAPTER XI

THE HILL TRACTS OF CHITTAGONG (*continued*)
1867–68

"WHY do the Khyoung-tha wear their hair like women," I asked, "in a coil at the nape of the neck?"

I was on a visit to the new Bohmong, Momphru, who reigned peaceably in his brother's stead at Bundrabun, and was my most devoted friend.

"My tribe is from Arracan," he replied. "Long ago, before the time of the English Sahibs, when the Moghuls ruled in Chittagong, my ancestors lived on the Koladan river, and owed allegiance to the King of Arracan. Now, the King of Burmah had a quarrel with the King of Arracan, and called together all the wise men to consult them how he best might subdue his enemy. Then one skilled in magic art rose up and said, 'I alone will go to the King of Arracan and will subdue him, if so it be ordered.' And the King of Burmah made answer, 'It is ordered.' So the wise man went alone to Arracan, and gave out that he was a fugitive before the face of the King of Burmah, because that cruel monarch had ordered him to turn all the houses of Burmah into gold and he had refused to do so. 'I could have done it easily,' he added, 'but the King was greedy and cruel, and I would not do it for his order.' When the King of Arracan heard this, he made much of the wise man, and assigned to him a house and slaves, and gave him an allowance for his daily subsistance and greatly favoured him. Now the wise man gained great influence over the King of Arracan, by flattering him and promising to make him invincible in war, both him and also his people.

"'Let us begin with the city,' said the King. 'First make my royal dwelling-place invulnerable.'

"'That is most just,' replied the wise man; 'for how should you go forth to conquer, or make great adventures, save from a prosperous and secure city. But your walls, O King, have been constructed without reference to the laws of magic art. They must be levelled and then rebuilt, when I will deposit a powerful charm at each of the four corners.'

"So the King ordered that it should be done even as the wise man said. So the strong walls were demolished, and he performed incantations at the four cardinal points, and the charm was so strong that the hearts of the people turned to water and cowardice prevailed. Then he filed the King's teeth, and changed the shape of the people's spoons, and ordered every man to wear his hair knotted in the nape of the neck; there was no end to the malicious things which he did.

"At last he proclaimed that he was going to perform a solemn incantation, so that the walls should be rebuilt by magic. And for this purpose he must shut himself up in his house, and none must disturb his meditations until he should give them leave. Then he went into his house, and put rice in a pot and sprinkled it with water until it sprouted, and in the night time he fled away to his master the King of Burmah.

"Day by day the King of Arracan sent to inquire for his friend the wise man, on whose advice he had come to lean in all things, and day by day grew more disquieted when the answer came back, 'The doors are shut.' At last, he called his guards, and they broke open the door and came and told the King, 'Lo! my lord, we found no one, and the wise man must have been personated by an evil spirit, for the rice was sprouting in the pot; and no man hath eaten thereof for many days.'

"And even while the King stood astonished, wondering at these things, there came a shout in his ears, for the King of Burmah had arrived; and he slew the King of Arracan, destroying his city, and carrying his family away into captivity. And the men of his tribe, who were my forefathers, fled away into these hills; and it is owing to that magician's wicked incantations that our young men are not so brave as others are, and we must still wear our hair knotted, like women, in the nape of the neck."

My visit to the Bohmong at Bundrabun having ended satisfactorily, I bethought myself of a visit of thanks which I owed to the Mong Raja, who had given me the guardian image of my bed-chamber, and who wished to entrust to me the care and education of his son. I went the whole way, some thirty-five miles, walking barefoot, and wearing the dress of the hill folk.

On reaching Maniksari, the chief's village, I was lodged in a large room in the Raja's own house, which was ordinarily used by him as a place of assembly or to transact business in. This was a mark of great and special favour, as no Englishman had hitherto been thus admitted into family intimacy, and on my previous visit I had lived in a small tent.

As far as possible I adopted the dress and customs of the country on this and similar occasions, with a ceremonial garb for the assemblies and evening gatherings, consisting of a rich crimson silk waist cloth, snowy white cambricover-shirt, and a turban of white silk with a flower stuck in it, sitting on a mat bare-foot and cross-legged.

Some of the customs were not altogether delightful, and my resolution to conform was sometimes sorely tried. On the present occasion, being an honoured guest, my dinner was prepared under the Rani's own supervision, and when it was served she herself pressed me to eat, and even selected and offered me with her own slender fingers certain specially choice and delicate morsels.

I had courageously consumed cane tops, bamboo shoots, with divers unknown comestibles, when my hostess appeared, smiling with hospitable intent, and bearing in her hand a small brass cup, which she placed before me. It contained four large white grubs, delicately fried in oil, and one of these she kindly took between finger and thumb and offered to my shuddering lips. I forced a somewhat ghastly smile of thanks, and bolted the creature; but while endeavouring to assure her of my appreciation, outraged humanity rebelled, and I retired hastily, to save my reputation for good manners. These large grubs, or maggots, are found under the bark of decaying trees, and are esteemed a great delicacy.

At the Raja's request I had agreed that his young son, Narabadi, should come and live with me, and that I would superintend his education, and treat him as my own son. I left Maniksari, taking the boy with me, and marched to the river

Huldah, a tribu ary of the Karna-phuli. Here my boat was waiting for me, and embarking, we rowed slowly down to the greater river.

The evening was lovely, and I lay on a mat on the roof of the boat, smoking and talking to Narabadi, and enjoying the coolness and beauty of the scene around us. My bearer Sonarutton brought me a piece of live charcoal for my pipe, and in doing so looked up at the sky with an exclamation; and then, removing his turban, he made a lowly salutation.

"What is it?" I asked.

"It is the new moon, Sahib. One must always salute the new moon if one wishes for good luck."

It was curious to find here also this old superstition among such primitive people. I looked up and saw the faint silver crescent outlined against the turquoise-blue of the evening sky, and wondered what I should wish for. I had power, position, money enough for my needs, and influence sufficient to carry out the work to which I had set hand and heart. But health—ah, there was the rub! So I saluted my lady moon, and wished most earnestly that I might have health and strength for the task I had before me.

I had to go down the river to Akyab to see after clerks for my office. The Bengali baboos having all resigned when they found the petitions and complaints against me had failed in their ends, I had obtained permission to go to Akyab in search of good Burmese clerks, as, thanks to the English educational system, many were to be found there. I also intended to visit and consult with my *confrère*, the Superintendent of the Arracan Hill Tribes, and to arrange if possible to unite our chain of frontier posts, and so get an effective police patrol without break along the entire frontier.

I went by the coasting steamer from Chittagong, and paid a most pleasant and successful visit to Akyab, meeting many old acquaintances, and among them my comrade Major M——, and his little dog, which we were so near eating in the Shendú country. Having satisfactorily arranged business matters and engaged my clerks, I determined to walk back to Chittagong along the coast.

The rains were at their height, and as there were rivers and swamps on the way, I determined to do the journey native fashion, barefoot. I was quite inured to this, the perfection of progress in a wild country without roads, and the freedom and surefootedness I had acquired by the absence of heavy English boots amply repaid me for the pain I had at first endured before my feet got hardened.

I was accompanied by Narabadi, the Mong Raja's son, and my boy Sonarutton, with one other servant. Our road lay chiefly by the sea-coast, along the white sands, which were fringed for miles by one grand continuous line or border of lofty casuarina trees.

At night we found lodging in native huts; but the daily march was arduous in the extreme, the monotonous flat smoothness of the sands stretching for miles and miles without any break, after the pleasing undulating variety of our hill travelling, made the feet ache terribly. By the time I reached Cox's Bazaar, after a three days' march of over forty miles, my feet were so swollen, and my skin where it had been exposed was so burnt and blistered by the heat of the sun, that I was heartily glad to hire a native boat and make the rest of my way to Chittagong by water.

On returning to Chandraguna, I was pleasantly surprised to find two large boxes with presents and supplies from England. Great was the excitement among my hill friends, and quite a crowd assembled at my house to see the opening of these mysterious cases, each article as it was extracted eliciting rounds of applause and exclamations of wonderment. I promptly opened two or three bottles of milk-punch, and we all drank the health of my mother who had sent out these good things.

The Chakma Dewan, Ishan Chunder, who was present, carried off triumphantly a tin of bacon and a pot of jam which I presented to him; the head officer of my police (a Portuguese gentleman named De Rosario) was made happy with a tin of haddocks; while Narabadi rejoiced greatly over some barley-sugar and a deer's-foot cheroot-holder. He desired me to convey to my mother his respectful thanks in the following terms:

"Atsak hrey-ji, phie khang-ji; atsak ta khoung hrey-li-ji de lak ma ka," &c., which, being interpreted, meant, "May your years be extended and no misfortune befall you; may your prosperity increase, and may each grain of your sowing bring forth a hundredfold."

In Bengal the sensation most keenly felt by an Englishman is that he is an alien in a foreign land; but among the hill folk one is among fellow-creatures. Wherever I went among the people, I was hospitably entertained, fed, and fêted; in return I kept open house for all who came to see me.

I devoted all my spare time to acquiring the different languages and dialects spoken in my district, being strongly impressed with the idea that no true justice can be done through an interpreter, and that the only key to the thoughts and customs of the people lies through their language.

In the Chittagong Hill Tracts there were spoken no fewer than four distinct languages. With the first of these, Burmese, I was now fairly acquainted; Bengali I knew before coming to the Hills, and so mastered the Chakma tongue, which is practically the same with the introduction of local words. The Tipra and Lushai languages were quite distinct, and difficult to acquire.

I had parted with all my Bengali "baboos" save one, and the people could now understand the working of justice in the court-house, or kutcherry, my Burmese clerks being in sympathy with them and understanding their customs.

Towards the end of the year 1867 the frontier became much disturbed, and I moved up, with all available fighting men at my disposal, to our most advanced frontier stockade at Kassalong. I felt more and more convinced that the chronic state of irritation which existed among the border tribes could not, without danger, be allowed to continue, and that, sooner or later, the Government must be driven to offensive as well as defensive measures.

The violent and cruel Lushais saw in a pacific policy only fear or cowardice, and would only be convinced of our power by stringent reprisals. Rutton Poia's tribe alone stood staunchly by their alliance with me, and gave me frequently private information which enabled me to frustrate intended or attempted raids on our territory.

During my stay at Kassalong I embraced every opportunity

of becoming better acquainted with the Lushais, who freely resorted to our market, and learnt all I could concerning their language and customs. They have a curious tradition concerning their genesis, which I heard from one of the principal karbaris of the Sylu tribe.

"Our ancestors," said he, "came originally out of a cave in the hills. This cavern may be seen at the present day near Van Huilen's village among the Burdaia clan. Strange noises are heard to issue therefrom, and no one willingly approaches the spot.

"At the first we had a great chief whose name was Tlandrokpa. He married God's daughter and was a very powerful chief. To prepare for the marriage all the animals were summoned to clear a road through the jungle by which to bring the bride home.

"At that time, which was longer than long ago, all living things spoke with one language, and all the animals obeyed the call except the sloth, his cousin the huluq monkey, and the earth-worm; therefore it is that to this day these animals are ashamed and hide themselves, not loving the sunlight.

"Then there were great festivities. Tlandrokpa gave Patien (God) his great gun; one can hear the sound of it often when it thunders, that is when Patien goes out hunting up there.

"Some time after the wedding Tlandrokpa quarrelled with Patien, and was conquered by means of the great gun and its fire. And the earth took fire and burnt with a great heat, and the whole race of men would have been consumed; but Patien's daughter counselled us, and we came towards the sea, where there was much water, and so our ancestors saved their lives.

"Here in the new country, there was great scarcity of food, for at that time men did not eat flesh; but at last, by reason of great hunger, they began to kill and eat the animals. Then the creatures spoke and begged for mercy in such pitiful words that it was hard to slay them, until at last Patien's daughter besought her father, and he took from the animals their power of speech. Since then food has been plentiful among us. This we have heard from our ancestors."

The Lushais resemble in many points our own Highlanders. Their chiefs wear mantles woven of a red and blue tartan;

their music resembles that of the bagpipes, with a gourd reservoir instead of the skin bag; they are split up into clans, which are often at feud one with another, and they cement friendship and foment strife by free indulgence in an ardent spirit closely resembling Highland whiskey.

Their chiefs are chosen from one ancient strain of royal blood; but it does not therefore follow that every chief's son shall succeed his father. He must first show himself worthy to be a leader before men will follow him. Although his rule may be set aside, the scion of a chief's house (or "Lal," as he is called) is held sacred as being of semi-divine origin, and must not be ill-treated or killed. The chief directs in war, and must be the first to attack and the last to retreat.

Once, in Rutton Poia's village, I noticed a drunken Lushai rudely push the chief out of his way. Rutton Poia said nothing, but gathered his mantle closer around him and continued his conversation with me.

"What is this?" I asked; "do you not punish disrespect in your followers?"

"Disrespect!" he exclaimed, "why the man is drunk and incapable of disrespect! But putting his condition aside, here all are equal. On the warpath, or in the chase, if he did not obey me he would die; but here he is as in his own house."

If any man is in want, he walks into the chief's house and takes what he needs. "He is a chief," they say, "and will receive plenty more gifts. All we have is his; so also his goods are ours. Who should give to us if our chief does not?"

For public purposes, such as feast days, receptions, the entertaining of guests, &c., the chief sends for anything that may be required to whoever has it. His house is built for him and his land cultivated by the unpaid labour of his followers.

The chief's house is a sanctuary, where all criminals may take refuge. Even the avengers of blood, pursuing a murderer red-handed, may not pass beyond the threshold with arms in their hands. But by thus seeking refuge under the chief's roof-tree the fugitive becomes *ipso facto* the chief's slave. He has other slaves also of those taken in war; by them he sends orders and messages, their authorization being the chief's own spear, which represents his sign manual. A piece of red cloth attached to the spear means "blood," a small piece of cane attached means "beating," and if to the same is added a piece of capsicum, then an offender knows that his punishment will be hot and pungent. Two pieces of bamboo tied crosswise accompanying the spear is a demand for black mail, the number of head of cattle required being indicated by bends in the bamboo; if the cross-piece be burned or charred with fire at one end, great danger and urgency are denoted. This last token is like the old token of the fiery cross on the Scottish border; it admits of no delay, and must be responded to by men fully armed, even if they have to go through the forest by torchlight.

In the house of a chief there is always drinking going on. The "seepah" or "khoung" (both names being given to the hill beer made from millet-seed) is either sucked up through reeds direct from the great earthen jars, or drawn off into mighty horns or great brazen bowls, by means of a syphon formed of two reeds jointed with lac and resin, and thence ladled out to the drinkers by a gourd spoon. Should there be an extraordinary gathering of guests, auxiliary cups are quickly manufactured from the joints of a bamboo.

My interpreter, Ramoni, who had formerly been a slave in Rutton Poia's house, and whose freedom was granted at my request, gave me a very graphic account of an expedition he had made with the chief into British territory. The raid was directed on the Bengali villagers of Cachar.

"The Bengali men," said Ramoni, "all ran away, except those whom we were able to spear. The young women and children also tried to escape, but we caught most of them. We killed all the men we met with, except healthy young lads of fifteen and under; these, with women of not more than thirty or thirty-five years, were tied by the thumbs, their arms being bound behind them. The women were kept together by a cord passed through the lobe of their ears; if the hole in the lobe were not large enough, it had to be widened by a knife or skewer.

"On the return journey one of the women sank down from exhaustion and could go no farther, her feet and ankles being much swollen. The chief halted, and after a short consultation, he said to me, 'Go, Ramoni, and spear her. I will stand by and see that you do it properly.' I felt much afraid, for I had never killed a human creature, and I was only seventeen years old.

"When the girl saw me approaching her with the spear in my hand she fell a-weeping and caught at my feet and my garments, entreating me. Then my heart beat and my head became giddy, so that I said to the chief, 'I cannot do it.'

"'Dog, and son of a slave!' replied he; 'never again call me by the name of father!' And all the young men of the war party laughed and jeered at me, saying they would tell the maidens in our village how brave I was, and would ask them to make a petticoat for me.

"Then I shut my eyes and rushed at her with my spear, but the blow was ill-directed; and Rutton Poia snatched the weapon from my hands and killed the girl with one blow. 'Here,' said he, giving me back my spear with the blood on it, 'lick this to strengthen your heart.'

"The blood of Bengalis is very salt," added Ramoni; "but since then I have not been afraid to spear anyone."

When going out on a foray the Lushais take with them as food, yam and rice pounded together, and rammed down into tubes of bamboo. On this meagre sustenance they can march enormous distances. They are very cunning in their strategy, sending out spies, and keeping their main body in ambush. On the only occasion when they surprised and destroyed one of my outposts they did so by means of a decoy. Late at night a loud knocking was heard at the gate of the stockade, and voices called out that a village of the Khyoung-tha, distant some four miles, had been attacked by a party of Lushais, and prayed for assistance. The guard promptly got under arms, and headed by the Jemadar, went off in the darkness to succour the distressed village, leaving only a few men to guard the stockade.

As soon as the main body of the defenders were at a safe distance the Lushais came out of their hiding place and escaladed the stockade, killing my men, carrying off the women and children into captivity, and taking the heads of the slain with them as trophies. It is to this latter practice that the Lushais owe their name, "Lu" meaning head, and "sha," to cut; so that "Lushai" would signify a "decapitator." The generic name of the whole nation is "Dzo."

It is customary for young men on their first expedition to eat a piece of the heart or liver of a slain enemy in order to confirm their courage. When successful in a foray, they are careful not to wash the blood-stains from their hands until they return home. On nearing their own village, they are met by the women and old men, who escort them to their houses with triumphant songs, beating of gongs, and blowing of reed pipes. A guyal, or two or three pigs will be slaughtered, jars of beer broached, and for two or three days the whole village is given up to rejoicing and feasting.

They are, however, on the whole, a grave and silent people, doubtless heedful of the old proverb, "My son, if you be wise, open first your eyes, then your ears, and last of all your mouth; for the Lushai sleeps, hunts, and smiles with his mouth closed. This habit undoubtedly prevents the admission of cold air and consequent tooth-ache and early loss of teeth. Also there is among them no croup, no teething disorders, nor lung diseases.

From early childhood they are taught to close the jaws and cover the head and face with their mantle while sleeping, in order to avoid the damp air and malaria of night. The Lushais, like most hill-dwellers, are a hardy and healthy race, and suffer mainly from disorders brought on by hard drinking. Cholera (which they call "the foreign sickness") and small-pox were unknown among them until the year 1861, when the former was introduced among them by some Bengali captives taken in a raid.

The contagion spread rapidly, infecting village after village and causing dire consternation. Men attacked with the terrible malady, in many instances, blew out their brains rather than endure the pain of the disease and their inevitable desertion by all their relatives. Thanks, however, to this inhuman practice of deserting the sick and dying, the disease died out after slaying its thousands, and has not since reappeared.

In ordinary cases of death, all the relatives of the dead man are called together, and a big feast is held. The corpse is attired in a fine mantle, and placed in a sitting posture, with his weapons near him, and is thus addressed by the eldest male relative: "Brother! you have a long journey before you; eat." Then he places food before the body, and the dead man's pipe is filled and placed in his hand, while all present bid him farewell.

On the second day, when all the guests have well drunken, the corpse is placed in a hollow tree by way of coffin and buried in the jungle. Among some of the tribes the curious custom prevails of drying the bodies of their chiefs or great men, over a slow fire, first sheathing them in pith, and then hanging them up on a tree.

In the Howlong clan, the body thus dried is hung from the rafters of the house for seven days, and during this period the widow must sit underneath the corpse spinning. On no account must she quit the spot, not even to take food, being dependent for her nourishment during this period of mourning on the kind offices of her relatives.

I found the idea of my position as a Government official conveyed but a vague impression to the minds of these uncivilized people; so I took my standing among them as a chief, paramount in the district, but subject to a yet greater white chief in Calcutta. I had obtained permission from Government to move my head-quarters from Chandraguna to Rangamati, a more central spot, a day's journey nearer the frontier, and I determined to test my position as chief, in the local fashion, by calling on all the Toung-tha in the vicinity to build me a house.

Accordingly I sent messages to all the Pankhos, Mros, and Bunjogi villages for twenty miles round, saying that I was moving from Chandraguna to Rangamati, and desired a house to live in there. I further informed them that numerous jars of beer and three pigs were waiting the consumption of those who laboured.

Within a week some three hundred men had set to work with a will, and built me a large house, Lushai fashion, on the spot I had selected. It was built entirely of bamboo, except the posts, which were huge logs of unhewn timber, and the floor, which was constructed of small saplings about two inches in diameter laid lengthwise.

The position of my new head-quarters was quite central. It was situated on a bend of the river Karna-phuli, which at this place makes a sort of loop. I had the land thus enclosed cleared from jungle. At the narrow part of the bend I placed the police barracks, thus defending the small peninsula from land attack, while the river, which was here very deep, protected the other three sides of the new settlement. My own house was placed on a lofty cliff overhanging the river, and commanding a beautiful and extended view on all sides. I named my new abode "Barn House," but had hardly settled myself comfortably in it when I had to start off again in hot haste for the jungles.

My new frontier police patrols had kept the district free from raids for many months; but I now got tidings from Rutton Poia that a party of the Howlong clan had started on the war-path, and might be expected to raid in the Southern Hill Tracts.

This timely information enabled me, by a rapid jungle march, to cut in between the marauders and the Bohmong's villages which were threatened, and, finding their plans discovered, they retreated without doing any harm. I followed their trail with my police for two days, but was unable to catch any of the party.

During this expedition I camped out with my party, sleeping under the trees at night; and I was struck by a peculiar custom of the hill men who accompanied us as coolies. They carefully notched the tree under which they intended to sleep, in upward nicks with their daos. I thought they were doing this in idleness at first, but at dawn I observed them reversing the process and notching the tree downwards, and inquired the meaning. They explained to me that by notching the tree upwards, the dew which falls during the night is absorbed by the leaves, and consequently does not drip on those who lie beneath; and that it was necessary to reverse the nicks in the morning in order to appease the wood spirits and avert misfortune.

Another interesting and useful piece of woodcraft I also learnt on this journey. Our road lay due south along a lofty hill range, and our camping-ground at night being far from any stream, we could find no water. On this one of my hill men took his dao, and with two sharp cuts severed a piece, about two yards long, of one of the many creeping plants which swing from branch to branch and from tree to tree in wild luxuriance all through these forests, and holding this up perpendicularly, about half a pint of clear water trickled out. The water did not come unless a piece of the creeper were cut right out, the air seeming to stop the flow if the plant were simply cut through.

Our only captive this time was a huluq monkey, a shy little beast, very rarely seen or caught. They have black fur with white breasts, and go about usually in pairs swinging from branch to branch with incredible agility, and making the forest resound with their strange cachinnatory cry. They walk erect on the ground, generally holding one long arm in the air, ready to grasp a bough if they are disturbed. They are wild creatures, and cannot be domesticated unless taken as sucklings, as they *pine and die in captivity.*

I grew quite attached to the one we now caught. It was curiously human in appearance, the hands and nails specially so. He slept at night lying at full length with one arm under his head as a pillow. He grew very tame, feeding on fruit and grain from my hand, and croodling in a most sympathetic manner if I pretended to be in trouble. His great delight was to accompany me in my walks, going upright and hand in hand with me in friendly fashion. I missed him much when he died of lung disease about six months later.

The Rani Kalindi remained as irreconcilable as ever, and when a new Commissioner was appointed at Chittagong, in place of my good friend Y——, she took advantage of the occasion to send her grandson and heir on a special mission to Calcutta, renewing all her old complaints, and again seeking my dismissal. She feared my increasing influence would diminish her power, and spent a considerable sum in providing her grandson with a suitable retinue and hiring advocates, accompanied by whom he presented himself before the Lieutenant-Governor of Bengal.

The ground now taken was that the late Commissioner had been my friend and partisan, and that no one had ventured to complain to him; but that if an impartial inquiry were held crowds of the unfortunate and oppressed hill men would come and bring forward their complaints.

A fresh inquiry was accordingly held at Chittagong by the new Commissioner, who carefully sifted the evidence, and ended by requesting me to return to my district, as he could discover nothing prejudicial to me except, perhaps, that "the Regulations" were not sufficiently observed. The sacred Regulations! How was it possible to fit them on such very irregular subjects as I had to deal with?

On my return to Rangamati I found messengers were awaiting me at Kassalong, from Savunga, the head chief of the great Sylu clan of the Lushais, who wished to meet and confer with me. I was greatly rejoiced, as, if I could only gain a hold on this clan, I might hope for peace, both on the northern frontier of my district and also in Cachar.

I therefore received the messengers graciously, and tried to arrange an interview with their chief. There were difficulties to contend with, as small-pox had broken out in the Hill Tracts, and the Lushais have such a terror of this disease that there was no chance of the chief venturing on British territory while the epidemic lasted; and at length I settled to go out a two days' journey into the forest beyond the frontier, and meet him on neutral ground.

The Sylu messengers told me that, three years before, my predecessor had been visited by some messengers from Savunga's village, and he, being desirous of cultivating friendly relations with the chief, had sent by the hands of the messengers a bank note, which was worth many rupees. Desirous of testing its value, the men showed it to a Bengali shopkeeper in the bazaar, who speedily offered them salt, beads, and salt fish to about a quarter of its value, which they accordingly accepted in its place and carried to Savunga. On reaching the chief's village, the messengers reported what they had done. "How?" said Savunga. "The Sahib gave you a magic piece of paper, and you have sold it? Cut them down!" So the luckless ones were slain.

The karbaris asked me to give them a magic letter that could be turned into money, such as had been given before, and I promised I would give it to the chief himself when we met. So I provided myself with a bank note, and, taking with me thirty of my best men, in case of treachery, I set off to meet the chiefs.

After camping in the evening, I took a quiet stroll with only a small walking-stick in my hand, when, without any sound of warning, a magnificent tiger slowly and majestically passed across the small stream up which I was proceeding. He did not appear to see me, and feeling much relieved as he passed out of sight, I thought it wiser to return to camp.

Savunga himself failed to appear at the rendezvous; but he sent some minor chiefs as his representatives, and with them I went through the usual formula of oath swearing, making them presents of cloth, beads, &c. They wanted gunpowder and bank notes, but these I refused, as Savunga had not come personally. I mistrusted them indeed, altogether, and put no faith in their oaths and protestations. They seemed to me simply to have come seeking for presents, not in any good faith.

To carry out my character of a hill chief, I determined this year to cultivate my jum at Rangamati; and in May, I and my servants set to work and cleared about half an acre of land. It was no child's play, but very hard work, and my hands got terribly blistered in the operation.

With the first rain I sowed my crop of grain, cucumbers, and melons, hoping that I might enjoy the fruit of my labour. Unfortunately I forgot that every hill man lives on his jum, with wife and children, weeding the young crop, whereas I had not only neither helpmate nor olive-branches, but was also constantly on the move, looking after all the irons I had in the fire; in consequence the fowls of the air devoured my seed, and I had to content myself with a scanty cotton crop.

I made an effort about this time to introduce silk culture, and for this purpose obtained a stock of cocoons from Assam. Silk fabrics were much prized among the wealthier sort of people, and raw silk was imported from Calcutta and woven into very beautiful fabrics at Cox's Bazaar and its immediate vicinity. The attempt failed, however; either the worm did not thrive, or the people could not manage it properly. I was more successful in the introduction of improved varieties of grain and cotton seed, the latter in particular being eagerly taken by the people.

I was now on good and cordial terms with all the chiefs of my district, excepting always the ever-truculent and irreconcilable Rani and her Bengali advisers. She, however, was silenced, at any rate for the time, as her last costly petition had again resulted only in strengthening my hands and bringing me the sunshine of official praise, both from my immediate superior, the Commissioner of Chittagong, and also from the Lieutenant-Governor of Bengal. I had worked hard, and the praise and sympathy accorded gave me fresh courage for my somewhat arduous undertakings.

I had on hand a comprehensive scheme for the re-settlement of the revenue system, which required very tender handling, touching as it did the influence and income of the leading men in the Hills. This I felt bound to see through personally, if possible, as I feared a stranger to my hill friends might involuntarily do them injustice.

Next I had to complete the establishment of the new head-quarters at Rangamati, removing the police barracks, the courts, the treasury, and the bazaar, forty miles further up the river from Chandraguna; and although my own house was built for me voluntarily in recognition of chiefship, the building of the further state accommodation was no small undertaking.

I had also set on foot primary schools at different central places; and no slight pressure was required to induce the people to send their children for instruction. I entered into negotiation with the Mission in Calcutta, hoping to obtain the services of a missionary, and being willing to pay half his salary myself, as I felt convinced that there was a wide field for religious effort among the simple nature-worshippers. The Buddhists I did not propose to interfere with.

My great desire was to help the people to raise themselves without introducing the evils of European civilization among them. But it was a difficult task. Living, as they did, a hazardous care-driven life; each chief set against his neighbour; each clan against the other; their arms of offence and defence alike inefficient; their ambition but shortsighted self-interest; their habits of life little removed from the wild creatures in the woods surrounding their villages: how long would it take to bring them to a knowledge of better things? However, the future can never be inquired into, and I could only act for the best in the space of time I was with and among them.

A party of Toung-tha visited me in September, bringing their offering of first-fruits—rice, melons, and cucumbers, with some bottles of arrack. I regaled them to their satisfaction with "Turkish delight" and English rum, and by special request exhibited my small galvanic battery. This little instrument was regarded as the highest manifestation of magic art and added greatly to my reputation.

One of my visitors with much misgiving, but more curiosity laid hold of the handles, while I worked the wheel. And then what moaning and contortions ensued, followed by much rubbing of hands and elbows, while those who had not tried the experiment were convulsed with laughter at their comrade's discomfiture, until their own turn came for groaning.

The climax of astonishment was reached when I placed a rupee in a brass bowl of water, and announced that whoever could hold the handle of the machine in one hand and take the rupee out of the water with the other should have it for his own. The other handle of the machine I placed in the bowl, and, of course, as soon as a hand touched the water the fingers doubled up and failed to grasp the coveted rupee. The discomfiture and surprise of even the most resolute among them was comical in the extreme, and I laughed till I was tired.

"L'homme propose, mais Dieu dispose," and towards the close of the year my health failed me completely, and I was advised that I must go for a year's leave to England if I wished to do any more work.

I set my affairs in the best order I could, and on the 10th of January went up the river to Kassalong, to send friendly words of farewell to Rutton Poia, and to personally assure his karbaris that I should certainly return to the Hills after a short absence, and also to make a parting inspection of the police out-post.

I landed, and sat writing in my small mat hut inside the fort on the river's bank, when suddenly the walls and roof began to shake violently. I thought that probably an elephant had got loose, and was amusing himself by pulling down my house, so ran out hastily; but there was no elephant to be seen. I gazed about me in some bewilderment. The bank was high, and commanded a considerable stretch of forest land on the opposite side of the river; and as I looked; the solid earth moved as if a wave were sweeping along beneath its crust, while the great trees bowed down and swayed their arms wildly, as though smitten by a mighty wind. But the air was perfectly still, and I knew it was a heavy shock of earthquake. In my district all houses were built of bamboo and mat, and suffered little or no damage; but the disturbance did much mischief in other parts of Bengal.

I paid one more visit to the Mong Raja; but this was perforce a hasty one, owing to severe dysentery and repeated attacks of fever. My parting from him and his people was very affecting, the women crying, and the men touching my feet and holding my garments.

"Do not leave us," they cried. "We shall never see your face again. Why must you go?"

I was greatly concerned, for the kindly simple folk were very near my heart. I felt that my efforts for their welfare had not been in vain; and I resolved that if it pleased God to restore my health I would soon return to my work among them.

CHAPTER XII

THE LUSHAI EXPEDITION

1871–72

I WAS absent on leave for nearly two years, and on my return to Calcutta, in January, 1871, I learnt that the south-western frontier was in a very disturbed condition, and I was requested by Government to return to my post in the Hill Tracts with all possible speed. There had been two raids during my absence, both upon the territory of the Bohmong, and both committed by the Shendús; with these two exceptions, the Hill Tracts had been at rest. My friends the Lushais, however, considered that their compacts with me left them quite free to attack other *districts*; and so, *uniting their forces*, they had *committed* a series of forays of the most aggravated character in the neighbouring district of Cachar, killing several Europeans, and carrying off Mary Winchester, the little daughter of a planter, with many other British native subjects, into captivity.

Before leaving Calcutta, I had interviews with both the Governor-General (Lord Mayo) and the Lieutenant-Governor of Bengal, and learnt that a punitive expedition was to be despatched at the end of the year against the Lushais. Lord Mayo's minute upon the subject, which I afterwards saw,* very admirably condenses the situation and the causes which led up to it, as follows:—

"It is with great reluctance that I have to express the opinion that it will be necessary to send, in the ensuing cold weather, an armed force into the country of the Lushais. The cruel raids that have been made for some years past upon various parts of our territory, more especially on the tea-gardens in the Cachar district, and the very unsuccessful and inefficient means which have hitherto been taken for the protection of our frontier, together with the partial mismanagement and want of success which has attended almost everything we have done, doubtless imparted to these savages the impression that we are either unable or unwilling to take active measures and to punish the perpetrators of such

* Hunter's *Life of Lord Mayo*, vol. i. p. 230.

crimes. Having expressed this opinion, it will be necessary to consider first what the character of the expedition is to be, and, second, the mode and means by which it is to be carried out.

"I cannot think that the expedition ought to partake of the character of those which have from time to time been undertaken on the North-Western frontier for the chastisement of a particular tribe or clan. It does not appear that whole villages or tribes take part in these Lushai attacks, and it is difficult to trace particular raids to any particular tribes the Howlongs, the Sylus, or others. This state of things renders the precise object of the expedition rather difficult to define. It would be impossible to send a force into the Howlong country, for instance, with orders to burn right and left, destroy villages and root up crops, a course which might be justifiable if we were punishing an Akkazai or Waziri village. I therefore agree with the Lieutenant-Governor, and am opposed to any measure of pure retaliation; if our advance into the country is met with opposition, our opponents must, of course, be severely punished; but besides this, it will be necessary to give the expedition a definite object, and here lies the difficulty. The restoration of the captives might be one; the infliction of a fine on certain villages whose inhabitants took part in the raids would be another; the carrying off hostages as pledges of good behaviour, a third; the surrender of undoubtedly guilty parties, such as leading chiefs, and others who were known to have taken part in the raids, a fourth; the immediate destruction of any village, with the surrounding crops, which offered any resistance, a fifth; but the main object would be to endeavour to enter into relations of a permanent character with the savages; to make them promise to receive into their villages from time to time native agents of our own; to show them the advantages of trade and commerce, and to demonstrate to them effectively that they have nothing to gain and everything to lose by placing themselves in a hostile position towards us. With this view it will be necessary that the expedition should be attended as much as possible by chiefs belonging to friendly tribes, and such use must be made of their people and followers as the circumstances of the case admit. I am not disposed to hamper the present enterprise with the task of making a road, as has been proposed, from Cachar to Chittagong; the success of such an undertaking is very doubtful, and some objection has been taken as to its policy. A road of this kind must be protected, and if its construction was resented by the tribes it would be a perpetual source of anxiety and expense. On the other hand if the road can be made with the consent and by the assistance of the tribes, it would probably be easily constructed and kept open at a small cost and at little risk . . . The expedition must not be looked upon as a campaign, for no formidable resistance is anticipated; it should be looked upon more as a military occupation and visitation of as large a portion of the Lushai districts as possible for the purpose of punishing the guilty where they can be traced, but more particularly for showing these savages that there is no part of their hills to which our armed forces cannot penetrate."

I confess to having felt very glad that the Government had come to this determination, for I had eaten much dirt at the hands of the Lushais for some time past in carrying out the conciliatory and defensive policy which had been hitherto prescribed. The expedition, in my opinion, might have been avoided, had discretionary powers been granted to the district officers to follow and punish all raiders found crossing the frontier; it would have been comparatively easy to deal with our enemies thus in detail, and quite in accordance, moreover, with their own customs: but to attack them *en masse* by a military occupation of their country was a very big thing indeed, and would cost a large sum of money. However, better this enormous cudgel than the perpetual sugar-stick which my unwilling hands had previously administered; and so, having received my instructions, by the month of February I was once more back at Rangamati, with the reins in my hands as of yore.

It warmed one's heart to see again all the familiar faces. I had a grand reception, and the stream of my visitors did not cease for at least a fortnight. I built out a gallery of bamboo from the summit of the lofty cliff behind Barn House, overhanging the river, and commanding a beautiful view. Here was always a cool breeze, if such a thing were anywhere to be found, and here regularly, at a little before sundown, fine mats were spread, and with a big pillow to lean upon, I took my seat cross-legged, and prepared to smoke and chat with such of the hill people as might look in. My servants handed round cigars and a silver dish full of betel and pán to all who came, and my gallery speedily became the popular lounge, where I gained much valuable local information, and heard stories and legends by the score. At seven my servant Nurudin brought me a glass of sherry and announced dinner, which was the signal for the break up of the party.

Nurudin entered my service first in an inferior capacity at Chittagong; but when I was appointed Hill Superintendent, all my servants except the faithful Toby refused to accompany me into the wilderness, for the place and its inhabitants had a bad name with the plainsmen. Nurudin, however, at last took his courage with both hands, and, disregarding the warnings and entreaties of friends and relatives, followed my fortunes to

Chandraguna, and served me faithfully until the close of the Lushai expedition. I then, as a reward for his fidelity, obtained for him the appointment of Bazaar Jemadar on the frontier, for which, indeed, he was well fitted. I had previously avenged myself upon his family by marrying him to a hill wife, and he became quite habituated to the country, attaining a fair knowledge of the Lushai language.

Meantime, at Rangamati I had not been idle in making preparations for the expedition. I arranged for guides and interpreters, and settled what coolies should be furnished by each tribe. I also communicated darkly with Rutton Poia, and assured myself of the stability of his alliance. Having made these arrangements, I was again summoned to Calcutta by the authorities, and in the month of May attended a conference there, to settle administrative details for the coming expedition. It was arranged that two columns should enter the Lushai country, one from Cachar on the north, the other from Chittagong on the south, and, if possible, the commanding officers of the two columns were to effect a junction in the Lushai Country.

I was to act as Political Officer in subordination to the General commanding the Southern column, while the Deputy Commissioner of Cachar was to accompany the Northern column in a similar capacity. Lord Mayo was very kind to me, and, in an interview I had with him, he listened with much interest to my account of the Hills and their people; and when I took leave of him, he desired me to do my utmost to promote the ends of the expedition, promising me that in case of success he would see that my services were adequately rewarded.

My frontier police were now increased in numbers, and their arms and general equipment improved; additional European assistants were placed at my disposal;—in short, rough things began to be made smooth in the Hill Tracts.

At the close of the conference, I was directed to proceed to Sylhet, to see the Deputy Inspector-General of Police there, who was in command of a recruiting depôt for my Hill Tract Corps and the Cachar Frontier Police, and to arrange with him questions of detail in reference to their pay and equipment.

My journey thither presented no difficulties. I was given a special train from Calcutta to Kushtea on the Ganges, and a free passage in the Government steamer which plied thence to Dacca; there I struck the regular line of steamers plying to Assam, and after a monotonous voyage up the mighty Brahmaputra, I was landed at the village of Chatak, where the small stream leading to Sylhet and Cachar debouches into the main river. From Chatak I hired a boat, which conveyed me to Sylhet, and having there concluded my business with the Deputy Inspector-General, and arranged matters to our mutual satisfaction, I returned as quickly as possible to Chatak, hoping to catch a return steamer from Assam to Dacca.

I took up my temporary quarters in a small mat house with a mud floor, and having discussed a meagre repast of rice, eggs, and water, I gazed anxiously up the great river, hoping to see in the distance the black funnel of the expected steamer. To my right lay the beautiful blue ranges of the Khasia Hills, their flanks streaked here and there with white lines, where the torrents foamed down to the plains in a mad leap of four thousand feet. There was no sign of the steamer, so I took a walk about the place—the small aggregation of mud huts called Chatak.

On the outskirts of the village, close to the great river, I discovered a ruined temple, or shrine, sacred to the goddess Kali, and, looking curiously into the dark interior, was somewhat startled at seeing a ghostly figure sitting silently near the central altar. It was a "fakir," or religious mendicant, nearly naked, as far as I could distinguish in the dim light, smeared from head to foot with white ashes, while streaks of added vermilion gave the face a ghastly grotesqueness.

The following dialogue ensued between us:

"Salutation! holy one. Why are you sitting alone in the Mother's temple?"

"Sahib, I am seeking wisdom."

"What wisdom, Maharaj?" No reply.

"I do not speak lightly. I also am a seeker after knowledge; even so, although my face is white and I wear the garments of the Sahib-log. I salute always all seekers after light. What wisdom, Maharaj?"

"I am repeating 'muntras' (charms). To-night I have to wrestle with the dead. I ask you not to interrupt me."

"I will leave you; but first tell me, father, before I go, what will you do to-night?"

"When I have sufficiently strengthened my muntra, I go to the grave of a boy, and, by the force of that charm, the dead one will arise and come forth. Then shall I wrestle with him. If I overcome him, I shall gain the wisdom I require; but if otherwise, I must go into the grave."

"Enough, O Maharaja! May you be successful!"

On inquiring at the village, I was informed that this fakir was a very holy man indeed, and that he had been alone in the temple for a week. The villagers placed food at the door, but had never ventured to disturb the meditations of the eerie occupant of the building. The steamer came down in the course of the afternoon, so I was prevented from learning the result of his undertaking.

On reaching Dacca, I was hospitably received by a friend, and forwarded the next day in a comfortable "budgerow," or pleasure-boat, reaching Comillah, the head-quarters of the Tipra district, the same evening. Here I put up for a couple of days, at the house of the English agent of the Tipra Raja, telegraphing to Chittagong for horses to be sent out for me. My host kindly furnished me with horses for the first thirty miles of my return journey, and a walk of fifteen more brought me to the banks of the Pheni River, the boundary between Tipra and Chittagong. Here I had hoped to find a horse-dâk laid for me from Chittagong; but a mighty rain had fallen, the floods were out, and the roads impassable for quadrupeds; so, as I had often done before, I had to trust to my own legs, and slipping off shoes and stockings, Nur-u-din and I trudged for three days, a distance of sixty miles, through mud and pelting rain to Chittagong, where I arrived somewhat fatigued and considerably washed out.

On reaching Rangamati, I worked hard drilling the Frontier Battalion, as the Hill Tract Police were now styled, collecting information, and making arrangements generally for the coming campaign; but my health began to fail, and doubts would now and then assail me as to whether I should be able to remain much longer in my beloved hills. My violoncello shared my depression, and fell to pieces from the damp.

They gave me now another assistant, and an officer was sent to act under me in charge of the Frontier Battalion. I received also complimentary letters from Government officials as to "the essential services" I should be able to render, and "the prospective advantages" which would accrue to me. In short, the quiet corner of the world where I had ruled so peacefully began to pass rapidly into the glare of publicity, and the process was not a pleasant one.

In July I completed and sent in to Government a collection of the proverbs current among the Hill Tribes, which I had been engaged in making for some time. Many of these proverbs were delightfully quaint and characteristic; but what was most forcibly brought home to me in making this compilation was, that even the widest differences of race and manners, of language and religion, are after all only superficial distinctions, and that underneath lies very much the same nature common to all humanity. Numbers of these proverbs were the common property of the world, the same thoughts, under a slightly different dress, being found among the most dissimilar races, Asiatic or European. The only explanation of this is, I think, that the proverbs of even the most civilized people date from the earliest periods of their history, and represent the time and feelings of pristine simplicity; for our crust of civilization, of artificial culture and conventionality, is, after all, very superficial: "scratch the Western and you will find the natural man beneath."

All was now hurry and bustle as the months wore on, and the time approached for military operations to commence. I had to visit the Bohmong and arrange for the frontier posts in his country being taken over and garrisoned by his people during the campaign, as the Frontier Battalion would be wanted to the last man, to keep open communications, furnish baggage guards, and act as scouts. No sooner had I returned from Bundrabun than I had to set out to the other extremity of the District to consult with the Mong Raja what was the maximum number of coolies for the expedition that could be squeezed out of his people. I lived as much as possible in my boat on the river, in order to avoid the jungle malaria, which I found myself less and less able to withstand.

The campaign commenced on the 8th October, 1871, by the arrival, as *avant couriers*, of the Deputy Commissary-General and the Assistant Quartermaster-General, who overwhelmed me with questions upon every conceivable subject connected with the country and its inhabitants, and who, having in twenty-four hours pumped me dry, set forth to the frontier to see for themselves what there was to be seen.

On the 28th of October I went down to Chittagong to meet General Brownlow, who was to command the right column. I donned full uniform to receive him, not wishing to lose my caste as a military man in his eyes. He was a gentlemanly, refined-looking man, in the prime of life, with a genial smile and a kindly blue eye, which occasionally shot forth an eagle gleam, that to an enemy or an offender might seem ugly. I liked him, and thought that I should have no difficulty in working under his command.

I had been desired to write demi-official reports of all that transpired to the private secretary of Lord Mayo; but I undertook to do so much against my inclination, as it was an invidious task, and I ran the risk of inadvertently saying something which might offend either General Brownlow or the Bengal Government.

In November I assumed my position as Political Officer with the right column, and made over charge of my dear Hill Tracts to a Bengal civilian, a very Irish man, who inspired me with no confidence whatever.

The Lushai expeditionary force was to assemble at Kassalong before entering the enemy's country, and thither I accordingly repaired. I had previously sent word to Rutton Poia not to be alarmed at any warlike preparations he might hear of, as I would guarantee his safety and that of his tribe, if they were true to our alliance. I had great hopes of utilising him and h's men as intermediaries in recovering the captives from the Howlong tribe. The expeditionary force slowly assembled at Kassalong, coming by steamer from Calcutta to Chittagong, and thence by boats to the frontier. The 2nd Ghurkha Regiment, commanded by Colonel H. Macpherson, arrived first on the scene; splendid little fellows they were, with an equally fine body of officers, quite a *corps d'élite*.

I sent on my assistant, Mr. Crouch, with one hundred and fifty men of the Frontier Battalion to build a stockade and clear a camping ground for the troops at Demagree, close to Rutton Poia's village.

Rutton Poia himself, with two minor chiefs, came in on the 12th of November and gave in his adhesion to our cause, offering all the assistance in his power. I introduced him to General Brownlow, with all due form, whom he asked to pay a visit to his village when opportunity served, which the General good-naturedly promised to do.

The great difficulty of the campaign, it was evident, would be the commissariat. All supplies had to be drawn from Chittagong, being carried from there by boat to Demagree, on a river broken in its upper course by frequent rapids.

The Khyoung-tha contingent of coolies sent by the hill chiefs now began to assemble, their chief employment would be to manage the dug-out canoes carrying supplies in the upper river. The small Ghurkhas, true hill men, like the Toung-tha or the Lushais, were utterly unable to manage a canoe; indeed, as we soon ascertained, some among them could not even sit in a dug-out without upsetting it.

On the 16th of November, the General, Colonel Macpherson, and I started from Kassalong to Demagree, in separate canoes, each manned by four hill men. We passed the night in our boats at Utan Chatra, and here I found some turtle eggs in the sand, which were not unacceptable at our frugal mess. We arrived the next day at Demagree, and were delighted to find a good stockade built and a large area of ground cleared for the accommodation of the troops. This had been well and quickly done by the men under Mr. Crouch's orders, to whom the General expressed his satisfaction.

A Lushai look-out station was discovered close to the Demagree falls, where the river came tumbling through a gorge into a large rocky basin; a cradle of cane, rigged up in a lofty tree on the heights, commanding a view far down the Karna-phuli. The night of our advance party arriving there, the Lushais had tried their vigilance by throwing stones into the camp, but otherwise they had been undisturbed. I had sent out scouts into the Lushai country beyond, and they now reported that the Lushais were in force on the Sahjuk stream (a northern tributary of the Karna-phuli), and were preparing to resist our advance.

The men were set to work preparing a timber slide up the Demagree falls, as, when once we had passed onward, every ounce of food would have to be dragged up the fall, which was of no great height, perhaps twenty feet.

On the 22nd of November the General visited Rutton Poia's village in accordance with his promise; he started early, taking a company of the 2nd Ghurkhas as escort, and I accompanied him to act as interpreter. The village was situated on the range of hills east of our camp at a distance of three miles; and midway on the road the chief met our party and conducted the General to the village, where we breakfasted on provisions which we had brought with us, and were regaled with hill beer. A guyal also was killed in honour of the visit, and two basketsful of the flesh were sent to camp for our consumption.

General Brownlow and his staff returned in the afternoon, but I remained at the village for the night, as Rutton Poia wished me to assist at a great council of his friends and relatives which was to be held there, to decide the course which the clan should take during the coming contest.

There was accordingly a big talk and a corresponding drink. Rutton Poia's desire was to maintain a benevolent neutrality; but this I assured him would not be allowed, and I pictured the ferocity of the General in unspeakable terms. The difficulty seemed to be that if Rutton Poia and his clan should take an active part in our favour, the hostile tribes on the retirement of the expedition would destroy him root and branch.

I promised that at the close of the campaign he should have a detachment of police in his village, if he desired it; and by judiciously waving in the background the wrath of General Brownlow, he finally consented to act with us. For the present, I undertook to leave fifteen men to guard the chief's village, as an open sign of British support, while he and his clan agreed to afford full and loyal assistance in whatever way it might be needed during the campaign.

At the close of our long and animated conference, which lasted far into the night, Rutton Poia's wife brought her young son, a boy of about ten years old, and solemnly placed his two hands folded between mine, in token of his recognition of me as protector and suzerain.

On returning to Demagree and reporting what had passed to the General, he expressed himself satisfied, and took the opportunity to say that, as my place for the future would be with him at the front, it would be necessary to appoint another officer to superintend the work of the hill coolies, and he purposed appointing Captain Hood to that duty. I accordingly assembled the head men of the coolie contingent and harangued them in their own tongue, directing them to work loyally under Captain Hood, and to pay the same respect and obedience to his orders as they would to my own.

We had something of a scare in camp a few days later, for news came that a large party of the enemy had occupied the river in rear of us, with a view to cutting our line of supplies and communication. The hill coolies at Utan Chatra (half-way between Demagree and Kassalong) had struck work, and talked of returning to their homes, for the Khyoung-tha feared the very name of Lushai, and even a report of being cut off would create a panic. The news reached camp at nightfall, and an hour or so later I was on my way, with twenty men of the Frontier Battalion, to see what was really the truth of the matter. There was no moon, and we had a narrow squeak for it in the rapids, one of the boats being upset and four rifles lost; but no further damage was done, and at daybreak I reached Utan Chatra.

My first care was to reassure the hill coolies, who after a while calmed down and departed with a convoy for Demagree. On inquiry I found that a party of armed men, said to be Lushais, had certainly been seen crossing the river by a ford a few miles down stream only the day before, and on going to the spot I soon found a trail. We followed the traces of the party through the jungle for two hours, until we came to a spot where they had halted and cooked food. Here on the ground some rice was discovered which had been spilt, and this on inspection proved to be our own commissariat rice, easily distinguishable from the hill grain; therefore, as none of our grain stores had been plundered, the party could not have been Lushais, and were probably some of our own coolies, who had absconded with their rations. Leaving my Subadar, Mahomed Azim, to follow the trail farther, I returned to Demagree.

The chief Vanpoia came in on the 2nd of December, and gave in his adhesion to our cause. He reported that the Sylus were killing and eating their guyals, and would most certainly oppose our advance. He, like Rutton Poia, made an attempt to get a guard for his own village, alleging that at the close of the expedition he and his would be eaten up by the Sylus and Howlongs for taking our side. I promised him that a strong guard should be left at Demagree when the campaign was over, which would protect him if necessary.

I was much worried by the hill coolies, who would do nothing without my personal orders; and none of the officers of the expedition knowing the language, I had not a moment's rest.

Our force was now augmented by the arrival of the 27th Punjaub Infantry, who had marched from Kassalong to Demagree through the jungle. It did one's heart good to see so fine a body of men come down the hill into camp, marching, like our Highland regiments, to the music of the pipes. They gave the "Pathan scream" as they entered camp—a strange noise that stirred the blood as if for fighting.

The captives, whose recovery was one of the main objects of the expedition, were for the most part in the hands of the Howlong tribe, between whom and us interposed the Sylus, and it was clearly desirable to secure the neutrality, if not the amity, of this latter tribe, if it were in any way possible to do so; they were, however, so suspicious and unapproachable that all my efforts had hitherto failed. It therefore became necessary to obtain the services of someone who would act as intermediary, and with this view, on the 8th of December, I went to the village of a small chief named Lengura, who was own brother to one of the principal Sylu chiefs, but who, from ill-luck or incapacity, was a person of comparative insignificance. To my disappointment, I found the village deserted; but my men in routing about discovered a pig, two guyals, and fifty maunds of unhusked grain, so it was plain that the inhabitants' departure was only temporary. I therefore left a party in ambush, and towards nightfall was lucky enough to capture the chief Lengura himself, who returned to look for the guyals.

I spent a long time in endeavouring unsuccessfully to secure his assistance; he remained obstinately deaf to all proposals, even casting on the ground at my feet the money which I offered in exchange for his pig and guyals. After a day or two of close confinement he at length consented to act as our ambassador, and accordingly I despatched him to the village of a Sylu chief named Vanlula, which was within easy distance of our camp, authorising him to say that if our advance towards the Howlong country were unopposed we would not harm the Sylu tribe.

In the evening I strolled in the same direction which Lengura had gone, towards Vanlula's village, hoping to gain admission; but I had not advanced far up the slope when a ball came whistling close by my head, and I therefore accepted the hint and returned to camp.

The head-quarters now moved up from Demagree, and occupied a fresh camp on the Sahjuk stream close to Vanlula's village. The General was not at all well; but this was not surprising, as the hill climate is very trying until the constitution becomes inured to it.

It was a remarkable sight at the close of a march to see the speedy and dexterous manner in which the hill men and the Ghurkhas would, in the twinkling of an eye, convert a dusky forest glade into a comfortable village. At sundown we would halt in some secluded glen; the arms were piled, and in a few moments the air would be filled with the cutting sounds of dao and kukri; the tangle of jungle would be cleared; huts built, thatched with leaves and walled with split bamboos; fires lighted, and everyone within a measurable distance of comfort in less than half an hour. There was not a tent of any sort with the whole force; every ounce of dead weight that could be carried was brought along in the shape of either food or ammunition. For houses we depended on our enemies, and in their default we were able to run up very cosy shanties ourselves.

On the 13th of December Lengura returned, and informed me

that no less than five of the Sylu headmen with their followers were assembled at Vanlula's, and that, in reply to the message which he had conveyed from me, they had desired him to request that the expedition should at once leave the country: on this condition only would they treat with us or assist in recovering the captives; if we advanced any farther they would attack us. Foolish folk! I rewarded Lengura, and communicated his intelligence to the General, whose practical reply was the issue of orders to attack Vanlula's village the following morning.

The advance was made in two parties under cover of the morning mist. The right attack under Major MacIntyre of the 2nd Ghurkhas was a feigned one; and while the enemy's attention was thus engaged, the main body of the 2nd Ghurkhas under Colonel Macpherson, crested the hill on which the village was built, and, charging with the bayonet, took the place at a rush.

The enemy bolted, leaving one man dead, and carrying away with them two or three more dead and wounded. At the very first shot fired Vanlula set fire to his village, which was almost wholly consumed before we got possession of it; among the burnt houses we established ourselves as best we might, and scouts were sent out to ascertain the enemy's movements. They returned at sunset, reporting that the Sylus had retreated northward, leaving signs of a precipitate flight in the shape of various articles dropped along the road and a dead body abandoned in the retreat. Among other things was found a coat belonging to a man of the Frontier Battalion who had been killed by the Lushais a year before; also a basket and other small things of Bengali workmanship. From this evidence we deduced that the Sylus had been concerned in the raids upon British territory which had caused the expedition; this in some measure explained their persistent mistrust and hostility towards us.

The General was still far from well, to the regret of all, for he was a true leader of men, and gained the confidence of everyone who was brought in contact with him; but his indisposition was not allowed to interfere with the work of the expedition, and he marched on foot and directed everything just the same as before.

It was determined to form a provision depôt at Vanlula's, and parties were sent out in all directions, to search for and bring in such hidden stores of grain and other comestibles as were discoverable, it being necessary to utilise, as far as practicable, the resources of the country.

My position as a diplomatist began to cause me considerable anxiety, for how was it possible to recover the captives, or to enter into relations of a friendly character with the Sylus, if they absolutely declined all intercourse with us and confined themselves to a sullen hostility. Rutton Poia, who was with me, was apparently on bad terms with them, as neither he nor any of his men could be prevailed upon to undertake an embassy. Moreover, we depended for our food chiefly on supplies from Chittagong, which had to be brought many weary miles before reaching us. What should be done, if, as seemed probable, the enemy retired before us, burning every thing save the standing crops, and carrying with them their live-stock and other comestibles ?

I went out in the early morning of December 19th to think over some new plan ; but sitting on the hill-top, some two thousand feet high, so beautiful was the sight before me that for the moment I forgot all my perplexities, and could only rejoice in the grandeur of the landscape spread out below.

The sun had just risen out of a wilderness of delicately purpled peaks, which stretched towards the east, and a keen cold breeze from thence seemed to whisper a message of defiance from our enemies, whose villages, perched like eyries on many an unknown hill-top, could be clearly seen all around.

The whole Sylu country lay within striking distance of our position, no less than six large villages being within a day's march. Beyond these lay the Howlongs, living on still loftier heights, never trodden by English feet, an undiscovered country, range upon range stretching far away in the distance, even to the confines of China.

Every valley around was filled with fleecy white mist, which, like soft snowy wool, hid all beneath it, and out of this rose craggy eminences covered sparsely with forest trees, while here and there, in the morning sun, some Sylu clearing gleamed golden with ripe corn. The far-off horizon was bounded by a clearly defined dark purple range of hills, perhaps twenty miles distant, and as the sun rose the mist came pouring over this ridge and through the clefts of the range like some gigantic ocean, another deluge dashing its waves in foamy cataract on an affrighted world. So real did this seem to me for the moment that I found myself thinking that had this white foam been water, between me and death there could have been but a short five minutes.

The climate, now that we had got up on the heights, was simply delicious, and the General's health began to mend rapidly. The air was bracing and dry, developing one's appetite to an alarming extent, the more so as from Dan to Beersheba all was barren. After my usual solitary life in the hills, I found the gay sociability of camp life very pleasant and much enjoyed the daily change and adventure, the nightly camp-fire with its round of song and story.

We were somewhat harassed by attempts on the part of the Lushais to cut our line of communication. One day they laid an ambush for the party bringing the mail, and shot one of our Ghurkhas; but they did not escape scatheless, for our men promptly retaliated and killed two of their assailants.

On the 21st of December Colonel Macpherson assaulted and took the village of Lal Hlira. We watched the attack with much interest through field-glasses, the village being on the next range of hills, three or four miles off as the crow flies. There was a great deal of firing, and the General was much relieved when Macpherson telegraphed by flag-signal that the attack had been made without any loss on our side, although the enemy had suffered, and large stores of grain had been captured.

At the same time, Major MacIntyre, with another detachment, was busy to the northward, where he burnt two villages and destroyed fifty-six granaries. One of these villages was strongly stockaded, but was abandoned by the Sylus without any serious attempt at defence. Some cattle also were captured, which proved a welcome addition to the commissariat.

I meanwhile busied myself in endeavouring to communicate with the Sylus. Conversations were sometimes held between us, across a valley, by shouting. The burden of my song was always, "Make submission, and we will cease from troubling you"; but I received no satisfactory reply, nor was any result attained.

Christmas Day was observed in camp in true English fashion. General Brownlow invited all the officers of the advanced column to dine with him, and to our great astonishment, among other good things, a miraculous plum-pudding graced the board. I obtained the recipe afterwards from Major East, Assistant Quartermaster-General, who had evolved the same from his inner consciousness, as follows: one pot of marmalade, one pot of black-currant jam, some guyal suet, and a sufficiency of biscuit pounded fine, together with a tablespoonful of essence of ginger; the whole boiled for two hours, and served with a few spoonfuls of burning brandy. Result, beatific!

The next day we moved forward and occupied the village of the Sylu chief, Van Hnoya, meeting with no opposition. This village was a large one, consisting of about three hundred houses, and was remarkable for having in its vicinity a large sacrificial altar of curiously carved stone, decked with a varied collection of the skulls of the different animals which had been offered thereon. I could find no human skulls among them.

Soon after our entry into Van Hnoya's village, the villages of Van Kunga and Van Hnuna, which were in sight, were set on fire by their inhabitants. I sent on a party of picked men, and some of Rutton Poia's Lushais, to parley with them, and prevent this useless destruction; but in vain.

Day after day passed by as we pursued our course, marching farther and farther into the bowels of the land, until by the end of the month we had reached the great Towrang Tlang range, where the General hoped to obtain some tidings of the other column. The enemy always pursued the same unsatisfactory tactics; they fought as little as possible, but burned their villages on our approach, retiring with all they could carry. They hailed us out of the jungle one day, saying, "Do not destroy our grain."

"Let your chiefs come in, then," I rejoined, "and make submission."

"No, no, no," was the reply. "Go your ways; leave our

country. We have nothing for you but powder and ball, and plenty of that." Brave words these! but nothing else.

At the General's request I caused proclamations to be prepared, written in Burmese and Bengali, setting forth that our object in invading the country was to effect the release of certain of Her Majesty's subjects, who were held in captivity by the Lushais, and inviting the tribes to send emissaries to treat with us. These proclamations were left, nailed up in conspicuous positions, at every place we visited; but as the Lushais could neither read nor write, I did not anticipate much effect from this step, unless their curiosity should induce them to employ some literary captive to investigate the mysterious magic papers which the invaders were sowing broadcast about the country. Otherwise, the proclamations would certainly be regarded as magical formulæ, intended to bring disease and pestilence among the people, and would be looked upon merely as an additional incentive to hostility.

One of our little Ghurkha soldiers was caught, while out scouting, in a Lushai deer-trap. The trap consisted of a stout young tree bent down as a spring, with a loop outspread. Into this loop the man unwittingly thrust his foot, and was at once jerked high into the air, kicking lustily. His comrades soon set him free by cutting the thong which held him, and he escaped with the fright and a bad sprain.

The weather grew colder and colder, the nights and mornings being truly Chrismatic; but the general health of the force was good, in spite of a very limited scale of diet.

On the 2nd of January the General and I ascended the Towrang range, hoping to discern some sign of General Bourchier's column; but we gained nothing by our climb, save a grand view of the surrounding country. Sylu Savung, the largest village of the Sylu tribe, and the residence of their head chief, Savunga, lay in full view not more than ten miles off, separated from us only by a deep valley, which was curiously intersected by the head-waters of three rivers, two of which ran northwards to Cachar, and the third bent south to join the Karna-phuli river. Far away to the east we saw the villages of the Howlongs, while about eight miles to the north lay the strongly-stockaded village of Lal Ngora, eldest son of Savunga, which the General determined to attack and destroy.

The following day, therefore, Captain Battye of the 2nd Ghurkhas, with two companies of that regiment, was sent to reconnoitre in the direction of Lal Ngora's village, and reported that it was held in force by the enemy, who apparently meant fighting.

The next day the attack was made by the whole of Colonel Macpherson's regiment, and the place taken by storm. Major MacIntyre led the assault, and was the first man over the stockade. We lost one Ghurkha killed, and nine wounded. Captain Battye also was slightly wounded in the attack. The village was burnt and a large quantity of grain destroyed.

That night the Sylus approached our camp in the darkness and held a parley with me. They said that their head chief Savunga wished to come in immediately with a peace-offering of elephants' tusks. I replied that he might do so with safety, but that until he did, the progress of the expedition would not be stayed. I added that their villages and crops would be spared if no resistance were offered.

Rutton Poia was with me during this nocturnal colloquy, and he promptly suggested that, if Savunga came in, it would be wise to chop off his head and put it on a pole. So much for Lushai faith! No wonder they were suspicious. We halted all the next day to see if anything would come of this overture, but the Sylus still made no sign.

We advanced upon Savunga's village on the 6th of January. The road was very difficult, being blocked by huge boulders, and leading ever up and down, first along a ridge, then plunging down a thousand feet into a valley, where we waded and stumbled for an hour or more along the bed of a torrent, then up once more to the heights, and so on.

On arriving at a "jum," or clearing, within about nine hundred yards of a small outlying village, we saw that it was filled with armed men, and the General thought this a favourable opportunity for showing the Lushais the force of our guns, which had hitherto not been employed. Fifty Ghurkhas were sent forward skirmishing straight to the front, while the mountain-battery (of which Colonel James Hills was the commandant) was directed to open fire over their heads. The small seven-pounder steel guns, unscrewed into two pieces, had been painfully carried along on the shoulders of coolies; but now they were quickly put together, and in an incredibly short space of time were making beautiful shell-practice at the village, which was crowded with armed Lushais.

Having never seen a big gun fired before, the enemy's consternation was great, and as the first shell burst over their heads all scattered helter-skelter, abandoning the village, and fleeing for their lives in all directions.

"It is wonderful!" remarked Rutton Poia. "You fire one gun out of another. No one could withstand it."

On mounting to the village, we found that the enemy had prepared for us an artful avalanche of rocks, which was to have swept the path leading upwards; and also a goodly store of spears, arrows, and other missiles, to be hurled upon our devoted heads; but they had reckoned without our seven-pounders, and their designs came to naught.

The same day some of my men, whom I had sent out scouting into the jungle, in the vain hope that they might capture some Sylu man who would serve as envoy, discovered and brought in to me four fine gongs of Chinese workmanship.

The next morning, early, the great village of Sylu Savung burst into flames. The encounter of the day before had apparently convinced the Sylus that they had no chance against us in fighting; and on the 11th of January we occupied the site of their chief village without any further opposition.

There was now but one village of the Sylu tribe left standing, that of Lal Jika, the youngest son of Savunga; all the rest had been burned by their own inhabitants, or taken by us. This tribe, therefore, might be considered as subjugated, and we accordingly turned our attention next to the recovering of the captives from the Howlongs, whose villages were now in full view, and within striking distance.

The Government of India had been pressing the General to avoid any unnecessary destruction of villages or crops, although I confess, I could not see how this could be avoided, or what could have been done other than what had been done. Still, the Governor-General's wishes were law, and I determined, at the General's request, to undertake a peaceful embassy to the Howlongs before the first blow should be struck against them.

I started, therefore, on the 13th of January, taking with me Rutton Poia and his Lushais, together with an escort of fifty Ghurkhas, bound for the nearest Howlong village, which was plainly visible from our camp. As we drew near, the inhabitants of the village discovered our approach, and, to my dismay, followed their usual procedure and set fire to the place.

Rutton Poia looked very grave at this unmistakable declaration of hostility, and forthwith declined to proceed any farther, saying that the only method of peaceful approach to the Howlongs was by the rear. He proposed that we should at once return to Savunga's, whence he would pass by a long detour to the south, and only thus be able to gain access to Benkuia and Sangbúnga, the two brothers who ruled the Howlong tribe. This proposal involved much delay ; but I saw no other course, and, to my regret, we had to return to Sylu Savung, and report the failure of our mission to General Brownlow.

Much against his inclination, the General agreed to halt at Sylu Savung, while Rutton Poia set off on his roundabout journey, accompanied by Subadar Mahomed Azim, one of the most intelligent officers of the Frontier Battalion.

The chief was directed to inform the Howlongs that the only basis upon which we would treat with them was the unconditional release of all the captives, together with free access for ourselves to the Howlong country ; otherwise we should attack. We had then to await the result ; and, indeed, both officers and men needed rest, for, although the campaign was not very arduous as far as fighting was concerned, still enormous distances had been traversed over the roughest ground, the soldiers carrying heavy weights in the shape of clothing and ammunition. Hard fare also had been our portion in this savage and inhospitable country, the English officers, for instance, having subsisted on a diet of chapatis, tinned mutton, and rum. The General himself fared no better than the rest of the force, and the general health of all began to suffer from want of change in the diet.

There was no grumbling, however, unless the universal and heart-felt aspiration to make an end of the business could be construed into a complaint. While awaiting the result of Rutton Poia's mission, the General turned his attention to the last remaining village of the recalcitrant Sylus, who had as yet made no sign of substantial submission. This was, as I have said, the village of Lal Jika, youngest son of the chief Savunga, and here, if anywhere, the tribe might be expected to show fight.

General Brownlow, having reconnoitred the place and determined upon his course of action, delivered the attack on the 21st of January. We started at 8.30 A.M. to avoid the mists of the early morning, and marching along, found our road stopped by a stockade. While the guns were being got up, an extension was made by both flanks to turn the enemy's position, perceiving which, the Lushais let fall about our ears an avalanche of rocks and stones which they had in readiness, but which fortunately did little damage. They then abandoned the stockade and retreated to their village.

Our advance was continued, and at a distance of seven hundred yards, Colonel Hills' small seven-pound rifled guns opened fire with shell and shrapnel. This made a clearance of the Lushais, who fled in dismay before these new and terrible projectiles, and we occupied the place without loss. It was a strong position, most elaborately stockaded, and, but for the guns, we must have suffered severely in capturing it.

Having destroyed the crops and granaries in the vicinity, we returned to our camp at Sylu Savung. Here I was met by the glad tidings that my ambassador, Rutton Poia, had effected the release of Mary Winchester, and had delivered the child into the keeping of Colonel Tytler, of the 4th Ghurkhas, who commanded at Demagree, by whom she had been despatched to Calcutta *viâ* Chittagong.

Mary Winchester was described as being a pretty child of about six years old, fair complexioned, with hazel eyes and European features. The officer who was sent by Colonel Tytler to take her over from Rutton Poia, found the little maid sitting on the log platform of the chief's house, having for clothing only a blue rag round her loins, and with a pipe in her mouth, issuing sententious commands to a troop of small boys who were disporting themselves before her.

She appeared, during her long stay with her kidnappers, to have altogether forgotten the English language; but on the officer fumbling in his pocket, and demanding whether she would like to have a sweetie, her memory at once responded to this ancient and familiar question, and she held out her hand, showing that she understood what had been said.

She was duly made over to her friends in Calcutta, and from there was sent to Scotland, where I believe her father's relatives resided. Ten years afterwards her name appeared among the list of those who had creditably passed an examination at the Royal Moray College. It was curious to consider that, but for a chain of unlikely events, she might have been the bride of some dusky Lushai chief, wearing a scanty kirtle and an amber necklace!

Further, I was informed that the chief Rutton Poia, having succeeded so far in his embassy, had departed with all speed to the Northern Howlongs, whose villages now confronted us, and he particularly requested that we would abstain from hostilities, as otherwise his safety might be jeopardised.

The General chafed like a caged lion at this forced inaction, which he was compelled to endure; for it would have been but poor satisfaction to undertake a military promenade through the Howlong country, as we had already done through Syluland, and then to have to retire without recovering the remainder of the captives; and as, moreover, I had pledged my faith to Rutton Poia, it was agreed to wait for one week more before entering the Howlong territory.

A night or two afterwards, as we were sitting in the General's hut playing a rubber after dinner, we heard two shots fired in quick succession, followed by the scream of a wounded man; then more shots, sharp and quick, as our men fired in reply. The whole encampment was astir in a moment, like a disturbed ants' nest. The hum of voices and the clank of hastily-donned accoutrements were heard on all sides.

We found that the Lushais had stolen up through the jungle, under cover of the darkness, and had shot one of our sentries, sending a charge of slugs into his chest at twenty paces distance, and then had promptly scuttled off. Our poor fellow was badly hurt, and at the time it was believed that medical aid could do nothing to save him.

Returning to the hut, we could not resume the rubber, but smoked an angry pipe, grieved at the loss of a good soldier in so cowardly a fashion. I may add here, however, that the little Ghurkha, who was shot through the lungs, did not die of his wound, his life being saved by the unwearied attention and skill of Dr. Allen, the medical officer of the 2nd Ghurkhas; but, as they say in the East, the lad's "kismet" was bad, for he had no sooner recovered from the charge of slugs in his lungs, than he was attacked by cholera, and died before the end of the year.

The conversation running on night attacks, General Brownlow related some of his experiences of that kind on the North-Western Frontier.

During the Ambeyla campaign he had been beleaguered one starlight night by countless Afghans, who yelled and fought for six hours, in their endeavour to turn him out of a small breastwork of loose stones held by a picquet of his old regiment, the 20th Punjaub Infantry, about one hundred strong. The position, on a commanding knoll, was a good one, and the enemy dashed themselves against it in vain, being driven back time after time with much loss. After one of the most determined of these onslaughts there was a lull and a silence, which was broken by a voice close to the picquet proposing a suspension of hostilities and a song. The object was probably to gain time to carry off the killed and wounded; but most of the men of the 20th happened to be Pathans, and the incident was so much to their taste that they broke into a shout of applause and begged the General to give the order "Cease firing," which he accordingly did.

Then from behind his sheltering rock the Bajowrie (for he gave his name and clan as well as a pledge to enlist in the 20th at the close of the campaign) immediately began a wild weird song of love and war, that indicated the throat and lungs as well as the heart of a free-born mountaineer. He had no sooner ended than two young Afridis of the regiment sprang on to the parapet of the breastwork, and sitting outlined against the sky, a target for a thousand matchlocks, replied in a duet of equal sound and melody, not a shot being fired at them.

As the last words of the song died on their lips they jumped back under cover, with the plaudits of both sides, and the promise of the Order of Merit as a reward for their music and their valour.

A few playful remarks of mutual defiance were followed by the warning from without that it was time to resume business, and emphasised by a storm of bullets and renewed attacks that lasted until daylight, when the enemy withdrew, and the exhausted picquet was relieved and returned to its bivouac below.

This same outpost, known to history as the "Crag picquet," and on which the safety of the whole camp depended, was twice subsequently carried by the enemy sword in hand, and on each occasion its capture and recapture cost the British force upwards of a hundred killed and wounded, Sir Neville Chamberlain (the General Commanding), and Colonel Hope, of the 71st Highlanders, being among those who were badly hit in the last of these Homeric contests.

Our Lushai opponents, however, were not of this kidney, but like the mosquito, although contemptible, they were annoying. On another occasion they came creeping up the hill-side to the house where I was sleeping, and fired through the floor (the house being raised on piles, Lushai fashion), without, however, doing me any harm. The campaign, we hoped now, would be finished in three weeks' time, for after the expiration of the week for which I had stipulated, the General intended to take a stretch out with a flying column, severing for the time being his communication with the rear.

General Bourchier, who commanded the left column, had set out from Cachar at the same time as the right column left Kassalong, and we had hoped ere this to have seen or heard some signs of his advance. Even if a junction could not have been effected, it would have cleared our brains, topographically speaking, to have opened communication with the other column. The country between us was unknown and unmapped, and it was impossible to say what distance apart we might be.

To tell the truth, as the days dragged their slow length along, we all became very ill-tempered. A soldier can endure anything better than inaction, and here, waiting at Sylu Savung, there was nothing to do, nothing to see, nothing to read, nothing to eat; there was not even any news.

Our clothes were worn threadbare; our boots were in holes; the shanties we lived in were bitterly cold, and the ground on which we lay at night was so hard that sleep was impossible; even the songs at evening were hushed in mournful silence, and the last good story had been told. So, *faute de mieux*, the whole camp began to look sourly upon the political officer to whose cursed diplomacy this deplorable condition of things was attributable; the Government, in letters from Calcutta, began to cavil at the delay in carrying out the objects of the expedition; and even General Brownlow (worst blow of all) began to regret *that he had yielded to my representations*.

I had, at any rate, acted according to the best of my judgment although success alone could justify my course, bringing with it the sunshine of official approbation and the star-shine of decoration on manly breasts. Surely the desire of "the moth for the star" is as nothing compared with that of the soldier for his bit of ribbon, and the monarch who first invented this mode of distinction must have been a keen observer of the weaknesses of human nature. For a leg lost in battle, a metal cross! the services of a lifetime repaid amply by a bit of tinsel frippery; and so long as a king has a yard of ribbon left he will always find men of the best and bravest sort ready to give their lives in exchange.

The end of the week came at length, and the General would wait no longer, nor, indeed, could I avouch that diplomacy had not received a fair trial. Nothing more was heard of Rutton Poia, and there remained now only the argument of the sword.

We started with our faces set against the Howlongs on the 12th of February, 1872. Our small force consisted of three hundred Ghurkhas, with the two mountain guns and half a company of Sappers. The path descended first some 2,300 feet into the valley of the Dalesari stream; then rose for 1,300 feet, leading along a ridge for some distance; then another plunge of 1,000 feet into the bed of another hill-stream, whence a final ascent of 1,600 feet brought us out on to a rolling upland—the country of the Howlongs.

When we had to march long distances through water it was my custom to go barefoot. This was at first regarded by the officers of the force merely as eccentricity, but experience, hard stones, muddy water, and long marches combined, proved potent arguments in favour of surefootedness *versus* shoe-leather, and convinced many of the expediency of following my example.

We camped for the night soon after our final ascent, and the next morning, Captain East, our Assistant Quartermaster-General, and I went out together reconnoitring; after proceeding some distance we saw on some rising ground to our left the smoking ruins of a village, which, in due course, had been burnt by its inhabitants on our advance the day before. The knoll on which the village had stood, however, was now crowded with Lushais, and on our hailing them a friendly dialogue ensued. To my infinite satisfaction, they professed a desire for peace, and said that their chiefs were quite willing to release the captives. "Go then," I said, "fetch your chiefs; let them bring the captives and arrange matters. We will do you no harm then."

Returning to camp, we reported the occurrence to the General, who was as pleased as we were at the turn things seemed likely to take. Our force moved on, however, in spite of fair words, to a village called Chongmama, to the east of which, at a distance of two days' march, lay the villages of Benkuia and Sangbúnga, the head chiefs of the Howlong tribe, and within easy striking distance of four other large villages, aggregating, perhaps, a thousand dwellings.

We found in the jungles round Chongmama numerous huts, which had been erected by the burnt-out Sylus, with stores of grain and other things. These we carefully left untouched, as sufficient punishment had been inflicted on that tribe. It was ascertained from the Howlongs that General Bourchier's column was distant about four day's journey to the east; our General, therefore, abandoned all hope of effecting a junction, or even communicating with the left column, as we were at the extreme end of our tether and lofty ranges of hills intervened.

On the 15th the General sent out two reconnoitring parties: one under Major MacIntyre, which returned after some hours with full information as to the roads and passes northwards; the second party, under Captain Battye, went east, and soon after sent back a messenger to the General, reporting that a mile below camp was a stream, the passage of which was barred by large bodies of armed Lushais. Were they to force the passage or not? The General ordered the party to return, and sent me down to parley with the enemy. I found the ford guarded by Benkuia's men, that being the direct road to the chief's village. I bade them go and fetch their chiefs quickly, and that I would be personally responsible for their safety. In my own mind I felt convinced that Rutton Poia's embassy by the rear had been successful, and that the Howlongs meant to submit; their own innate treachery, however, made them suspicious of us.

That night, as I lay asleep in my hut, a voice came to me out of the darkness, close to my head.

"Thangliena!" (Lushai paraphrase of Tom Lewin) "Thangliena! Is it peace?"

I made no reply. The voice continued—

"The great chiefs will be at the Tuldung stream to-morrow at dawn, but you must come alone, without any soldiers." A pause; then—"Thangliena! do you hear?"

"I hear," I replied, groping for my revolver, and cautiously emerging from my shelter to hold further parley with the mysterious speaker, but there was nothing. All was silent, and there was only the dark night and the keen wind, with the sound of my own men snoring. The messenger, a Lushai, evidently had crept past our sentries, done his errand, and was gone; so I lit a pipe, and sat down to think over the situation.

I knew that the General would object to my going alone to the meeting as proposed, for if it should turn out to be a ruse, and I were captured and carried off as a hostage by the Lushais, the last state of things would be worse than the first. Again, if I went to the rendezvous with a body of soldiers, the chiefs would suspect treachery and probably would not appear.

However, I had been successful before, in my dealings with the hill men, even when I had no avenging force at my back; and now my necessity was greater, for I had my policy to justify. The mere thought of failure was insupportable. My whole experience led me to believe that these people could not understand or realise a complex governing machine like ours. They needed personal dealing, personal authority, personal promises. After all, I had played with my life for much smaller stakes, so I determined to go.

In the early morning, before the camp was well awake, I set off down the hill path leading to the Tuldung; after going about half a mile I heard a sound behind me, and glancing round, found that I was followed by an armed Lushai; a little farther on, another man issued from the jungle and joined the first, then another, until at last I was followed by ten or twelve of the Howlongs.

I took no notice whatever of my following, but marched steadily on; down went the path, steeper and steeper, until at length I reached a black slow-flowing stream, the Tuldung. Across this a rough bridge had been thrown by felling a large tree, the trunk of which lay across from bank to bank a distance of eighteen or twenty feet. On the opposite side of the stream the ground rose again abruptly, and I saw standing there tier on tier of Lushais, in serried crowd, armed with guns and bristling with spears.

My heart was beating a good deal faster than it should have done; but there was only one course possible, so I tightened my belt with a hitch and went on steadily over the bridge. The passage of that narrow slippery tree-trunk across the deep dark stream, with the rows of strange hostile faces looking down on me, I shall never forget.

As I reached the other side, a venerable white-bearded Lushai met me and took me by the hand; two other men bearing light canes, made a passage for us through the crowd, striking the people, and chiding them back, and so I was led to the chiefs.

They were sitting in a circle, a little distance back from the stream, in a small forest glade, and around them surged myriads of Lushais; the jungle was like an ants' nest. As I was led forward by my white-bearded conductor, there was a cry from the crowd of "Thangliena! Thangliena!"

The chiefs rose and received me. I inquired which was Sangbunga; he came forward, and in an agitated manner put his own gun into my hands, while his brother, Benkuia, took a short sword from his waist and hung it about my neck. Fortunately I had on me some valuable arms, a sword and a silver-mounted dagger taken long before in the Mutiny, and these I presented gravely as return gifts. Then we seated ourselves.

I felt inexpressibly relieved; they were evidently in a great fright, so I consequently ceased to be nervous. The game was won; the campaign was at an end.

I was able to speak some Lushai myself, and the chief's "karbaris" were acquainted with bazaar Bengali, so I had little difficulty in communicating to Sangbúnga and his brother the terms on which alone peace could be concluded. It was necessary, I told them, first that they should give up all British subjects whom they held captive, or account for them, according to lists which I had in my possession; also free and friendly access to their villages both now and in future must be granted to us; and further, I required them to take a solemn oath to abstain from making any raids in future upon British territory. If they complied with these conditions our force would be withdrawn.

After some consultation, the chiefs replied that they had heard my words with satisfaction, and that their desire was to have peace. They promised to send a definitive answer to my demands on the morrow.

Just at that moment I heard the tramp, tramp of our Ghurkhas coming down the path on the other side of the stream, and some of the Lushais ran up shouting that the soldiers were coming. For a moment a look passed round the circle, just a glint of the eyes, which gave me a cold feeling down my back. But I explained that the soldiers would not cross the stream, and had probably been sent by the great General Sahib to escort me back; and so we parted with many expressions of amity and good will.

On my return to camp I had infinite pleasure in reporting to the General all that had passed, and he, with the generosity which is his chief characteristic, after expressing his satisfaction at the turn matters had taken, was so good as to say that he left the entire management of the affair in my hands. This was just what I desired, for by personally concluding a treaty with the Howlongs, backed by an avenging force, I felt that my influence would be greatly enhanced in any future dealings I might have with them after the expedition was over.

On the 18th of February I swore the indispensable oath by blood and steel with the Howlong chiefs, and they presented to Government a peace-offering of elephant tusks, home-spun cloth, guyals, &c.; and the day following the first instalment of captives was sent in, with the promise that the rest, who were scattered in distant villages, should be collected and delivered up as soon as possible.

The camp now swarmed with picturesque Lushais, men, women, and children, bringing for sale eggs, fowls, cloths, pipes, and other local wares, and gazing with infinite curiosity on their quondam enemies.

In accordance with our newly-made agreement, the General at once despatched a detachment of Ghurkhas and an officer of the Survey Department, to visit the village of Benkuia and others in the neighbourhood, and thus assert our right of free entry. The Survey officer took with him the necessary instruments to map the country that was to be visited.

Everyone was in high good humour, for the expedition was practically concluded, having gained nearly all the ends which had been proposed for it. But alas! our sunshine was soon heavily clouded, for on the 18th of February the news reached camp that the Governor-General, Lord Mayo, had been assassinated while visiting the Andaman Islands.

We could hardly realise it. Nothing else was spoken of; nothing else filled the thoughts of all. The remembrance of this cruel deed, the outcome of a madman's vindictive broodings, rose at every moment to dash the satisfaction which we should otherwise have experienced in the successful conclusion of the campaign.

The General issued a Brigade Order on the subject, and it is not too much to say that the brief but sorrowful notification found an echo in the heart of every man in the command. It was, indeed, the Governor-General's own campaign, determined on and watched over by himself, and, only the week before, our General had received a kindly telegram from Lord Mayo, personally congratulating him and his force on the success which had attended their efforts.

Except for this misfortune, all went well with us. The Sylus came in and made terms, delivering up their captives (for they too had some), and swearing perpetual amity. They had suffered heavily, they said, and were now afraid that, when the expedition withdrew, they would be attacked and broken up by the Howlongs. This fear of theirs was soon after confirmed, as Benkuia sent word to me that he had expelled all fugitive Sylus from his country, and that, if we desired it, he would forthwith attack Savúnga.

The detachment which had gone to Benkuia's village returned on the 22nd, having been received with effusion in all the Howlong villages they had visited. Provisions of all sorts had been profusely supplied to them, and they had even been serenaded at night with sweet music.

There was nothing to detain us any longer, and accordingly, the whole force returned to Demagree, whence the General made a demonstration against the Southern Howlongs, forcing them also to give up some captives, and to make submission; and this ended the campaign.

The outward appearance of the whole force at the conclusion of our work was eminently ridiculous, emulating, indeed, the plight of Billy Barlow, who, as the song records, had but one boot and one shoe. Many had purchased cloth from the Lushais, and made themselves garments of home-spun, of curious cut, while rags and tatters were the order of the day with the majority.

The General was, on the whole, favourably impressed by our late enemies, the Lushais, and expressed his opinion in a despatch as follows:

> The Lushai will bear comparison with most eastern races in physique, natural intelligence and character; their thews and sinews and their well-turned limbs indicate health and freedom from want or excessive toil; their faces indicate a happy genial disposition without any expression of cruelty or want of courage.

What struck me most among them was the contentment and well-being of their lives, as compared with the feverish anxieties of civilized life. Involuntarily I contrasted their ignorant happiness with our own laboured learning, and their simplicity with the vices which are to be found in even the most polished European society.

They occupy a country of wood and dale, having an almost Italian climate. Every man is equal; the chiefs only having rule in matters relating to the general good; indeed, should a chief attempt to enlarge his authority, he is speedily brought to his senses by the desertion of his people, who at once seek some less ambitious leader.

They cultivate the earth sufficiently for their wants, and, with less labour than a Bengali peasant undergoes in a month, they can raise enough food for a year. Bound are they by no code of laws, for the chief end of law is to secure property, and they have none which they fear to lose, nor do they desire more; for them, therefore, to submit to laws would be to undergo an obligation with no prospect of reward.

They require no knowledge other than what they have; they know how to sow and when to reap; they have their own pharmacopœia of simples, herbs and roots; their women weave warm cloth; and cunning are the snares by which they entangle all sorts of animals, few there be that escape the pot.

In a word, they know what is necessary for their happiness and well-being; to know more than this would make them unhappy.

Ignorance is the happiness of the poor. We English people are like some good old country dame with a turn for doctoring, who is always trying to force her nostrum down people's throats. With us, civilization is the antidote for all earthly ills, and to all with whom we come in contact we preach diligently the gospel of chimney-pot hats and Poor Law Boards, forgetting that these things, like all else in this world, have a genesis and slow progression of their own, which must be painfully followed from the beginning.

No Oriental race can be pitch-forked to the august altitude which we have ourselves attained, and neither competitive examinations, nor School Boards, nor Municipal Government, nor Acts of Parliament, are sufficient to alter the laws of nature, which, depend upon it, will prevail unto the end—even to the end of the Liberal or all other Governments.

The campaign was ended, and the last days of March saw the General and all his officers on their way to Chittagong, *en route* for Calcutta. I had been so closely connected with them all, for the last four months, that I felt rather solitary when I bade them good-bye, and prepared to resume charge of my own duties as Deputy-Commissioner of the Chittagong Hill Tracts.

The results of those four months may be summed up very briefly: We had recovered Mary Winchester, and released from captivity upwards of one hundred British subjects; two powerful tribes had been effectually subjugated, and twenty of their villages which had offered resistance had been destroyed, while the principal chiefs of those tribes had personally tendered their submission, and entered into solemn engagements with us for future good behaviour. These were no inconsiderable results to have attained, and it was probable that the frontier would, in consequence, have peace for some years to come—might, indeed, be permanently pacificated, if the effects of the present expedition were fostered and allowed to take root in men's minds, instead of dying away, as they certainly would if we merely withdrew to our old position again; but of this I shall speak more presently.

The General was pleased to speak highly of my services during the campaign. He has given me permission to quote his letters, and, as these pages are mainly written for my children and my friends, I may, perhaps, be forgiven for thus publishing my own praises. I have this further excuse, that these pleasant words of praise were my sole reward; and, as not only the leading officers in the expedition were either decorated or promoted at the close of the campaign, but the political officer with the left column, who held a precisely similar position to myself, received the Star of India for his services, many of my friends thought and said that the omission of my name in the roll of honour must have arisen from some fault of omission or commission on my part. I crave indulgence, therefore, and, as I have faithfully set down the admonitions and rebukes which from time to time have fallen to my share, so now I venture to record the words of kindness and approbation which were accorded by the General under whom I served.

General Brownlow's despatch, reporting to Government the results attained by the expedition under his command, contained the following paragraph:

Political and military considerations have been so mixed up in the conduct of this expedition that, though I have been compelled to refer a good deal to the former, the very able civil officer with whom I have been associated, in endeavouring to carry out the objects of Government, will submit in his own department a full report, showing the important part he has so successfully played. It is due to Captain Lewin's strong personal influence over these tribes, his knowledge of their language and habits, added to his patience and sagacity in dealing with them, that a single chief submitted or a single captive was recovered. In expressing my thanks and acknowledgments for the assistance I have received from him, I am bound to record my belief that, if he were located with two or three hundred men for the next year on the Demagree range, while the impression of our power and the friendliness of our intentions are still fresh, he would bring the Sylus and the Howlongs into the same relations with us as Rutton Poia and his men, to the permanent pacification of at least a portion of this frontier.

The remarks of the Indian Press also upon the expedition gave the public impression at the time. I record one extract only, from the "Observer," a Calcutta paper of high repute:

About the middle of February, when General Bourchier's column was reduced to four hundred, and General Brownlow's to a still smaller number of fighting men, not a single blow had been struck against the most powerful and numerous of all the tribes the Expedition had been directed to operate against, viz. the Howlongs; who, having burned their villages and removed their herds and other property beyond the reach of our troops, were awaiting them in armed array in the passes and ravines that led to their country.

General Brownlow did not attempt the conquest of this tribe; he had neither troops nor time to do so, and General Bourchier, by detouring so far to the east as he had done, put it out of his power to co-operate effectually or at all with the Chittagong column.

Now this quandary, and quandary it certainly was, would have been altogether obviated had the Chittagong column been originally made so much the stronger of the two that one portion of it could have pushed east into the Howlong country, while the other was advancing northwards beyond Savúnga. As things turned out, the Howlongs did send in their submission, or, at least, professions of amity, but even that much they would not have consented to but for the influence over them, not of our columns, but of a political officer, Captain Lewin—but for whose tact and good luck on the occasion, both the columns would have had to return to quarters with the satisfaction of knowing that they had left the work of the Expedition unfinished, and perhaps so much so that another expedition to reduce the Howlongs would still be a necessity.

The military commanders did their work well, but assuredly it was the political officer with the Right Column who gave to the Expedition its claim to be considered to have completely effected all that had been expected of it.

So much for my own justification. Had Lord Mayo lived to see the successful conclusion of the campaign which he himself inaugurated, doubtless he would have remembered the words of encouragement and promise which he vouchsafed to me. But it has been well said: "Truly I am an unprofitable servant. I have done that which it was my duty to do."

CHAPTER XIII

CONCLUSION

It was pleasant on the breezy heights above Demagree, with the slumberous murmur of the bees around me, and the odour of the wild thyme floating in the air, to lie on a soft couch of husked-rice straw, in the shadow of an old "jum" house, looking far away out over the winding reaches of the river, which wound like a silver ribbon through the valleys below. A beautiful azure and black butterfly came for a moment and settled on the stock of my rifle, which lay beside me, and then flew away, scared by the approach of some Lushais who came grunting up the path with their loads, in true hill fashion.

All things are finite, from the softest and most rosy-hued dawn to the longest and most wearisome of nights. The expedition was over! I had said farewell to the General and bade adieu to the officers of the 2nd Ghurkhas, pleasant fellows, with whom I had served for so many weeks; and now, far away on the white-gleaming reaches of the Karna-phuli I could see the boats which were carrying them all away, down stream to Chittagong, leaving me once more alone in my hill solitudes.

It was time, indeed, to have done with campaigning, for the heat was growing apace, and the sun beat down so fiercely that the ground grew too hot for even the hard and horny feet of the hill men; the glossy dark-coated guyals sought the shelter of the densest thickets, moaning to each other in sympathetic anguish at the torment of the forest flies; the smaller hill-streams had begun to threaden from the heat, sadly straitening their finny tenants, so that the shallows swarmed with fish, and many a savoury mess was to be obtained by roaming along the sandy banks at night armed with a torch and a dao, with which latter weapon effective chops could be made at the unsuspecting fry.

Not long, however, was I allowed to indulge in idleness or idyllic retrospection, being speedily summoned to Calcutta, where a council was held to decide on future frontier policy in regard to the Lushais. The campaign was the talk of the moment in Calcutta, and I made many acquaintances in consequence when I went there in April, 1872. General Brownlow was specially good to me, and lost no opportunity of praising my services and enhancing their value.

He was my ideal of a true English gentleman, and I took a great enthusiasm for him; not, assuredly, because he spoke well of me, but because he always thought of others first and of himself last. I considered, and do still consider it, a great piece of good fortune to have served under his command. With a rough and domineering or even an unsympathetic commander I could not have worked so well; therefore, indirectly, whatever good work I did in the campaign was mainly due to my General.

The opinions I had formed as to our future frontier policy were given very flattering consideration by the Lieutenant-Governor of Bengal. I returned to the hills with orders to establish a permanent post at Demagree under an English officer; and for this purpose Lieutenant Gordon was appointed my additional assistant.

He and I returned to Chittagong together on the 25th of April, and at once proceeded to Rangamati, where I resumed charge of my own district, setting out immediately afterwards for Demagree to introduce him to his new work. We had no time to lose, for the rains were expected to set in at any moment, and before we left Kassalong the monsoon burst upon us, and the river came down in flood with a rush and a roar, giving us uncommonly hard work to get along. The current was so rapid in places that our boats made head against it with great difficulty; every little rapid became a foaming torrent, into which Gordon and I had to step waist-deep, with our men, to haul the boats through. At night, to make our case worse, we were attacked by swarms of sandflies, creatures so minute that they penetrated the finest mosquito-curtains, and whose bite was so venomous as to cause sores. The only way to baffle these small but malignant enemies was either to adopt the native mode, and muffle oneself from head to foot in a thick cotton mantle, or to sleep in the smoke of a sort of ants' nest, which was plentiful in the jungle, a piece of which if lighted would burn slowly, giving out an aromatic fume which was abhorrent to the sand-flies. In either case success was only partial, and the result was a restless and disturbed night, with the bright stars overhead, their light partially defining the dim hill ranges, while the monotonous roar of the rushing river smote the ears in never-ceasing reverberation.

In olden times I used to think of these hills as beckoning me eastward; now, how many and varied had been my experiences among them, how unforeseen the events which had occurred. Truly nothing occurs but the unexpected.

At Demagree I chose the site for our new permanent post, and made the necessary arrangements for the men's food. I was the better able to do this as I had in hand a considerable quantity of surplus stores, left behind by the expedition. From this stock, also, I was glad to be able to befriend the Sylus, who, in consequence of the havoc we had wrought with their granaries, were now hard pressed for food.

I paid a visit to my friend Rutton Poia in order to introduce Lieutenant Gordon to him. We found the chief in fine feather: his power and importance had been wonderfully increased by the part he had played in the recent campaign, and he consequently beamed as upon a benefactor.

There being no adequate accommodation for the rainy season, I did not propose to remain myself or to leave Gordon at Demagree, but intended moving up there permanently in October or November. Having put matters in order, therefore, and left a strong guard over the stores and munitions, we returned to Rangamati. This little station was now quite gay and lively, as compared with the time when I had lived there alone like the bumble-bee. Now there was Gordon, who was Assistant-Commissioner, together with Messrs. Knyvett, Crouch, and Bignell, who had been appointed to the Frontier Battalion under my command. It was strange to think that not so long ago I cut my way through the dense forest growth that then clothed the ground where our houses now stood, while a flourishing bazaar occupied the site of my old "jum." The formerly jungle-clad hills around were gradually becoming soft sweeps of grass whereon cattle grazed, while the country was thickly dotted with small homesteads and cultivated fields. My mission in the country evidently was to act as pioneer; for, having established this comfortable settlement at Rangamati, I was now, during the ensuing cold weather, to move forward to Demagree and there undertake the same work again.

The Lushai expedition had whitened my head and brought me much ill-health; the doctors strongly advised my seeking change of air by a voyage to England, or at any rate that I should apply for some other district, but I could not tear myself away from my dear hills, where the work became more and more absorbingly interesting.

This was, in truth, a wonderful year for me. Almost every measure of reform or improvement which I had advocated was sanctioned by Government. Chiefest among these measures, was the permission to advance small sums (aggregating, however, £4,000) to the hill people, as loans with which to purchase ploughs and cattle, and so enable them once and for ever, as I hoped, to abandon their old nomadic system of "jum" culture and to settle down to own, and hold land, as permanent cultivators. This movement, if successful, bade fair to change the face of the country and to permanently ameliorate the condition of the people.

Numbers of our quondam enemies, the Sylus, came in to visit me, for my name had become great in Lushai-land: they called me father, and named children "Thangliena" after me, it being, as they averred, a name of power and good fortune. I thought sometimes of King David's psalm, "A people whom I have not known serve me: . . as soon as they heard of me they obeyed me; but the strange children dissembled: . . the strange children failed and trembled in their hill forts"; and I thanked God, very humbly and sincerely, in that He had strengthened my hands and prospered my work.

The cold weather came on apace, and we began to prepare for action. Lieutenant Gordon, with Mr. Bignell, and a strong detachment of the Frontier Battalion, were sent to take charge of the Bohmong's country to the south; this part of the district was chiefly subject to raids from the Shendús, who came from the Arracan hills, and they, having been unscathed by the expedition, would probably be as "peart" as ever. Mr. Crouch went to take command of the Demagree post, while Mr. Knyvett remained in charge at Rangamati. For myself, Government had directed that a thorough exploration should be made of the Southern Frontier, and had directed me, if possible, to lay down a line which might serve in future as the boundary from Demagree to Arracan. For this purpose, a special officer of the Survey Department had been deputed to accompany me and map the country through which we passed, it being entirely unknown and said to be uninhabited.

I took with me fifteen picked men, well armed, and ten hill coolies to carry our food. The Government Surveyor, on his part, moved with a guard of military police and a number of coolies to carry his baggage and heavy surveying implements. Altogether his party numbered ninety souls.

My own notion was to do the journey as light as possible, in rough frontier fashion, our only road being the wild elephant tracks; but much against my judgment, the party was increased in numbers until it reached the above unwieldy dimensions.

We set forth accordingly at the end of November, and dragged this weary tail after us for nearly a fortnight, until the Government Surveyor decided that his instruments could be conveyed no farther, and, as food was running short, and he had succeeded in mapping a very considerable extent of hitherto unsurveyed country, he determined to return to Demagree.

On the 17th of December, 1872, I parted company from my companion and plunged joyfully into the pathless solitudes of the primeval forest, the home of the tiger, the rhinoceros, and the wild elephant. Once we lost our way, and our food supply ran dangerously low; once a tiger steadily followed our small party for two days and two nights, mewing round the camp in the darkness like a gigantic cat, but not otherwise molesting us.

Christmas Day dawned upon us through the gleam of interlacing branches and tangled underwood, seven days' journey at least from any human habitation. My Christmas dinner consisted of boiled rice and spring water, with sundry unknown roots and berries; my tobacco fortunately held out, or I should have indeed deemed my lot a hard one, for there is no slavery like that of the votary of nicotine.

We marched one hundred and fifty miles through absolutely unknown country: here and there we met with great cleared spaces in the jungle, the elephant's parlour, pillared by enormous forest trees, and the ground as smooth and well-beaten as a threshing-floor. Here Behemoth had made his sport, for hard by, great trees were uprooted and crushed, the branches being thrown hither and thither as by a gale of wind, while the earth showed great tusk marks and the print of huge rolling sides.

One morning, as we marched along, a large rhinoceros trotted playfully in front of us for some distance, and on another occasion a monster snake, full twenty feet long and as thick as my thigh, slid his slow gleaming bulk across our path.

We slept on the ground every night under the trees, and a very hard bed Mother Earth afforded. In camping out thus, I generally found it impossible to sleep later than three or four in the morning; either the increase of cold at that hour, or the turning of night towards day, brought back consciousness, and one sat up and gathered together the embers of the dying fire, shuddering at the dense sea of mist and darkness and the unknown unknowable forest that beleagured us round.

Sometimes in our day's march, which averaged about twenty miles, we had to pass along the edge of, or to scale, precipices, where a downward look meant vertigo and destruction, and at evening we had only our rice and roots to comfort us; but at length the journey was successfully accomplished, and that portion of the frontier roughly demarcated.

We reached our southernmost outpost at Chima, in the Bohmong's country, and thence to Gordon's head-quarters on the Sungu river, arriving very worn and ragged, with prodigious appetites. After inspecting Gordon's posts, and arranging matters with him, I returned by river, *viâ* Chittagong, to Demagree as fast as possible, and settled down once more to my work there.

The Lushais now resorted in crowds to the small bazaar which had been established at Demagree. Here my faithful servant

Nurudin had, on my recommendation, been appointed Jemadar, or trade superintendent, on a salary of £60 a year. His future was thus secured, and his fidelity well merited the reward, the more so as he was in every way fitted for the post.

My mother had sent him out from England a double-barrelled gun, with good store of ammunition, as a reward for faithfully following me through the campaign, and a few days after receiving the present he brought me a carefully-penned missive, which he begged me to forward to his honoured patroness. It ran as follows:

MADAM,—With most respect and humble submission I beg to acknowledge the receipt of your favourable reward of one musket and seven hundred ammunitions. For this I am much thankful to you the kindness which is always awarded me by you and my master I shall be remembrance in my life.

(Signed) NURUDIN.

My experience during the campaign had added greatly to my knowledge of the Lushai language, and I occupied my leisure in preparing a hand-book of dialogues in that tongue, with a large vocabulary, which was afterwards printed and published by Government.

My residence at Demagree opened out quite a round of fresh occupations. At one time it would be a Lushai chief, with a score of followers, who came to pay a visit to Thangliena, and who would sit drinking silently, with no apparent intention of ever removing himself; or there were the hundred and one questions to be attended to, concerning the drill, discipline, food and equipment of my small force.

The food question was, in truth, the greatest difficulty I had to contend with, for the Lushai villages in the neighbourhood had no surplus for sale, and consequently everything required for the sustenance of my garrison of one hundred and fifty men had to be brought in boats from Chittagong, a distance of one hundred and eighty miles. Then there was the hospital, where I, poor physician, had to prescribe for fifteen or twenty sick men, until later on, when, much to my relief, Government sent us a native doctor.

Beside all this, there were trees to fell, ground to clear, and houses to build, together with twelve elephants to superintend;

not to mention the writing and, more tedious still, the copying out of the copious official reports upon every sort of subject which were required by Government, such as frontier policy, codification of law, vaccination, revenue settlement, education, survey, &c.

All sorts of curious cases came to me for decision. A girl fell at my feet one day, and sued for a divorce because, she said, her husband beat her mother every morning. But perhaps the most original and difficult case which came before me for decision was as follows.

I was walking up and down one evening, taking exercise in front of the mat house which sheltered me at Demagree, watching some of my men playing at quoits, when of a sudden there appeared a fugitive, like Man Friday coming to Crusoe. Bare-headed, bare-footed, with his clothes in disorder, one of the Frontier Battalion soldiers approached, running for his life. He was a simple, good-natured fellow, who had been sent to carry letters to the outpost on Sirthay Tlang, the hill-range above Demagree. This was his story:

" Sahib, I was going along with the letters "—here the quoits were abandoned, and a crowd of listeners pressed around us—" I was going along with the letters which I had received from your highness, and had reached the small water-fall halfway up the hill, where I stopped to drink. After I had drunk I proceeded on my way; but I had not gone above a musket-shot, when a great tiger came out and stood in the path. Then I feared for my life; and the tiger stood, and I stood, and we looked at each other. I had no weapon but my kukri (a Ghurkha knife), and the Government letters. So I said, ' My Lord Tiger, here are the Government letters, the letters of the Honble Kumpny Bahadur (the Honourable East India Company), and it is necessary for me to go on with them.' The tiger never ceased looking at me, and when I had done speaking he growled, but he never offered to get out of the way. On this I was much more afraid, so I kneeled down and made obeisance to him; but he did not take any more notice of that either, so at last I told him that I should report the matter to the Sahib, and I threw down the letters in front of him, and ran here as fast as I was able. Sahib, I now ask for your justice against that tiger."

This was a new mode of stopping Her Majesty's mails, so I sent out a party to prepare a trap for My Lord Tiger. It was most unreasonable behaviour on his part, for, as my men said, we never interfered with him. This stoppage of the road was a declaration of war, and we killed him not long afterwards.

The Chittagong Hill Tracts proper, of which Rangamati was the head-quarters, were managed during my absence very ably by Mr. Knyvett, the Superintendent of Police, who was vested by Government with the powers of a magistrate for the purpose; while the Bohmong's country, or, as it was now called, the Sungu Sub-Division, was in charge of Lieutenant Gordon. The whole, however, was under my charge, and required constant supervision.

I had formed a high opinion of the little Ghurkhas, who, under Colonel Macpherson, had done the fighting of the expedition, and I obtained permission to send to Nepal and get emigrants from there to colonise my frontier wastes. These Ghurkha colonies were established on the Myani river, a northern affluent of the Karna-phuli, and early in 1873 I set out from Demagree to visit them, and see how the settlement was progressing.

The country where these villages were located had previously been uninhabited, through fear of the marauding Lushais, and my idea had been to establish there good stockaded villages of courageous, stiffnecked people like the Ghurkhas, who should serve as a buffer between the Mong Raja's territory and the independent Lushai tribes to the east.

As I poled up the Myani, my dug-out canoe was brought to a standstill in a somewhat novel and unexpected fashion. A wild elephant (a big tusker) was taking a bath, and filled up the whole of the small stream with his huge body. Now the water was too shallow for us to effect a retreat with any speed, so that, had we insulted him in any way, he could easily have caught and punished us. I had with me, moreover, only a light double gun, which was of doubtful efficacy against such a mountain of flesh. There was nothing for it, therefore, but to wait patiently until His Majesty had concluded his ablutions, when he solemnly stalked up the bank into the forest and we were able to pursue our journey.

That same day I witnessed another equally curious and unusual spectacle. The banks of the stream rose on either hand, high and steep, the margin, however, affording a pleasant, passable path. I had got out of the boat to stretch my legs, and, more from idle curiosity than any other reason, I climbed the steep slope on the right to see what sort of country lay on the other side of it.

As my head topped the bank, I found myself looking into a small, grassy, basin-like clearing, on the opposite slope of which, facing me in the sun, lay a most beautiful tigress, with two small cubs tugging lustily at her teats. It was a fascinating sight, and fortunately, as the sun shone right into her eyes, I was able to observe it at my leisure.

Presently the two little ones left off sucking, and began to play in the most graceful and fantastic manner possible, until the sound of my boatmen singing, as they poled the boat up-stream, put an end to my enjoyment, and I retired as quietly as I had come, lest Madame might resent the intrusion on her domestic privacy.

I stopped for breakfast at a small Tipra settlement on the bank, on the chance of getting some milk or eggs, and as I rested for a while in the headman's house, a beautiful ribbon-snake, of the most vivid grass-green, slender and long like a whip-lash, slowly wound its way through the bamboo of the roof over our heads. The good man informed me that it was quite harmless, and was never disturbed, as it was thought to bring good luck to the house which it visited.

After inspecting the Ghurkha settlements, and also visiting some villages of Tipra immigrants who had settled under their wing, I made my way to the camp of my friend Captain Hood, the Superintendent of Government Kheddas—in other words, " Elephant-Catcher Extraordinary to Her Majesty "—who was out, in pursuance of his function, and from whom I had received an invitation to share in his sport.

The wild elephant is found in all the remoter valleys of the Hill Tracts, in herds of from thirty to forty, or, where food is plentiful, in still larger numbers, and once every two or three years the Khedda Superintendent organizes a big hunt to catch elephants, which are afterwards tamed and broken for the Government service.

The males seldom exceed nine or, in rare instances, ten feet in height. Twice round an elephant's foot gives the measure of his height at the shoulder. They are said to live to the age of one hundred and fifty years in a wild state, but no hill man that I ever met could remember to have seen a dead wild elephant. Probably when their powers fail them they retire to die in some very secluded spot. The domesticated elephant does not, as a rule, live more than eighty years.

There was an abundance of elephants in the forests at the head of the Myani river, and on my way to join Captain Hood we fell in with a herd of the great beasts. They were walking calmly along the ridge of a hill, the females and calves in advance with the tuskers as rear-guard. When we came in sight they halted, and I did the same, expecting that they would disperse and fly, as wild animals generally do at the sight of man; but instead of doing so, the herd huddled together, and a large, solemn tusker came to the front with uplifted trunk and flapping ears, charging us without more ado, and scattering my party hurriedly down the slope.

The only way to escape from an elephant who charges, if you have not got an heavy rifle with which to stop him, is to run down-hill, for if you attempt to run up-hill he has you in a moment, but down-hill his bulk baffles him, and he must perforce move with caution.

The herd which we thus met had probably been previously disturbed by Hood's scouts, for elephants do not usually seek the heights at that season, but keep to the valleys and streams from November to April, mounting to the high lands in May, to visit the salt licks, and to avoid the flies and ticks which render the forest uninhabitable during the rainy season.

I once went out elephant-hunting with Rutton Poia, and, as the Americans say, we had a high old time, so high, indeed, that I was thankful when it was over. The Lushai mode of elephant-hunting consisted in surrounding the animal, perhaps about fifty of us in a circle, and then blazing away to the centre. The consequence was that the bullets flew about as in a general action. We killed the elephant, it is true; but two of the

The khedda was surrounded by men, some holding spears, others fire brands, whose duty it was to prevent the more adventurous of the captive elephants from approaching or injuring the khedda. The big tusker made several attempts to descend into the inner ditch in order to pull down the stockade, but was driven back by lighted fire-brands and the firing in his face of blank charges of powder.

The sun was now westering, and the process of tying-up commenced: an operation that to me, as one of the uninitiated, seemed by far the most dangerous part of the business.

The tame elephants entered the enclosure, each bearing two men on her back, one of whom guided the tame elephant, and engaged the attention of the wild one which was to be tied, while the other man slipped off behind and dexterously tied together the hind legs of the newly-caught creature. The most combative and largest of the wild elephants were the first selected to be thus disabled; the smaller ones were attended to afterwards. The magnificent tusker was accordingly first tied, and when thus hampered was led out of the enclosure between two tame elephants (another pushing him from behind when necessary), and was securely picketed with strong ropes to two great trees in the vicinity. It was a wonderful sight, and one never to be forgotten. Night set in before the work of tying up was concluded, for it was necessary to secure safely each captured elephant before the men were permitted to rest from their labours; but when all was over, Hood expressed himself as satisfied with the result, having obtained twenty-one fine elephants.

The next morning we went to look at the captives, chief among whom was the majestic tusker aforesaid, evidently the king of the herd. Some food had been given him, grain and plantain shoots, but he would have none of it. There he stood, swaying his body backwards and forwards with a restless never-ceasing movement, looking thoroughly untameable.

"Don't go too near him," said Hood, "he is still dangerous, I think."

As the words left his lips, the elephant seized the stem of a plantain-tree which had been given him for food, and hurled it at us with surprising force. Fortunately neither of us were struck, and we retired promptly to a more respectful distance. This grand creature, I afterwards learned, refused all food, and finally starved himself to death, but never gave in !

Captain Hood intended making another khedda, and subsequently captured nine more elephants ; but I could remain with him no longer, and returned with all speed to Demagree, having to superintend the establishment of the new stockaded

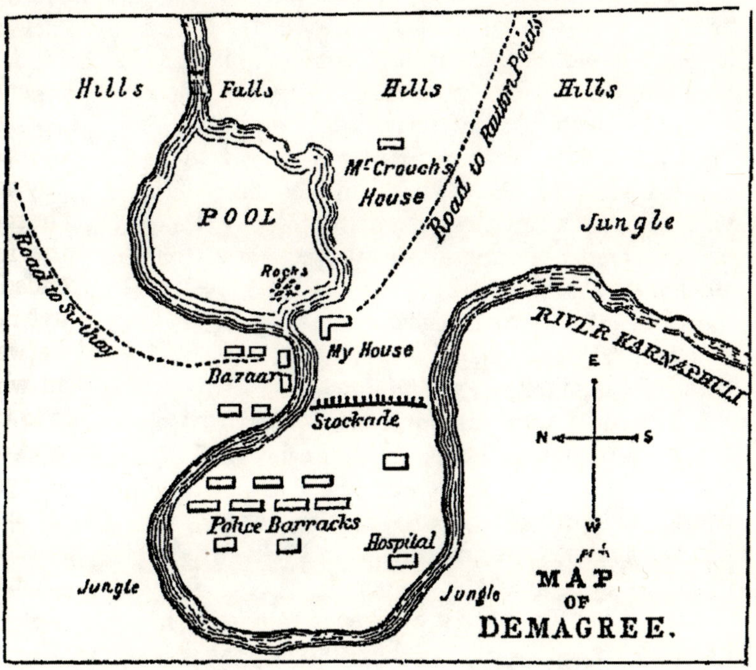

post on Sirthay Tlang, the hill-range in the immediate vicinity of our new settlement.

I had found by the experience gained during the last rains that the valleys were only healthy during the colder season of the year, and I was consequently anxious to move as many of my men as possible to the heights.

Demagree itself was very picturesquely and conveniently situated, and was well calculated to serve as a depôt and storehouse of provisions, which could thus far be brought by water. The river Karna-phuli here breaks through a hill-range by a narrow gorge of black rock, over which it foams, in two small falls, down to a still basin of clear green water of about half a mile in circumference.

The hills, which rise in long ranges to the east, trending north and south, shielded the place from the cold winds, while the level shores of the basin offered facilities for building. On the south-western side of the basin a bed of rock deflected the river, causing it to make a bend, and thus to form a small peninsula surrounded on three sides by deep water; a strong stockade across the neck of this peninsula rendered it an easily-defensible position, and here, consequently, were placed the police barracks, hospital, and provision depôt. My own house was built on a small eminence outside the stockade, commanding a good view of the bazaar on the north side of the pool, whence a path ran steeply up the Sirthay Tlang, a lofty peak of the Ohepoom range, where I proposed building a strong stockade, together with a house for myself. Here, also, I hoped eventually to establish the headquarters of the Frontier-Administration, Demagree serving as a trading centre and a place of disembarkation and storage.

I had some time previously intimated to Rutton Poia that I desired to have a house built for me on Sirthay Tlang, and the men of his tribe had speedily constructed there a rough but comfortable house, in Lushai fashion, where I intended passing the rainy season. Accordingly, in the month of May, I moved up to my eyrie and took up my abode on Sirthay Tlang.

It was curious what a difference was made in one's comfort by a rise in altitude of a thousand feet or so. At Demagree I had been overpowered by the heat and devoured by sand-flies, while at Sirthay I had to clothe myself warmly and keep the doors shut. The house which my Lushai friends had constructed for me was made of rough unhewn logs, plastered outside with mud, and the walls inside covered with bamboo matting, very comfortable in its way, but decidedly savage. This was afterwards christened Uncle Tom's Cabin by my assistants, and was dear to me, not so much as a dwelling, but as an emblem of diplomatic triumph and recognition of chiefship by the Lushais.

I must needs confess, however, that the wind whistled at

times very keenly on my lonely hill-top, and I gazed enviously at the crested falcon which perched on a dead tree near the house, wishing that I had a warm suit of feathers like his, instead of some thin old English garments which kept out neither wind nor weather. I missed also the care and attention of my servant Nurudin, who was at the Demagree bazaar as Superintendent.

My household, which consisted almost entirely of hill-men, became demoralized without the major-domo Nurudin; they lost my clothes, they broke my lamps, they dropped my concertina into the river, so that I was never able to play on it again; and, as a crowning misfortune, they selected a fine conical black rock, and from the back of one of the elephants they dropped upon it the box containing my stock of wine and beer, newly arrived from Calcutta.

Just two days before I moved up to Sirthay I had received by post a cookery book, from the study of which I promised myself both pleasure and profit. The keen air of Sirthay also gave me a fine appetite; but, alack! my faithful cook took this opportunity for going on leave, while his hill-deputy came to me smiling, with the intelligence that the bottom of my best saucepan had burned itself out, and that the store of potatoes and onions was entirely exhausted.

"Allah Akbar!" I said, "who can struggle against Fate?" So, after a month's comfortless sojourn on the mountain, I returned to Demagree, where, at any rate, one could keep dry. It was most cool and pleasant at Sirthay, but as the rains gathered power the clouds literally filled my house, everything becoming as wet as if I had inhabited a cavern at the bottom of the sea. It was impossible, with the rain falling in sheets, to get about much, so I occupied my time in putting into Burmese Professor Max Müller's translation of the "Dharma-pada: the Path of Wisdom or Virtue." This I afterwards had printed for distribution among the Khyoung-tha of the Hill Tracts, by whom its sententious philosophy was highly appreciated.

I busied the men in planting a thick cactus hedge along the stockade at Demagree, and also, whenever a break came in the rain, I practised them in rifle-shooting. It was as well to be prepared for any emergency. Small parties of Lushais frequently visited me during the rains, bringing presents, such as fresh vegetables from their "jums," the leg of a wild pig, or a quarter of venison. I was able by this time to converse with them pretty freely, and amused myself by collecting from their lips a variety of stories and legends. These visits involved, of course, the consumption of much drink, and I devised a plan whereby I was able to hob-nob with them to their heart's content, for while they drank undiluted rum I quaffed freely from a decanter of toast and water. The necessary appearance of roystering was preserved, and all parties were pleased.

I moved up again to the heights of Sirthay Tlang as soon as the rains abated somewhat of their fury, for the loneliness and wild grandeur of the place had a strange attraction for me. I carried with me two Lushai cats, and treated (unsuccessfully) for a parrot, feeling it necessary to preserve the "Crusoe" *ensemble* as much as possible.

I remember one afternoon standing on the verge of a mighty brown rock that crowned the hill close to my house on Sirthay; I knew that beneath me the valley fell in a sheer dip of hundreds of feet, but instead of the usual fair woodland landscape, there rose up, striking me dumbly in the face, a mighty wall of grey mist, blotting out earth and sky alike. Piled up to heaven, and stretching far away on either hand, it rose before one, dim, white, mysterious, and, as if possessed of an individuality of its own, there would come now and again a slow uneasy movement in the white mass, as if something were stirring in its folds, like a snake in its coils. One could not look long enough; "Krey ma wak," as the hill folk say. The sight was fascinating, and gave one an impulse to spring out into the soft white fleece. And this mist would pass away as quickly as it came. That same evening it was quite clear, and there was a glorious sunset; so I scrambled down a neighbouring ravine, and watched the rushing torrent cast its masses of topaz-coloured water over the dark rocks, foaming, raging, roaring, and tumbling headlong down, with such an uproarious outpouring of living strength, that I shouted aloud in sympathy with the wild water.

The day was dying peacefully as I climbed back to my cabin. The light faded away off the far-away purple hills in the Howlong country, lingering last, for one tender moment, on the scarped scaur of the great Mui Fang Tlang, the range of hills which had stood between the right column and the column commanded by General Bourchier. Far down below in the valley twinkled a light from the dwelling of some savage householder, and on the evening air floated the mournful wailing cry of the guyal, as they slowly wound their way home from the woodland to their master's house, where a handful of salt awaited them. I sat long, looking eastward, dreaming of fresh explorations, new adventures (dreams never, alas! to become realities), until nightfall compelled me to seek the warmth of the cheerful wood fire which I found burning on my earthen hearth in true Lushai fashion.

I had much at heart a plan for inducing the principal Sylu and Howlong chiefs to accompany me to Calcutta, there to pay their homage to the great ones of Government and to see the glories of the metropolis, and I had to this end frequently thrown out feelers while conversing with chiefs who came to see me.

It was, however, no easy task: the entire ignorance and simplicity of the Lushai mind freed them from the inducements which would influence men in general. What, indeed had they to gain? and had they not their lives to lose? In asking them to place their lives and liberties in my hands, to undertake what in their eyes would be a long and perilous journey to a foreign country, over unknown "lakes," and in strange and wonderful steam-vessels, it was perhaps hardly to be expected that they would readily lend their ears to the voice of the charmer. Still, I lost no opportunity of urging the idea upon the attention of such chiefs as came to visit me.

One day, the chief Saipoiya, a leader and influential man among the Southern Howlongs, came to see me with a numerous following, and to him I forthwith propounded my scheme in glowing colours: he would receive presents from the Governor-General; he would see such wonders as none of his ancestors had ever seen or ever dreamed of; and, moreover, he would be quite safe, for, as I pointed out, his brother-in-law, Rutton Poia, had agreed to go, and this he would not have done unless assured of safety. All this and much more I pressed upon the chief, who was evidently much tempted by the proposal. His followers, however, did not at all relish the idea, and a wily old karbari put forward the views of the opposition, in logical form, as follows :—

" It is true, and we believe all you say, Thanglicna ; we have known you for a long time, and your tongue is straight. Your words are very good words, but it is wise to look at both sides of a matter. Is it not so ? "

A murmer of assent from all, in which I joined.

" You say," continued the karbari, " that the Big Chief in Calcutta, the Gubnor Gendel, is more powerful than you are. Is that the case ? "

" Yes," I replied. " He is very great ; certainly more powerful than I am."

" Well, then," rejoined the karbari, " suppose he orders Saipoiya to be speared ? " Sensation.

It is needless to say that Saipoiya did not go to Calcutta. He took leave of me, asseverating that, although he was indeed my brother, yet he was no relation of Lord Northbrook's, and would not, therefore, visit his village. I had many such interviews to go through, and arrangements to make with the authorities at the other end ; for I had set my nets on as large a scale as possible, and wished to take with me to Calcutta a fairly representative troop of my wild men. If one had to play the part of showman it was well at least to have a good show.

I had to arrange so that the chiefs should remain as short a time in Calcutta as was compatible with their seeing everything and being seen by those in authority there ; for, should the health of any member of the party suffer, I should have been personally responsible to the tribe, and should have to compensate his relatives with blood-money, for the *lex talionis* prevailed to an alarming extent amongst my barbaric friends.

After a good deal of manœuvring I at length started for Chittagong accompanied by seven chiefs with a select number of followers, the party numbering altogether twenty-seven. From Chittagong we went by steamer to Calcutta, the journey being performed without any noteworthy incident, save that I was struck by the impassivity of the Lushais, their astonishment, if they felt any, being expressed by an apparent increase in the stolidity of their demeanour. Throughout the journey they steadily maintained an attitude of suspicion, which chiefly manifested itself by a pertinacity of attachment to myself, never allowing me to be out of their sight.

On arriving at Calcutta, tents had been pitched for the accommodation of the party on the "maidaun" or large grassy plain which forms the lungs, as it were, of the city; and I had hoped to take up my quarters at the Club hard by, in my usual fashion; so, after putting them in a carriage at our place of disembarkation, under charge of Nurudin, I was entering another vehicle myself, when I felt my coat-tails firmly clutched from behind; turning, I found the chiefs, who refused to return from following after me. Vainly I expostulated, and explained what was proposed for their comfort; but the fear of Lord Northbrook was upon them, the great white chief who was more powerful than I, and they would not let me go. Another tent, therefore, was pitched for me in their camp, and I remained with them during their stay in Calcutta.

They went in due course to pay their homage to the Lieutenant-Governor, as the head of the Bengal Government, to whom they gravely bowed as to an equal, presenting him with the usual offerings of elephants' tusks and home-spun cloth. They objected, however, to visiting Lord Northbrook, and were not taken there.

The magnificence of the City of Palaces did not apparently impress them, nor the dwelling of the Lieutenant-Governor, palatial as it was, although a solid silver sofa, supported by silver lions, which occupied a conspicuous place in the drawing-room of Belvedere, held their attention for a brief space. Two of them lost themselves in the streets one evening, and were brought back late at night by a friendly policeman, much to the relief of the remainder of the party, who had become very silent and depressed through fear of Lord Northbrook. After this they never wandered far from the tents, unless under my charge, or with Nurudin.

They slept very little, but sat together in the tent, talking and smoking far into the night. On the whole, the balance of their minds inclined in favour of their own hill-tops, where there were no mosquitoes (the plague of Calcutta), and where the ceaseless jostling of strange men troubled them not. They were not disturbed by the crowd of idlers which daily thronged our camp to gaze at them ; perhaps because this was in accord with their own customs, for in the Lushai villages I was mobbed to death, and never enjoyed a moment's privacy.

Once, and once only, were they roused to enthusiasm, and that was when I took them a mile at full speed on a fiery, snorting locomotive engine, which was placed at my disposal for the purpose by the Traffic-Manager of the East India Railway. This fairly frightened the dignity out of them, and when safely arrived on the earth again, they shook their heads, confessing that the power and wisdom of the Sahibs was altogether wonderful.

They remained in Calcutta a fortnight, and then departed to their hills, under the charge of Nurudin, laden with a variety of presents and purchases. They were well pleased with their visit, and more than well pleased that it was safely over, and they bade me farewell with effusion, begging me to follow them with all speed. Doubtless, in after ages tradition will hand down the wonders seen by these chiefs when they went with Thangliena to visit the Lord Sahib in Calcutta.

This visit of the Lushai chiefs to offer their homage personally to our Government formed a fitting sequel and, as I regarded it, a culmination of the Lushai incident. To the Calcutta idlers who came to stare at the wild men encamped on the "maidaun," they seemed but a handful of barbarians, with unkempt hair, clad in curious tartans, and armed with strange weapons ; but to me, who had lived among them, and knew the nature of these men, and the authority wielded by them among their own people, it seemed a wonderful thing that I should ever have succeeded in pursuading them to trust their lives in my hands.

Honest fellows they were, and true, in their own wild way. I never saw them or their hills again, for the Home Government refused to sanction the proposals made by the Government of India for the reconstitution of the Frontier administration, and I saw no chance of being able to carry out efficiently the work on which I had set my heart, to which I had pledged my faith, and for which I had worked so long.

I think, also, I was out of spirits, as I certainly was out of health. The life which I had led in the hills was one involving the extremest hardship and personal responsibility. Without friends, without society, and (until the last year or so) without the companionship of a fellow-countryman, and now, added to this, the lack of any recognition of my services, filled me with such a chill sense of disappointment, that I felt it impossible to renew work on the old terms.

I had disregarded the doctor's advice at the end of the Lushai campaign, in order to complete and consolidate the effects of the expedition; but I could hold up no longer, being really ill; and so, once more, somewhat weary and broken, I returned to England, and, a few years later, left the service, with the honorary rank of Lieutenant-Colonel, and a pension of £190 a year.

Looking back now, with the wider philosophy which years have given, I can see that the Indian Government is perhaps wise in not encouraging individual effort. A public servant's idiosyncrasy must not be too strongly developed, even for the *good* of those under his charge. Things may go better for a time—for his time—but the difficulty of replacing such an officer, when removed by death or promotion, is an insuperable objection. A high Indian official once brusquely but pertinently remarked in my hearing, "We don't want personal influence; we want men who will obey orders."

Talleyrand's maxim, "*Surtout point de zèle*," is, perhaps, too cynical as applied to our Indian bureaucracy; but a zeal that involves the outlay of Government money, and risks lives that may have to be avenged, is to be deprecated rather than encouraged. I knew and loved my hill people. I lived among them and was their friend. They admitted me into their homes and family life as few Englishmen have been admitted. I ate with them, talked with them, played music at their feasts, and joined in their hunting expeditions. They concealed no thoughts from me; I had their confidence. They gave me their sons to educate, and invited me to the marriage-feasts of their daughters. I was ready to spend and be spent in their service. But, after all, I was only "a fly on the wheel"; they were not *my* people. I did but represent and make known to them the impartial justice, the perfect tolerance, and the respect for personal freedom which characterise the British rule in India, gaining for it the respect of all creeds and all classes, and making it, in spite of many blunders, misunderstandings, and mistakes, the strongest and wisest Government, since the old Roman Empire, that this world has known.

Look not mournfully into the Past. It cometh not again.

Wisely improve the Present. It is thine.

Go forth to meet the shadowy Future without fear and with a manly heart.

L'ENVOI

THIS book, the record of the life of a young man in the service of the Government of India in the last century, has found favour with many, and a new edition has been called for.

Those who read it may like to know what has happened in Lushai-land since the Author took his departure, and this can best be told in the words of the subjoined letters.

From the officer in charge of the South Lushai Hills to the Secretary of the Government of Bengal :—

(*Extract from Diary for the week ending 27th October*, 1896.)

"I reached Sangliena's village of Paileng the afternoon of the 20th, and had to decide a divorce case between Mongthoma Seilo, chief of Kongleeng and his wife, Thomkungi, daughter of Sangliena Seilo deceased, chief of Paileng. As both belonged to the royal caste, I was called on to settle the case, which was brought at the instance of the wife. I found on enquiry that Mongthoma persistently ill-treated his wife and that there was no prospect of their living amicably together, so I made out an order of separation; Mongthoma to give the wife's family two guyals. This decision satisfied both parties. On the 21st I reached Lallouva's village, after a march of 18 miles, and halted the next day, as Lallouva wanted to kill a guyal in my honour. This was duly done and a great feast held: much rice-beer was drunk, my escort materially assisting the festivity by song and dance. I picked up much information as to old habits and customs, some of which was extremely interesting. A funny thing occurred at Lallouva's, at the drinking party: some of the old men took to calling me 'Luan Sahib.' I asked them why they did this, and they said that I was much greater than formerly, I had become like the great Luan Sahib. I then grasped the fact that they referred to Captain Lewin, whose name lives green over the South Lushai Hills."

From the Rev. J. Herbert Lorrain, Missionary to the Lushais, to Colonel T. H. Lewin, dated 25th April, 1899 :—

"DEAR SIR,—I have for many years had a great desire to write to you, but, until lately, I did not know your address. My friend Mr. Savidge and I have had the great privilege of being the pioneers of the Gospel in a land which I am sure has a warm place in your affection, even after so many years. I refer to the country of the Lushais. Having read your book, 'A Fly on the Wheel,' we know that your love for these wild hill men was very real, and we feel sure that you will be glad to receive some news about them. It was in 1891 that we determined,

God willing, to go to the Lushais, and, after residing some time in Eastern Bengal, we went to Chittagong. It was here that we came across some books on the Lushai language written by you. War was then going on up in Lushai-land, and the authorities would not allow us to enter the country, but we were permitted to reside at Kassalong, and went there hoping to perfect ourselves in the Lushai language. In this we were disappointed, for the Lushais had all taken fright at the expedition which was working farther inland, and the few who visited Kassalong would not converse with us, being suspicious of our intentions. We spent some time in Rangamati with no better results, and, after undergoing much hardship in the jungles of the Chittagong Hill Tracts, we both fell ill, and were obliged to return to Calcutta. A few months afterwards we determined to try to enter Lushai-land from the north instead of from the south, and we, accordingly, went to Cachar. The country was still in a very unsettled state, and twelve months passed before the Chief Commissioner of Assam (Sir W. Ward) gave us permission to start. We left Cachar in a country boat on Boxing Day, 1893, and after nearly three weeks journey we arrived at Fort Aijal in the North Lushai Hills. During our stay in Cachar, we had come across your vocabulary and folk-lore, and this we learnt by heart. We also got some help from a little book, published by the native doctor of Rangamati. On our arrival, therefore, at Fort Aijal we were able, though with difficulty, to make ourselves understood, and from the first the people treated us as their friends., We were unarmed, and we trusted the Lushais entirely, and never once found them false to us. We built our house about a mile from Aijal between two Lushai villages, and set about learning the language in real earnest. From the time when we began to speak fluently the people looked upon us as members of their own community, and we became fast friends. We spent two years in this way, ministering to the sick, advising the people, and, generally speaking, identifying ourselves with their interests. They called us 'Mizo Sâp,' the Lushai Sahibs, or perhaps more often 'our Sahibs,' for they looked upon us as their own particular friends. In this way we got to know their manners and customs, which knowledge stood us in good stead afterwards. Meanwhile we began to teach the young men and children to read and write, adopting Sir William Hunter's system of transliteration, and they proved most intelligent pupils, soon beginning to teach others, so that the new, strange and wonderful art of reading and writing spread over the whole of the Northern Hill country. The Government officers always stood by us in our efforts to benefit the people, and, after a time, the Political Officer, Major Shakespear, opened a school for the Lushai people. Little houses were built near the Fort, and every chief who came in to learn was provided with board and lodging free for three months. This plan worked well, and a considerable number of chiefs and influential men became learners. By this time we had begun to translate portions of the Scriptures into the Dulien dialect, and we spent two years on this work, with short preaching tours now and then among the adjacent villages. The way in which these people received the Gospel was truly wonderful. They were as prepared soil for the good seed. We did not baptize any of them, as we knew that we were pioneer missionaries, and should probably have to leave the country to others after a few years, but there were many among the Lushais who loved our Saviour and trusted in Him for salvation. After we had been there some time the Welsh Presbyterian Mission expressed a desire to commence work there, and as we were only two private missionaries, we felt that we must not be like dogs in the manger and keep them out. The gentleman who had supported us while in Lushailand would only allow us to work in places where there were no other societies, so that when the Welsh Mission arrived we had to leave. It was a great sorrow both to us and to the dear Lushai people, but we were cheered by the knowledge that we had commenced a real work in their midst, and we brought away with us our manuscripts of the Gospel of St. John and St. Luke, and the Acts of the Apostles, which have now been published by the British and Foreign Bible Society, and are by this time, we hope, in the hands of the Lushai people. Our Grammar and Dictionary were kindly published by the Assam Government, and are proving a great help to the missionaries who have taken up our work. I have with me a newspaper called *The Highlander's News* (*Mizo chanchin Laishuih*), which is written by a Lushai and circulated by Government in the villages. It gives the news of the different hamlets, and conveys the orders of Government to the various chiefs. The other day there appeared in it a long account of a visit which some of the Lushais had paid to Calcutta. It was only five years ago last Christmas since we started for Lushai-land from Cachar, and during that time the change that has been wrought in these wild people is little short of miraculous. We cannot help seeing the hand of our all-loving Father in this work. But I have further news to tell which will gladden your heart even more than what I have written above. Your own influence upon the Lushais is still felt. I do not think there is a man or woman in all those hills who does not know the name of Thangliena or Luan Sâp. It is handed down from father to son, and they are never tired of singing your praises. We have sat for hours and listened to them talking of the bye-gone days and the wonderful white chief, who has become to them the ideal sahib or Englishman. Some few we have met who could boast that they had actually seen the great Thangliena in the flesh. One of these you will I am sure remember, the chief Savúnga. He was very old, when first we knew him, and died about two years ago.

"Just before his death I visited his village, and I shall never forget the time I spent with him. He was a grand old warrior, and retained his faculties to the last, revered even by his enemies. His grandson, Khamliena, is a fine fellow, one of our staunchest friends and best pupils. He still cherishes the double-barrel gun which his father, Lal Ngura, received from you when he accompanied you to Calcutta.

"I am,

"Yours sincerely,

"J. HERBERT LORRAIN."

From Colonel J. Shakespear to Colonel T. H. Lewin, dated 3rd December, 1910, from Imphal, Manipúr State, Assam, East Indies.

"My dear Colonel Lewin,—I send you a photograph of Nepuitangi, the widow of Vatasa, whose name you probably recollect in the old days when you ruled the Border. The old lady was well when I left the Lushai Hills in 1905, but quite blind, and I had great difficulty in getting her to sit for her picture, only persuading her to do so by agreeing to include in the photograph two other women older than herself. I thought that this picture might be welcome, to show you that you are not forgotten in these parts. I have taken the liberty of dedicating my monograph on the Lushai people to you, under your hill-title of 'Thangliena.' The monograph is one of a series brought out by the Government. The volumes on the Miris, Garos, Manipuris and Khassyas have already appeared. Mine is far from complete, but when you consider that twenty different clans, scattered over 20,000 square miles, are dealt with, you will not expect too much. I was interested in coming across your name, and that of an ancestor of yours in Dr. Busteed's 'Echoes of Old Calcutta.' I was transferred here in the spring of 1905, and hope to stay here for another three years, when I shall retire. Thank God we have no High Court here, and in consequence the people are quiet, peaceful and contented. My last news from Lushai-land is that all goes well. My successor, Major Cole, who has been in charge there for a long time now, is a great agriculturalist, and has introduced new crops into the country, such as potatoes and rubber; also has improved the breed of poultry. You know how very nomadic the Lushais used to be; very soon after I took charge of the Hills I found that much of this desire to move constantly was due to the fear that some neighbour would seize upon a coveted site, so I set to work to give each chief a certain number of sites, all included within fixed boundaries, well defined. The effect of this has been most satisfactory. The number of moves is reduced to a minimum, and some chiefs have established permanent villages, which 'joom' round certain sites in rotation, while they themselves have built houses in some central spot controlling the whole area. Khamliana, a grandson of your old friend Savúnga, the head of the Sailoo tribe, wrote to me to say that he had now over 2,000 rupees in the Government Savings Bank. The Thengawl valley, where you had your interview with the captors of Mary Winchester is now all cultivated. Two years ago they took 10,000 maunds of rice off Champhai, the goal of the Cachar column in 1871–72, which, when I first saw it, was all grass and swamp. Yet with all these changes I am glad to say that the old village system has been maintained, and the people have been allowed to work out their own salvation in their own way.

"With kind regards,
"Yours sincerely,
"John Shakespear."

BRADBURY, AGNEW, & CO. LD., PRINTERS, LONDON AND TONBRIDGE.

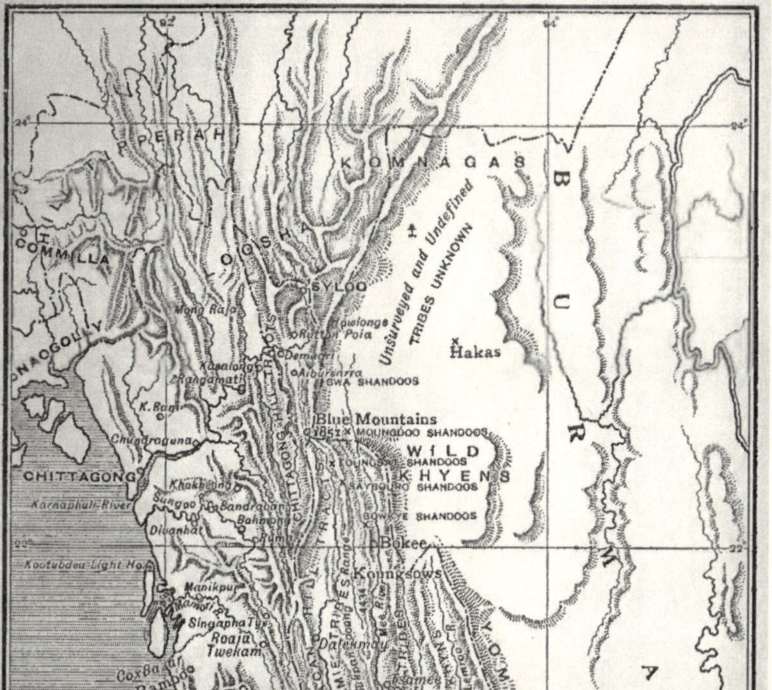

MAP OF THE CHITTAGONG DISTRICT